T0330406

# Alternatives to Capitalism in the 21st Century

*Series Editors:* **Lara Monticelli**, Copenhagen Business School, and **Torsten Geelan**, University of Copenhagen

Debates about the future of capitalism demonstrate the urgent need to envision and enact alternatives that can help tackle the multiple intertwined crises that societies are currently facing. This ground-breaking new series advances the international, comparative and interdisciplinary study of capitalism and its alternatives in the 21st Century.

## Forthcoming in the series:

*Capital to Commons*
By **Hannes Gerhardt**

## Out now in the series:

*Politics of the Gift*
*Towards a Convivial Society*
By **Frank Adlof**

*The Future is Now*
*An Introduction to Prefigurative Politics*
Edited by **Lara Monticelli**

## Find out more at

bristoluniversitypress.co.uk/
alternatives-to-capitalism-in-the-21st-century

# Alternatives to Capitalism in the 21st Century

*Series Editors:* **Lara Monticelli**, Copenhagen Business School, and **Torsten Geelan**, University of Copenhagen

---

## Advisory board:

## Find out more at

bristoluniversitypress.co.uk/
alternatives-to-capitalism-in-the-21st-century

# ALTERNATIVE SOCIETIES

## For a Pluralist Socialism

Luke Martell

BRISTOL
UNIVERSITY
PRESS

First published in Great Britain in 2023 by

Bristol University Press
University of Bristol
1–9 Old Park Hill
Bristol
BS2 8BB
UK
t: +44 (0)117 374 6645
e: bup-info@bristol.ac.uk

Details of international sales and distribution partners are available at bristoluniversitypress.co.uk

© Bristol University Press 2023

British Library Cataloguing in Publication Data
A catalogue record for this book is available from the British Library

ISBN 978-1-5292-2966-0 hardcover
ISBN 978-1-5292-2967-7 paperback
ISBN 978-1-5292-2968-4 ePub
ISBN 978-1-5292-2969-1 ePdf

The right of Luke Martell to be identified as author of this work has been asserted by him in accordance with the Copyright, Designs and Patents Act 1988.

Cover design: Liam Roberts Design
Front cover image: 'Murmuration' by Zualidro
Bristol University Press use environmentally responsible print partners.
Printed and bound in Great Britain by CPI Group (UK) Ltd, Croydon, CR0 4YY

FSC
www.fsc.org
MIX
Paper | Supporting
responsible forestry
FSC® C013604

# Contents

# List of Tables

# About the Author

Luke Martell is Teaching Fellow and Professor of Sociology at the University of Sussex. His interests are socialism, social democracy, social alternatives, and global politics. He is author of *Ecology and Society* (Polity Press, 1994), co-author of *New Labour* (Polity Press, 1998), co-author of *Blair's Britain* (Polity Press, 2002), and author of *The Sociology of Globalization* (Polity Press, 2010, second edition 2017).

# Introduction

We often evaluate and criticize existing society. This book is less about criticism of how things are and more about alternatives. In times of terrible global problems and great gloom, it examines how things could be better. It is an exercise in idealism, but rooted in reality, in the now as much as the future. It is about realistic ways of getting to a better future, also how that future might be organized. It is about alternative societies, how to get to them and what they can be.

There are some key emphases or angles of the book. First, it looks at alternatives in current society and the future, alternative societies across the board, and it tries to branch out in its plurality and breadth. The book brings alternatives together and explores the synergies and tensions between them and is inclusive rather than just focusing on individual alternatives, say, utopianism, prefigurative experiments, socialism, or global politics. So, I hope the book will be of interest to those who want wide coverage. I have tried to be up to date on the alternatives covered. Of course, not every possible alternative is covered, and some are given more space than others. I include critical assessment of the alternatives, but that is not the emphasis. The emphasis is on positive outlining of the alternatives. By 'prefigurative' I mean experiments that can be the beginnings of a wider future alternative society: they prefigure broader future social change based on their experiments and lessons. (On prefiguration, see Swain, 2019; Raekstad and Gradin, 2020; Jeffrey and Dyson, 2021; Monticelli, 2022.)

Second, I try not to resort to simplifications or too clean arguments for one thing over another. I do not believe clear oppositions or dichotomies work intellectually or politically. So, I make no apologies that the book argues for pluralism and complexity. However, it does not advocate just a mix-and-match approach. I have genuinely not started with a predetermined perspective, but I think many of the alternatives I look at imply socialism. So, the pluralism and openness end up within a socialist perspective, in an undogmatic but definite framework. I look at how to make that framework work well, rather than how to just mix it up alongside many others as an equal partner.

Third, and relatedly, much of this book comes to a commitment to a socialist society, but in an open-minded way and such a society that is pluralist and complex in its ends and in the means of getting there (see also O'Neill, 2002, 2003). The aim of the book is not to persuade anyone of socialism; there are lots of books that try to do this. This is more about how to do socialism, and in a democratic, liberal, and complex way; more about what form an alternative socialist society, and getting to it, could take than about justifying socialism. In the process of doing this, though, 'why socialism?' is something that gets discussed. You do not have to be a socialist to read this book. It provides an outline and assessment of many alternatives open to whatever your political perspective. Not all alternatives discussed in this book see themselves as socialist or are socialist. Some may resist the imposition of abstract or western socialism – for example, some of the concrete, plural, localist, bottom-up, ecological social reproduction approaches from the Global South that are discussed.

Fourth, the book is not just an equal overview of all alternatives. The opening two chapters of the book take a broad remit, but I feel that key issues they throw up are utopianism, socialism, economic democracy, and localism and internationalism as key dimensions of an alternative society. So, the later parts of the book focus on these, fleshing out their details and complexities in more depth.

Fifth, the book is international in scope. It discusses alternatives in global politics, and a chapter is devoted to this. Throughout, I discuss local, national, and international approaches to alternatives, Global North and Global South, that respond to the context of global capitalism. If the discussion does not explicitly highlight the Global South, that does not mean the discussion is relevant only to the Global North and not the Global South, and, of course, vice versa. The alternatives looked at can be found as realities or aspirations all over the world.

I think this book will be relevant to students, tutors, and those outside formal education interested in areas such as politics, sociology, political economy, and international relations, and in topics like socialism, utopianism, civil society alternatives, economic democracy, and globalization. In addition, I hope this book will join with others (for example, Parker et al, 2007; Dawson, 2016; Parker et al, 2018; Kothari et al, 2019) to encourage people to set up topics and modules on social alternatives, following courses initiated in this area in universities already. At the same time, I have tried to write this book in an accessible way, and on alternatives being practised as well as theories about them. I hope readers outside academia and institutional education, including those who have never been to university, will find it readable. I have deliberately not written the book in a polemical or rhetorical way. My aim is not to inspire the sympathetic, but to talk to the unsure. I think the latter are more open to logical and analytical argument, which sometimes has to go into detail. So, I have gone down this route rather than a passionate journalistic one that appeals more to the already amenable. Yet, as I have said, I hope I have done this in a way that is readable more widely than to experts. Each chapter has a table summarizing key themes and a section on recommended further reading.

Chapters 1 and 2 outline a range of types of alternative economy and society – in the past, now, and in the future; macro and micro; in civil society and politics. In Chapter 1, these include alternative economies of communism; co-ops and other forms of alternative and participatory economy; non-work and slow society; eco-localism, especially in the Global South; and tech and digital alternatives. In Chapter 2, I look at social alternatives in education, intentional communities, food countercultures, alternative social centres, alternatives to prison and policing, and political institutions of welfare and social democracy. In these cases, I look at the ends and means of change. These chapters raise themes and examples, some of which are mainly discussed there while others are expanded on in the remaining chapters.

Many alternative societies are regarded as utopian. While giving talks about alternatives and discussing them during the writing of this book, I was confronted with fierce criticisms of utopianism, often from people committed to political alternatives. Chapter 3 looks at common criticisms of utopianism from Marxist and liberal perspectives, arguing that it is very defendable against their judgements, and that this is possible from within these perspectives rather than by rejecting them. Utopianism as materialist and not idealist, and as liberal rather than totalitarian, is advocated.

Chapters 4, 5, and 6 focus on issues about alternatives that I feel demand closer and more in-depth attention. I think socialism is implied by many of the alternatives being proposed and tried. The theory and practice of socialism have been much criticized, often in an ill-founded way, though not always. In Chapter 4, I look at criticisms of socialism from liberal, neoliberal, green and feminist perspectives. I think the most telling concerns about socialism can be found in questioning from these approaches. I argue that sometimes these viewpoints give reasons for socialism expanding, as a good way to tackle their concerns. But sometimes I believe they lead to socialism needing to limit itself to some extent, where the points critics make hit home. Criticisms of socialism lead to both arguments for socialism and arguments for a more pluralist socialism.

For me, the most defining aspect of socialism is democratic and collective ownership in the economy, which has come back more into mainstream politics in recent years. Chapter 5 looks more closely at this, focusing especially on proposals for, and practices of, local, decentralized, and democratized social ownership, about which there have been new thinking and experiments, often localized but relevant also at levels above the local. I sympathize with such proposals and trials of the democratic economy but see dangers in localism and in optimism about winning support for them. I argue for national public ownership in a democratized form and well-planned strategies for political actors so they can be ready to fight back against resistance and opposition from interests like international capital and the political Right.

Chapter 6 looks at the global dimension, discussing the way anti- and alter-globalization movements have gone, their energies channelled more into national and local forms, and what promise these may hold. It looks with hope but pessimism at proposals for political globalization in support of social democratic and social policies, arguing instead for a sub-global internationalism. I argue that hopes in global change for a better world rest more with opening borders to the free movement of people. I believe there is a very strong case across the board for open borders and more positive hope and possibility for them than both critics and supporters often see.

The concluding chapter ties together what I have been arguing for. I draw together arguments about globalism, sub-global internationalism, national and local approaches, and experimental, prefigurative, and political approaches to change towards, and organizing of, an alternative society. I argue against dichotomous and polarized thinking about different levels and approaches to social change, and against false oppositions between materialism and idealism, utopianism and Marxism. I make the case for socialism and reiterate that socialism can deal with approaches like liberalism, feminism, and ecologism by both expanding and limiting itself. I discuss socialism in terms of democratic collective ownership and a democratic economy, in theory and practice, and challenges to be overcome. I argue for a complex and pluralist approach. This is not pluralism alongside socialism, but a pluralist socialism and socialist pluralism. What this means is discussed throughout the book and in the conclusion.

This book is based on grounded theory, looking at concrete alternatives and then developing analytical, theoretical, and political discussions founded on this. The concrete alternatives come in Chapters 1 and 2 before the more theoretical and analytical Chapters 3, 4, and 5. This follows the learning process that happens in many of these alternatives, and the one that I went through in studying this area, writing this book, and coming to its conclusions. I also think starting the book with concrete alternatives is the best way to make it accessible to less academic lay readers. The two parts of the book, on concrete alternatives and then more theoretical and analytical discussions, are not separate; the first leads to the latter, and they go together and are one whole.

There is some minor reiteration across chapters because while the whole book makes a case with all the chapters together, some will read just parts. So occasionally something mentioned in an earlier chapter or section is brought up again briefly in another one where it is important for someone not reading the whole book. Where this happens, I point this out, so readers of the whole book can skim issues that may have been discussed earlier.

**Further reading**

At the end of each chapter, I suggest further reading on the topic of that chapter. The emphasis is on reading for people new or relatively new to the topic. These are personal suggestions and, of course, others would recommend different readings. I also suggest more reading within the text of the chapters. I have tried as much as possible to provide suggestions for readings that are freely available. The browser extension Unpaywall helps find legal open-access versions of publications behind a paywall.

Good overviews of alternative forms of social organization can be found in Martin Parker et al's (2007) *The Dictionary of Alternatives*, an accessible introduction to relevant ideas, and in more depth in Parker et al's (2018) *The Routledge Companion to Alternative Organization*.

Ashish Kothari et al's (2019) *Pluriverse: A Post-development Dictionary* is a great overview of alternatives with an emphasis on Global South post-development theories and practices. There is a free download of this book from the website of Radical Ecological Democracy. The Global Tapestry of Alternatives website outlines alternatives globally and especially in the Global South. You can sign up for email updates, and it has a regular newsletter. The Vikalp Sangam website documents grounded alternatives in India. Laura Basu's short (2020a) 'How to fix the world', on the Open Democracy website, discusses alternatives globally, including green, feminist, and Global South perspectives. These resources with a Global South perspective are relevant to topics throughout this book and are freely available online. The Society for the Advancement of Socio-Economics has an Alternatives to Capitalism network, which can be found with an internet search, and it has a mailing list, events, publications, resources, and an associated book series, which this book is part of.

Matt Dawson's (2016) *Social Theory for Alternative Societies* outlines suggestions for alternative societies by sociologists and social theorists. Other good overviews on alternatives include the neo-Marxist Erik Olin Wright's (2010) *Envisioning Real Utopias*. See his website (realutopias.org) and his short book *How to Be an Anti-capitalist in the 21st Century* (2019), especially Chapters 3–5. There is an article version of the book (Wright, 2015). The more libertarian and anti-politics John Holloway (2010) discusses alternatives in *Crack Capitalism*, especially parts I–III. There is a short version of Holloway's argument in 'Crack capitalism – "we want to break"' (2012) in the online journal ROAR. Dada Maheshvarananda's (2012) distinctive and international *After Capitalism* includes spiritual and green principles and is inspired by P.R. Sarkar's progressive utilization theory.

# 1

# Alternative Economies

I will outline alternative economies and social alternatives in this and the next chapter. I will be discussing alternatives in both theory and practice, and ones that have been tried beyond current societies as well as within them. I want to raise some key themes. Some will come up in more depth in the rest of the book, but I will highlight some initially now. One is about socialism after the failure of so-called communism. Another concerns utopianism, not just in the future but also here and now. Another is about goals like human needs and self-determination. Implicit in all these is capitalism. I do not think capitalism is oriented to human goals and self-determination. It is about money and profit rather than human ends. And it is organized around capitalist and managerial power rather than self-determination. This is not to say you cannot achieve human ends and self-determination within capitalism. One of the things I want to say in this book is that you can. But they are not the ends of capitalism.

I will come back to utopianism in more depth in Chapter 3, but I will say a few words about it here as this chapter and the rest of the book are in many ways about utopias. The word 'utopia' is usually used to mean somewhere that is good, desirable, or even ideal but that does not exist. It may never exist, or it may do sometime in the future. Take feminism and the women's movement, the civil rights movement, the movement for working-class representation in politics, the movement for worker representation in employment, by which I mean trade unions, the movement for the welfare state, and the movement for independence from colonial domination – all of these seemed radical and utopian in their early days. But people pursued them and these past utopianisms became real. Critics of radical protest and utopianism today often sympathize with these historical radical and utopian movements and their achievements, yet are negative about radicalism and utopianism now. There is an inconsistency and lack of history in that perspective.

There are Left-wing, anti-racist, feminist, ecological and Right-wing utopias, some of which I will come back to in Chapter 3. Karl Marx was a critic of utopianism, especially utopian socialism. He said the problem with utopian socialism is that it has dreams about the future that are not embedded in current economic and social developments and contradictions, in tendencies in society now. I sympathize with Marx's critique. But I want to look at utopianism that *is* embedded in present contradictions and at utopianism now, not just in the future.

Manuel Castells talks about alternative economic cultures (Mason, 2012; see also Westra et al, 2019). He says people cannot wait for the revolution. They want to live differently now. So, Castells discusses alternative economic cultures such as bartering (like the Freecycle network and skills sharing groups; see Parsons, 2014), co-ops, and mutual aid. The latter, outlined by the anarchist philosopher Kropotkin (2007), has a long tradition and played an important role during the COVID-19 crisis (see Preston and Firth, 2020; Sitrin and Colectiva Sembrar, 2020; Firth, 2022). Castells made his name with theories about networks in society, as opposed to hierarchies, and he talks about the alternative economic cultures as being organized in network forms. People sometimes opt for alternative economies out of choice. They are ideologically committed to things like co-ops or mutualism. But sometimes they opt for them out of necessity. They do not have any money, so they have to use bartering. Or they experience hell at work, so they get out and form co-ops where they have more control. Or they cannot live off paid work or welfare, so they organize around social reproduction of their life rather than production.

I will look in this chapter and book at multiple experimental utopias, where people are trying out types of alternative society in different places, as much as total utopias that cover all of society, and localized and fragmentary utopias as well as society-wide ones. I will discuss utopias as a process being tried presently as well as an end to be attempted in the future and utopias that are spatial, happening in spaces today, as much as temporal, at a time ahead of us. In this chapter, I shall look at alternative economies of communism, co-ops, participatory economics, non-work, slow society, eco-localism (especially in the Global South), and online and digital alternatives. In the next chapter, I will look at social alternatives of free education, countercultures in communes, food and social centres, alternatives to prison, and welfare as a social alternative. Then in later chapters, I will go into more depth on key themes that come up in Chapters 1 and 2: utopia, socialism, and democratizing the economy.

## Communism

Although Marx criticized utopianism, communism is often seen as the biggest attempt at a utopia. I will come back to communism in Chapter 4 but will outline it here as it provides a context for the economic and social alternative societies that I will be discussing in this chapter and the next.

Communism was a project to create an ideal society that has not yet existed. So, this fits with the definition of utopia I mentioned earlier: a good place that is not yet in existence. If capitalism is the society we live in now, then the most obvious alternative to look at is communism. Communism is about collective ownership of the economy, for the production and distribution of goods and services according to need, as opposed to private ownership for making private profit, which is what capitalism is about. With collective ownership, exploitation of workers by capitalist owners can be overcome, as we would all be the owners. Alienation from each other and our work would also be overcome, as we would now own and determine that collectively with our fellow humans. We would also be freer, because as a collective entity we would be in control of the economy that previously dominated over us. (For Marx's communism, see Marx and Engels, 1968; Evans, 1975; Marx, 1975; Levin, 1989.)

Marx believed that once the proletariat seized power from capitalists and concentrated it in their hands, it could gradually be dispersed to the people via a system of communes and collectives, replacing the state. The main class division in society, between workers and employers, would be abolished, as we would all be part of collective ownership without employer–worker divides between us. The state, as a site of ideological conflict between classes, would wither away, because there would be no classes to use it against one another, and no major ideological disputes along class lines to be fought over in the state. All that would remain would be an administrative machinery for planning for need. A very strong criticism of this is that it does not pay enough attention to conflict and power that happens in other less directly economic structures, like patriarchy and colonialism, through, for example, divisions of gender, ethnicity, nationalism, and sexuality (see powerful statements by Carmichael, 2018, on race and by Fanon, 2008, on colonialism).

Marx was not primarily interested in an equal distribution of things; he was mainly concerned with collective power over production, and then that could be used to decide on distribution. However, he did envisage that on the way to communism, distribution would go to people according to the labour they put in rather than according to power or market demand, as under capitalism. Then, as communism develops, people would contribute according to their ability and distribution would be done according to need. Not all people will need the same things, but you would imagine distribution according to need would be much more equal than the unequal distributions under capitalism. This raises a classic criticism of communism: if the distribution of goods, services, or income is not linked to the work you do, and you get these according to need, why should people work hard and come up with great innovative ideas in their job? You will get paid the same however you perform. So, there are likely to be incentives or motivation problems under communism.

One Marxist response might be to refer to the two-stage approach to a post-capitalist society envisaged. The first stage, where what you get is based on labour, would assume that people need reward to be willing to contribute. Then a more communist mentality could grow, where people would be ready for the second stage of 'full communism', based on need. The communist retort is that at this point, communism would have its own incentives system based around contribution to the collective good, people being not just individualistic but also altruistic in their motivations.

### Attempts at communism

In practice, societies that called themselves communist, from the Soviet Union to China and Cuba, and claimed to follow Marx did have state ownership and planning for some conception of what people needed – rather than just acting in response to market demand – reducing the role of private ownership and the market, and having perhaps greater economic, if not political, equality. But they had centralized states, dominated by communist parties, and the state penetrated society in a way we are not used to under capitalism, at least not to the same extent. There was an official ideology that determined the content of the media, education, art, and culture, and the suppression of religion and criticism. Surveillance was spread throughout society via systems of paid informants in the institutions of everyday life. You never knew who the spies were, and this created a climate of terror where dissent was inhibited through fear and repression. But as we shall see later, surveillance is also very intense in contemporary capitalism, in fact more extensive and detailed than anyone dreamt possible under state socialism (as pointed out by Véliz, 2019a, and Solnit, 2022), a lot of it done by private corporations seeking profit.

At first, planning had successes; but over time, problems with collecting the information needed to plan, reliably and without distortion, affected the efficiency of this economic approach. Although these societies had state ownership and planning, they never achieved genuine dispersed collective ownership or the disappearance of the state. After initial successes, they suffered from stagnation, perhaps due in part to the incentives problems mentioned earlier as well as the information ones. They were not free, as Marx had promised. Defenders of communism would say, rightly, that these were not communist societies. But the problems they had could be (if not inevitably be) what happens if, with the best intentions, you try to pursue communism.

Defenders of communism say these societies failed in their communist promise because of their lack of internationalization. Capitalist states were able to stay a major threat to them. Most communisms attempted socialism from peasant societies, so they skipped the capitalist stage that Marx said could provide the development of technology and the collective consciousness of the proletariat that can be preconditions for communism. Or they had socialism imposed on them, as in Eastern Europe after the Second World War, rather than it being created through revolution by the people. They were statist, not communist. Others would argue that communist theory cannot be absolved for what happened in practice. Communist societies had a minimal blueprint for communism, so it was easy for people like Stalin to claim they were being communist when they were not. The revolutions got stuck at the repressive transitional stage and did not disperse power more communally. Perhaps it was naïve of Marxist theory to believe the latter would happen. Communists were overconfident about communist incentives replacing individualist capitalist incentives. Without a new incentives system developing, there was economic stagnation. Collective information about needs became impossible to collect and was often distorted by corruption at different levels of the system. The result was that needs had to be decided top-down. Non-class divisions were not overcome.

## Assessing communism

I do not believe, like some on the Left, that you can look at so-called actual communism and say it had nothing to do with socialism or communism, and that we can just continue being socialist without paying attention to what went wrong with those attempts. Marx saw communism as a society where state power has dissolved, and that is very different to what actual communism was like. But actual communism did try to do planning for need, which is a communist aim, and state ownership on behalf of the people, which is one type of collective ownership. So, I do not think you can say that socialism can just carry on regardless, unaffected by learning from what happened in these societies. If we are interested in alternative societies, we need to look at what happened in such cases and see if we can learn from that. One lesson is that so-called communist societies got stuck at the statist, repressive transitional phase. Marx said we would have to go through such a stage to get to communism, to fight against attempts at counter-revolution and people trying to defend private property. But these so-called actual socialist societies got fixed at this stage. So, we need to consider whether this is the right means to alternative societies.

Also, Marx said it would help (if not be necessary) to go through capitalism for the preconditions for communism to be built. One of these is collective consciousness, which you need for a communist society to work. This can develop under capitalism, which creates a proletariat with a collective consciousness, and this sort of mutual, communistic sensibility can be the basis for a fully developed one under communism, where the loss of individualistic gain does not matter because people are motivated by altruistic social concern. Actual communism – in places like the Soviet Union, China, and Cuba, where there were revolutions – happened in peasant societies, not capitalist ones, so these societies had not gone through the capitalist stage. One of the problems that people like Che Guevara and Mao Zedong tried to address when they were building communist societies was that the required social consciousness had not come to fruition, and they were concerned about how to build that.

So, there are (at least) two lessons we can learn from actual communism if we are thinking about alternative societies. One is about non-authoritarian means for getting there. And another is about developing collective consciousness now and not leaving this to a later date when the alternative society exists (see Raekstad, 2018). Many of the alternatives I look at in this book provide possible means of addressing these issues.

One person who criticized communism was John Stuart Mill (1989). Usually seen as a liberal, Mill also wrote positively about socialism in his *Chapters on Socialism*. He was writing before communism had been tried in the Marxist sense. He said revolutionary communism was irresponsible and too confident in its infallibility in trying to create a whole new system that had not been tried and tested, and where its details are unknown. Marx quite openly said he was not going to lay out in detail what a communist society would look like, because that would depend on history and had to be collectively decided by people themselves. Mill favoured gradualist experimental socialism now, where you try it out here and there, and see how it works before attempting to implement it on a whole-society scale. And he favoured a pluralist society with private property rights alongside other forms. What Mill said is relevant to some of what I am going to say in this chapter and later in the book. (See also Calnitsky, 2022, who argues that the risk involved in revolution will lead people to prefer reform.)

So, I have raised the issues of utopianism and communism, and I will return to these in later parts of this book. Following from what Mill said, I want to identify, in this chapter and the next, types of alternative society you can find within capitalism, so forms of utopia now, or empirical utopias. I wish to look at ones that are practical and feasible, despite being utopian. In the next chapter, I will focus on social alternatives, and in this one, alternative economies. Some approaches that seem to me to be key in planning for an alternative society will be discussed in more depth in subsequent chapters.

## Co-operatives

If there have been problems of communism on a society-wide scale, can it be pursued at a micro level, more experimentally, from within capitalism, on a basis of trial and error to see what works and how to overcome problems, and in a less top-down repressive way? There are lots of kinds of co-op, such as consumer co-ops, community co-ops, housing co-ops, and credit unions (see Cutcher and Mason, 2018, on credit unions; there are more references on other types of co-op later). In each case, the members own and control their enterprise. One of the most interesting types is worker co-ops (see Ness and Azzelini, 2011, on workers' control and Webb and Cheney, 2018, on worker co-ops). This is where businesses are owned collectively by workers. I have raised communism as collective ownership, and co-ops are collective ownership on a smaller scale at the company level.

People who get into co-ops do not necessarily do so for very ideological reasons. Some do it because they believe in co-operation. But when people are asked what got them involved, some say they had a terrible job and they wanted out of it so they started a co-op. This is a human well-being issue, and I have indicated human needs as a positive goal. Others say they had a horrible boss and they wanted collective self-determination. I have highlighted self-determination as an objective. I have also mentioned that Castells says opting for alternative cultures can come through choice or necessity, and there are some examples where it comes more out of necessity (as Kasparian, 2022, outlines in relation to Argentinian co-ops).

A key concern of co-ops is that the business is run in the interests of its members, such as workers and consumers, not external shareholders. As such, decisions can be made that are not about maximizing profits, but other goals. Many co-ops are, nevertheless, profit-making. Key values of co-ops are: democracy – members own and control them; equality – there is no longer a division between owners and workers, at least in the case of worker co-ops, and the possibility exists for income to be shared more evenly rather than accumulated disproportionately by some; and solidarity and community – co-ops are run collectively rather than by one group employing another. Some hope that such values will be strong enough in co-ops that they will spill over into wider society, spreading norms and practices of democracy, equality, and community (on the spillover thesis, see Carter, 2006).

Co-ops can have many benefits (Sutton, 2019, provides a concise summary). If you collectively own the business, then alienation from each other and your work should go, as should exploitation by the bosses, as you become the boss together; as I discussed earlier, this should also be the case in society-wide communism. People can have self-ownership because they are not owned during working hours by an employer, and consequently they are empowered. Employees have the power to make their work more meaningful, fair, equal, and ethical, and to ensure better pay and conditions. They can share responsibility with fellow owners, rather than the burden being carried on fewer shoulders. Collective ownership could enhance commitment to the company because as a co-owner, you believe more in the project you are involved in.

But co-ops face challenges (Cornforth et al, 1988, discuss how to overcome these). What problems they experience can depend on the co-op type (see Cornforth, 1983). Defensive co-ops, set up when a business is about to go under and the workers take it on from the employers, start with economic problems and so are likely to continue to have them. The main motivation is saving the business, rather than democratic ownership, so the democratic side may suffer too. Alternative co-ops (see, for example, Zaunseder, 2022, on radical Scottish co-ops) that are set up more with an ideological commitment to shared ownership do better in making the democracy work, because that is a priority from the start. They may not be hugely profitable economically, but that need not matter, because making big profits is not usually their main aim (Kasparian, 2022).

Members of co-ops may not initially have great business and management skills. Workplace democracy can be beset by conflict and slowness, as members must work through decisions collectively before they can be agreed on. Slow decision-making disadvantages co-ops against fast-moving and dynamic private companies where the boss can make a decision without having to agree it with everyone. To compete with capitalist companies, co-ops can adopt more top-down management or less co-operative decision-making. But then they lose some of their co-operative character. If they employ people from outside the co-op, albeit treating them better than a more capitalist organization might, then the co-operatives become employers and so, to some degree, capitalist (unless such employees then become members, which can be the case). If they do not go down this road, they stay more co-operative but may suffer in capitalist competition. If they are less competitive in capitalist terms because they stress co-operation, their income may be lower, and wages and conditions might suffer. Some studies show that co-operative values inside the co-op are affected by the outside world: in individualist and competitive societies, wider values may damage the co-operative and egalitarian ethos of co-ops. Co-ops adopt a business mentality (Greenberg, 1981; Masquelier, 2017a). But co-ops can be more efficient than other types of enterprise because of factors like greater commitment and co-operative teamwork (Arando et al, 2015). And, contrary to the criticism that co-ops are forced to become capitalist, they can resist capitalist profiteering priorities and still survive and be successful (Kasparian, 2022).

Certain factors can affect internal democracy in co-ops (Greenberg, 1983; Carter, 2006). Larger co-operatives find it harder to make participatory structures work because of the numbers involved, and some have to adopt more representative forms. Formal structures for participatory democracy are not necessarily accompanied by actual participation: some members may skip the meetings and let others make the decisions. A famous thesis about co-ops is the degeneration thesis (Cornforth, 1995). This suggests that to succeed, all organizations must adopt centralization in the face of external market pressures. If they do not, they will fail. This does sometimes happen, but co-ops can use democratic participation, democratic and egalitarian values, contestation, critique, and discussion to respond to degeneration. They can regenerate – for instance, by retraining in their co-operative and democratic ethos and orienting back to this. Another way is adopting centralization that retains co-operative aims and control over leaders – for instance, by rotating the higher management roles and making sure they stay democratically accountable (Noorani et al, 2013; Langmead, 2016; Diefenbach, 2019; also Kasparian, 2022, in a study of Argentinian co-ops, discusses how they have both oligarchic and democratizing tendencies at the same time).

For Gradin (2015), co-ops are non-capitalist in their departure from private ownership, profit, and competition. She argues that even where there are profit and competition aspects, these can be overridden by non-profit dimensions (through surplus sharing and income caps) and co-operative characteristics (through co-operation and sharing between co-ops). I will come back through the book to wider collective ownership and whether non-capitalist alternatives in capitalism, like co-ops, can lead to change towards alternative societies. For now, it is noted that contributors like Jervis (2022) make the case that co-ops in capitalism can be socialist and part of transition to socialism. Despite the scepticism of some Marxists about co-ops (for instance, Mandel, 1975), Marx and Lenin, as part of their nuanced views on this subject, said the same as Jervis, if co-ops are part of a wider political movement, rather than atomized and competitive (see Elliott, 1987; Egan, 1990; Jossa, 2005, 2014, 2017; Sharzer, 2017; Ji, 2020). This type of combination has been the case in practice in the co-operative movement. Civil society activists, individually and collectively, are often also political. This mix is argued for more generally in this book and pursued in the US case I turn to very shortly.

Sutton's (2019) survey of 'cooperative cities' in the US looks at how municipal government supports the growth of co-ops through measures such as legislation and budget initiatives. She categorizes approaches into three types of interaction between politics and civil society. First, 'developer' cities like Cleveland and Preston, which I discuss in Chapter 5, take a proactive, top-down catalytic approach, often because co-ops are not very developed in their area to start with. Second, 'endorser' cities have a more enabling and validating approach in response to bottom-up pressure, sometimes because there is already a co-operative ecosystem locally. Third, 'cultivator' cities mix active top-down and reactive bottom-up approaches, with the grassroots leading the way and local government taking the role of strengthening and expanding. I will be discussing municipalism throughout this book, and an initiative that facilitates co-operatives is discussed next.

## Cooperation Jackson

Cooperation Jackson is an ambitious initiative in Jackson, Mississippi, US, a city that has a poor and 80 per cent Black population in the Blackest and poorest state in the US (their website, cooperationjackson.org, is a good resource for what they are about; also see Akuno, 2017). Launched in 2014, it aims to build co-operatives and a solidarity economy, inspired by Black collectivism and self-defence and survival programmes, and by co-operative networks like those in Mondragon in Spain and those in the Emilia Romagna region in Italy. This economy would be based on self-management, self-determination and economic democracy, universal access to common resources, co-operation, sharing, social responsibility, sustainability, and social justice, rather than competition and profit. Cooperation Jackson's foci are addressing exploitation, racial inequalities, poverty, and ecological crisis.

Part of the work of Cooperation Jackson is the formation of co-ops; these include Freedom Farms (growing organic vegetables), the Green Team Landscaping (for gardening and composting), a café and catering co-operative (designed to fight obesity and diabetes), and the Center for Community Production (for 3D printing). It is planned to have a network of co-operatives, a co-operative incubator, a co-operative education and training centre, a co-operative bank or financial institution, and an eco-village on a community land trust (CLT) – all making up the basis for a solidarity economy separate from the capitalist economy, reducing racial inequality. The aim is that self-organizing and the growth of self-management can be the basis for wider democratization of the economy.

From 2008, Cooperation Jackson members started to purchase land, which was put into a CLT. They aim to use this to build affordable housing with locally sourced materials – with ecological crisis also being a key concern of the project, the co-ops aim for local production to reduce carbon emissions. The housing will be accompanied by compost toilets, solar panels, and grey water recycling, purchased through time banking and labour input. Some houses have been built on one street. Many in Jackson cannot afford even low-income housing. So, CLTs remove land from the market to avoid property speculation, which inflates prices. CLTs are run on a collective non-profit basis, and property built on the land must conform to the land trusts' rules, which keep property affordable.

A wider Jackson-Kush Plan is emerging from the Malcolm X Grassroots Movement and the Jackson People's Assembly, aiming for participatory democracy, an alternative economy, and sustainable development alongside political participation (Akuno and Nangwaya, 2017). The plan is to establish people's assemblies, political candidates, and a solidarity economy – the latter is where Cooperation Jackson fits in. It has a dual power and an in-and-against-the-state approach that fits with the emphasis of this book against polarizations and dichotomies between different approaches to change.

## Participatory economics

There is a website and set of books associated with what is called 'parecon', a project for participatory economics (see, among many other sources, Albert, 2003, 2006, 2012; Albert and Spannos, 2006). Following what I have discussed about communism and co-ops, supporters of parecon fill in details and add more to what a co-operative democratic economy could look like. I will outline these here and then come back to other proposals for democratizing the economy in Chapter 5, devoting all of that chapter to this topic. Parecon advocates lay down some key principles for a participatory economy. First, on the self-management of companies, which is what co-ops are about, they argue that people should influence business decisions in proportion to the extent that they are affected by what a company does. So, we must work out who is affected and how much in each case, and then allocate votes accordingly. This means all affected interests (see also Devine, 1988) have a say – not just single groups like workers or consumers or the local community – and influence should be proportionate to how affected you are.

Second, remuneration to individuals should not be based on power, property, or output, as in capitalist economics. People should be paid, in part, according to need, as under communism. But pay should also consider how long and hard people work and how onerous the work is, so adding some moral recognition for hard and responsible work and keeping more of the sort of incentives system that people say communism lacks. Parecon supporters also argue that people should be paid more for socially useful work. These criteria introduce more incentives but also a bit more of a complex moral basis for pay than just need. If you work hard or do useful work, you get paid more.

Third, parecon advocates say jobs are currently split, with 20 per cent involving skills, increasing knowledge and confidence, and empowering people in decision-making, while the other 80 per cent are disempowering. The latter fragment workers from each other and from decisions. Work activity can be repetitive and lead to a decline in skills, knowledge, and confidence. Parecon supporters say this divide should be replaced with 'balanced job complexes' where people do what they are expert at but everyone does a mix of tasks, so all are more equally empowered. This avoids a split into two classes and so leads to classlessness. The proposal relates to a critique of the division of labour that Marx gave. He argued that people should do a variety of jobs and have more time off from work so that more of the activities they pursue are outside paid work – something I will come back to later.

Fourth, advocates of parecon say that decisions about the economy can be done through either the market, planning, or self-regulation. They propose collective self-regulation, where worker and consumer councils make proposals about matters such as production, inputs, outputs, and prices. These include social costs and benefits, not just economic considerations, in decision-making. Workers and consumer councils negotiate their respective proposals, refine them, and come up with agreements in a process that will produce solidarity among actors in the economy.

## Critique of parecon

Some criticisms have been made of parecon from a more anarchist perspective (see a debate in Evans and Kay, 2009). First, it is argued that co-ops cannot out-accumulate capitalist companies. They are under pressure to compete with capitalist firms and so take measures such as cutting costs, which means they have to compromise on some principles. Conditions of workers in co-ops are, it is argued, sometimes worse than in capitalist companies. This may be in part because the class conflict in capitalist companies gets results and co-ops may be less dynamic economically. So, maybe a better approach is class struggle in capitalist companies, rather than opting out for co-ops.

Second, democratizing work is desirable, but this accepts that work exists. There should be abolition of work – not of productive activity, but of work as a different category. So, say my street needs regular cleaning. Currently, a street cleaner is employed to do this, and it is her job. However, the members of my street could take up cleaning it as a communal activity, just as something that needs doing. We could set up a rota and take it in turns to do it, or we could all come out once a week and clean the street together. The task needs to be carried out and still gets accomplished, but it is done as part of our lives and not as a separate activity. It is merged into the rest of our lives as a collective task and something we do for free because it must be done for ourselves, self-provisioning and do-it-yourself (DIY), not a distinct activity for money. This fits with the view that work should be abolished.

A third criticism is that the remuneration system proposed by advocates of parecon should be abolished. If you need wages to provide incentives to work, then there is something wrong with work. It cannot be very appealing if you require money to reward and motivate people. Changing the basis of remuneration, as parecon proposes, does not change this basic situation. One function of wages is as rationing in response to scarcity. There are not enough goods and services to go around for everyone. So, we are given a certain amount of money so we can decide what to buy and what not to. However, there are alternatives to this form of rationing. One is production for need.

This also eliminates waste, because you only produce what is needed and do not overproduce things that people do not end up buying. There could be needs testing and distribution based on that. Another is distribution on the basis of first come, first served. A third possibility is equal shares for all, and a fourth is a lottery to decide who gets more luxury things. If we do not pay people for a separate category of work but collectively self-provision, and if we get rid of remuneration for work and ration by allocation, then money is no longer necessary and can be abolished.

Fourth, and connected to this, a criticism of parecon is that the participatory planning system advocated is too complex and just would not work. An alternative is distribution not by push but by pull; this responds to consumption, with production done according to what is consumed, limited by the maximum output that is possible in the time available. If pull factors change, then workers can be reallocated from one sector to another. This is giving people what they want, limited by what can be produced.

## Leaders and participatory democracy: five cases

In this section, I will put participatory economics into a wider context, discussing concrete cases of participatory democracy internationally. In line with my argument in this book against polarizing approaches, these cases involve combinations of leadership and diffusion of power. They include participatory with common democracy. There are parallels between the cases of localist communal democracy discussed in this section and that of Rojava in Syria, which I will return to later in this chapter, as well as the Cooperation Jackson project in the US, discussed previously.

### Participatory budgeting

Participatory economics has been pursued in participatory budgeting (PB), initiated in the Brazilian city of Porto Alegre, subsequently spreading around the world (for a condensed overview, see Wampler et al, 2017a, 2017b, 2017c). It involves, as with other examples outlined in this book, party or state politics and greater citizen participation working together. So, there is not an opposition between state and popular participation; rather, both are combined. The Workers' Party (Partido dos Trabalhadores) in Brazil initiated PB in Porto Alegre in the 1980s, based on the idea that electoral democracy is not the whole of democracy but can be the start of its wider expansion. Governments incorporate citizens into decision-making about the allocation of budgets, making this more open to democratic control by people and taking more account of information on the ground.

The usual approach is that in different districts of a municipality representatives work with government officials on the budget. Citizens make proposals on different budget areas, and these are fed in to the process. Then citizens are involved in deliberative discussions with representatives to decide on the budget. The budget is subsequently voted on by the public. This is often an annual process. So, rather than the government just deciding on a city budget, there is much greater popular involvement.

After being introduced in Porto Alegre, PB spread across municipalities in South America, the more mainstream non-governmental organization (NGO) world, and Africa, Europe, and North America. It has expanded from mainly municipal to national levels. Information technology and online voting help the process work on a larger scale. Of course, the form PB takes varies a lot according to local contexts and factors such as government support, the strength of civil society, and resources.

Research suggests that PB may lead, unsurprisingly, to greater accountability to people, who are more able to make demands leading to greater sensitivity to the people by government. It can empower poorer people, women, and people of colour, who tend to be more excluded from elite decision-making, so leading to greater political equality but also economic equality as their interests are taken into account more. So, it has both democratic and social gains. It provides fora where people learn through material practice about deliberation and government, giving them a better understanding of politics; in doing so, they gain greater political confidence. It gives people greater belief in political parties that support this approach and are willing to hand over power to citizens, and more faith in party and state politics in general and increased confidence in the possibility of effective government. So, it benefits both popular democracy and party and state democracy. There is greater transparency of politics and people have more political knowledge, both of which lead to better oversight by citizens of government. Civil society tends to flourish with more groups and activities and partnerships with governments.

PB has led to resources being channelled to poorer areas and health, education, and sanitation. It involves budgeting that is more sensitive to needs on the ground, so there is better government, and social outcomes are more responsive to marginalized communities – and, as such, facilitative of greater social justice. In Brazil, at least, research suggests that PB has led to improvements in these areas, especially for the poor.

## Barcelona en Comú

In the vein of participatory democracy, the Guanyem (let's win) process has spread across Spain, a key centre being Barcelona en Comú (Barcelona in Common), an attempt at a movement party, with electoral power combined with popular democracy. Barcelona en Comú originated in part from the Indignados anti-austerity protests in Spain, which led to wider Occupy and anti-austerity bottom-up protests internationally. One view was that the movement should continue to seek electoral power while retaining its roots in social movements and radical democracy. The political party Podemos in Spain was another response to similar bases. Ada Colau won the mayoralty of Barcelona with Barcelona en Comú in 2015. Barcelona en Comú created a code of political ethics through participatory means using two days of open debate and an online platform. Assemblies covering different neighbourhoods and themes are used to allow municipal input from below into policy. Emerging position papers are then negotiated with other parties. Neighbourhoods and local assemblies are key for developing analyses, feedback, and proposals based on on-the-ground knowledge and bottom-up input on needs. This involves bringing together what are sometimes seen as contradictory or in tension, local participation and the state, and the smaller and larger scales, all within the aim of taking back control for the people of the municipality. There is co-production and co-responsibility in decision-making, which requires dialogue and consensus.

Thompson (2021) sees Barcelona and other cases discussed in this book as types of 'new municipalism', transnationally networked, urban based, political but beyond the nation-state, and countering neoliberalism. He distinguishes between platform municipalism (Barcelona), autonomist municipalism (Rojava, discussed later in this chapter, and Cooperation Jackson, outlined previously) and managed municipalism (Preston, discussed in Chapter 5). Of course, these are conceptual distinctions and different municipalisms show aspects of more than one of these forms. Platform cases like Barcelona are social movement driven, urban based, and act in, against, and beyond the state. They involve participatory assembly democracy using socialized digital platforms. Autonomist municipalism in places like Rojava and Jackson are also social movement driven, with democratic eco-socialist and libertarian approaches, but also oriented to political institutions. They encompass confederalist self-governing co-ops, anarchist, feminist, and anti-racist inputs, and an emphasis on social reproduction (on the latter, see the discussion of concrete utopias in Chapter 2). Managed municipalism (for example, in Preston) is more politically managed, about economic regeneration, co-ops, rooted in municipal socialism, and focused on localized supply chains.

## Fatsa

A less well known experiment in local participatory democracy occurred in the Turkish city of Fatsa in 1979–80 (see Eliçin, 2011; Acaroğlu, 2019). Fatsa is a small town in the Black Sea area of Turkey. In the October 1979 local elections, Fikri Sönmez, known as 'Fikri the tailor', supported by the Revolutionary Path, was elected mayor. He introduced direct democracy in the town through neighbourhood committees and neighbourhood meetings. The aim was to be more responsive to popular preferences and, as with PB, for local government and citizens to work together with a sense of commonality. As with the example of Marinaleda, to be outlined shortly, a charismatic leader – the mayor in both these cases – was key to the initiative. In such instances, leadership and popular democracy work together rather than in opposition.

Sönmez divided the seven neighbourhoods of Fatsa into 11 sub-neighbourhoods, with a committee for each and large assembly-like meetings of citizens of the neighbourhoods. There was a high level of participation in such meetings. Here, the municipality presented work programmes, open for discussion by citizens. Financial accounts were also presented at the meetings. The decisions of the committees were taken on by the municipal council. Numerous other issues were brought to the committees, to do with personal and property disputes, family issues, drugs, gambling, and so on. They worked to resolve the disputes, and there was an emphasis on greater participation by women, gender equality, and tackling violence against women. Stockpiles of goods for the underground market were seized by the municipality and sold to the people. The distribution of hazelnut shells, used for heating, was taken over from private families, who had trapped workers in debt, and carried out by the municipality. The committees were charged with distributing these more fairly. Roads in Fatsa were drenched in mud, with sanitation and health problems resulting. Experts said that dealing with this would be a long and expensive process, so Sönmez consulted with the community on the issue. The municipality took over the problem and tackled it through a common participatory process. Surrounding neighbourhoods and municipalities were asked to help, and in a short period the mud was cleared by ordinary citizens taking it on themselves, with visiting supporters being housed in the homes of Fatsa residents. The public meetings also advanced the idea of a popular cultural festival, which was held with great success.

Fraternity and a commitment to common work and mutual benevolence were important to the initiatives, together with mutual trust and belief in the government. At the same time, as a result of the municipal government's participatory policies, the hegemony of the state was reduced in favour of popular participation and self-governance. Democratic participation and deliberation were thrown open, and accountability and transparency increased. Political leadership and popular democracy worked together rather than being opposed. The initiative, however, was seen from above as a threat, and in July 1980, just months after Sönmez's election, the military moved in and brought it to an end. Sönmez was imprisoned and died in jail five years later while only in his forties.

## Marinaleda

In Marinaleda, a small village in Spain, another charismatic mayor, Juan Manuel Sánchez Gordillo, has overseen a combination of political leadership with participatory democracy and local collectivism, labelled a communist utopia (see Hancox, 2013). Changes in Marinaleda grew out of a situation of poverty and landlessness in the 1970s. Characterizing himself as effectively an anarchist kind of communist, Sánchez Gordillo, a schoolteacher, was elected mayor in 1979 (the same year as Sönmez in Fatsa). Decades later he was still being re-elected. A campaign to gain ownership of uncultivated land belonging to a local landowner, through means such as occupying the land and holding strikes, led eventually to the regional government handing the land over to the village. Now, rather than being run for efficiency and profit, the land is run co-operatively and cultivated using crops that require intensive labour, so creating employment. The village created a processing factory for the farm's output, further increasing employment. Surplus from the village co-operative is not taken as profits but reinvested, and everyone in the co-op earns the same salary. The village holds general assemblies, open to all. These make decisions by direct democracy.

This is not only not top-down communism, because of its participatory co-operative democracy, but also liberal communism that permits small-scale private ownership (for instance, of several local cafés and bars) and many people to work outside the co-operative (for example, in schools and social work). In this book, I argue for such a pluralist approach to socialism. There is substantial government-owned housing: 350 houses in a town of 2,500 people. The government provides the building materials if citizens participate in the construction of the houses, so there are reductions in the cost of the house in return for their time. The mortgage is very low – about 15 euros a month – and to avoid property speculation, the house cannot be sold, though it can be passed on to children. On Sundays, residents carry out voluntary work for the community – for instance, repairs, cleaning, and painting. Unemployment is lower than in the rest of Spain because of the commitment to employment, and many of the facilities, housing, and more are cheap or free. Marinaleda has its own TV and radio channels. There are no municipal police.

## The Zapatistas and Chiapas

Perhaps the best known of the cases I am discussing in this section is that of Chiapas, a poor state in Mexico with a large Indigenous population. On 1 January 1994, the day Mexico joined the North American Free Trade Organization, the Zapatista Army of National Liberation (Ejercito Zapatista Liberacion Nacional, EZLN) initiated an uprising in the Chiapas region.

The EZLN were the armed wing of Chiapas Indigenous communities seeking autonomy from the Mexican government, which was seen to be taking their land, extracting natural resources, urbanizing the population, and undermining local agriculture through free trade agreements. The uprising was short-lived and pushed back by the Mexican army. However, there ensued an initiative in autonomous, bottom-up, democratic self-organizing, independent of the national state, across justice, healthcare, education, and the co-operative economy, in expanding territories of the state of Chiapas (Forbis and Brenner, 2014; Gottesdiener, 2014; Briy, 2020). The Chiapas system is based on the principle of leading by obeying. There are political leaders, but they make decisions not as representatives, rather as delegates expressing the wishes of the community. Leaders are chosen based on Indigenous traditions of serving the community; they are unremunerated, and their mandate can be revoked if they are seen to fail to fulfil this obligation. Another key principle is the refusal of outside aid from the government, or even some international organizations, with the Zapatistas instead providing justice, education, healthcare, and production. The Zapatistas have resisted accommodations with centre-Left politicians.

Assemblies in Chiapas exist at the village level. The assemblies elect delegates to municipal councils. Then, on a regional level, municipalities are represented on councils. At this top tier, members serve for a total of three years on a rotating basis, in terms as short as a few weeks. Decisions at higher levels are put out to consultation with the community and municipalities. The emphasis is on consensus decision-making. The EZLN exists in parallel to the three levels of autonomous democracy, giving political direction, so there is a mix of direct democracy with political leadership. The EZLN is a hierarchical organization, but its highest body is made up of civilians elected by assemblies, and its role in community affairs is limited, to ensure democratic self-governance. Some communities are Zapatista and some a mix of Zapatista and non-Zapatista. In the latter, autonomous services are open to all. There is a law protecting women's rights in the guiding principles of the Chiapas autonomous communities, with women strongly involved in all areas and levels. Feminism feeds into the Zapatista/Chiapas system alongside other influences from the peasant leader Emiliano Zapata, from whom the movement gets its name; these influences are anti-capitalism and Marxism, anti-globalization, anarchism, direct democracy, decolonial perspectives, and Indigenous traditions (see Hopewell, 2018; Klein, 2019).

Economically, there are co-operatives and land collectives, whose income funds autonomous services in education and health. To provide opportunities, confidence, and participation for women, some collectives are women-only. The aim is to achieve economic self-sufficiency and equality. Alongside collective production, there is openness to family and individual enterprise, in line with my argument later for pluralist collectivist socialism.

Banks make low-interest loans to members for collective projects. Agriculture free from pesticides and genetic modification is practised.

Education is based in the community, with schools autonomous from the state and run by 'education promoters', mainly local youth who teach. They are unpaid, and while they work in education they may be assisted by other members farming their fields. They are under the authority of education committees elected by a local assembly, drawing on the expertise of solidarity groups, NGOs, and the local population. The community plays a role in shaping the curriculum, an element of which is preserving local traditions and knowledge. Classes are taught in Spanish and Indigenous languages, and they cover governance, self-sufficiency and autonomy, history, agroecology, veterinary medicine, and skills in areas such as electrical work and crafts. Similarly, the Zapatistas have their own health system, assisted by non-Zapatista experts, with local, trained, voluntary health promoters providing basic healthcare. More advanced care is available in higher-level clinics. Health committees exist at each tier, and communities participate in them.

The Zapatista justice system is based on restorative rather than punitive justice, an approach often rooted in Indigenous practices. This is used in many other places internationally and discussed in more detail in the next chapter. It is free, conducted in Indigenous languages, and based on finding a compromise that works for all parties. At the lowest level, less serious disputes are resolved by elected authorities or the communal assembly, based on customary practice. There is mediation to find compromises, in contrast to adversarial, penal, and retributive approaches. If things cannot be sorted out here, they go up to the municipal tier and are dealt with by an elected justice commission. Sentences usually involve community service or a fine. Prison sentences are often not more than a few days and are served in a room accessible to visitors. Issues concerning women and domestic disputes are dealt with by women on the commission. The highest council level deals with justice issues involving non-Zapatistas or other political or government authorities (covering, for instance, disputes over land) and is accessible to non-Zapatistas with grievances. The police are elected and unpaid, and members do not serve permanently; they are unarmed and do not wear a uniform. Communities have their own police.

There are, of course, challenges, such as ongoing patriarchy, enduring inequalities, and poverty, as well as people leaving, tempted by incentives offered by the state to undermine the Chiapas projects. But the system is built on bottom-up democracy and participation, communal justice, co-operation, and the pursuit of community well-being over profit and individualism. The experiment attempts to provide a self-organized, autonomous alternative to the state. The Zapatistas are outward-looking. In the early days, they made imaginative use of the emerging internet to make their case outside their community, and they spread the word by accepting visitors and researchers, and hosting conferences. They tour internationally to explain their project, learn from other experiences, and build alliances (Castillo, 2021; Vidal, 2021; for anti-colonial ideas for alternatives inspired by the Zapatistas, see Gahman et al, 2022).

## Less paid work

I have mentioned the possibility of abolishing work (see New Economics Foundation, 2010, Spencer, 2014, and Bregman, 2017, on society with less work). Rich societies have high consumption and production to produce profit. They fetishize work, seeing it as noble, and refer to people who do not work as idle and workshy. But this leads to long hours of labour. In rich countries, this is especially the case in states like Japan, the UK, and the US. The distinction between paid work and unpaid work is not an eternal one. Historically, families and communities have had tasks that needed doing and they have done them; these tasks range from raising children to growing and harvesting crops, making craft goods, and cooking and eating. These have all been part of sustaining life and livelihoods, without there being such a clear a distinction as we have now between one sphere of life – paid work – and another, between home and another place that we go to work for pay. In contemporary societies, people work long hours, even if the hours have been coming down in some places. Life is dominated by labour – for many people, more than 50 hours a week (UK further and higher education staff report working 50 hours a week, including two days unpaid overtime; UCU, 2022) – with the spare time outside work spent on recovery and renewal, so still defined by work. This is the case internationally, and in poorer classes and countries the pressure is higher and added to by greater necessity. In post-industrial society, it can be difficult to escape from work, because it invades home time through information technology (like email and social media). At the same time, there are inequalities between work-rich and work-poor families, so while many work a lot, others do not have enough work.

Work has positive meanings and functions for people. It brings income, economic independence (especially for women), structure and purpose, social ties, recognition and self-worth, identity, and fulfilment. But it also brings problems. Some of us say we like our jobs, but when asked to keep a diary of how we feel about them throughout the working day, we are often negative: well-being at work in the moment is not always the same as well-being at work as perceived overall when standing back (Bryson and McKerron, 2013). Work can bring stress and reduce time to do other things, and it can be pointless (Graeber, 2018), a means to an end rather than an end itself, and based on economic compulsion in that we have no choice but to do it. At work we experience domination, control, and loss of autonomy and human capacities, and as Marxists have said, work under capitalism involves exploitation and alienation. One study on work and depression suggests that the boss, not workload, is the problem. Of all the things we could dislike about work – pay, conditions, hours, load, and so on – it is low levels of control that have the most crucial effect on health and well-being (Sjøgren, 2013).

One way of dealing with problems of paid work – and this is a big theme of this book – is to bring it back under democratic collective control. So, we get rid of that boss and become, ourselves collectively, the employer. But another way is to question work itself and to abolish or at least reduce it. Greens and anarchists have often seen the merits in reducing working time. The Left has had an ambiguous relationship with work. Sometimes they see it as honourable and the path to collective identity, pay, and security. Yet socialists have also fought to reduce the length of the working week, and one of the great victories of trade unions has been (for some) the weekend. While Marx saw collective ownership as a way of overcoming alienation and exploitation at work, he also saw the reduction of working time and more free and autonomous time as a goal for communism.

Marx saw technology as leading to the possibility of less work: machines could do the work people used to do and so reduce their working week (see also Bastani, 2020). He was for de-alienation in the realm of necessity – meaning work – but also de-alienation through increasing the realm of freedom, away from paid work. The economist John Maynard Keynes and the philosopher Bertrand Russell also saw technology as leading to less employment, maybe not in a good way in the case of involuntary unemployment, but more positively if work can be willingly reduced. Technology has been used to raise production and so profits, but it could be used to sustain production at steady (or even reduced) levels while reducing working time. André Gorz (1982) was a Marxist who turned post-Marxist and bade 'farewell to the working class'. He was concerned with the interests and agency of non-workers, who, because they do not work, are not a class – class usually being defined by occupation; they are, then, a non-class of non-workers. They, he felt, have less of an investment in the system than the working class and so are more likely to be revolutionary agents. He argued for reducing work for all so that the unemployed could have work distributed to them, but *all* could work less and have greater freedom.

The reduction of working time intersects with a range of other issues: consumerism, ecology, time, freedom, equality, technology, well-being, culture, commodification, and welfare. We work to earn the income to consume, and for many people, consumption is a means through which they project their identity to others. Often the wants we have in consumption are artificially generated, created by advertising and consumer society, rather than essential. Satisfying those wants can be unsatisfying. Consumerism creates a division between those who are consumers and those who are excluded from consumption. It is linked to ecological problems and climate change because it involves resource depletion, pollution, trade, and transport to make and distribute goods. Ecological needs require a reduction in consumption and a less consumerist society. So, the reduction of work, and thus the income to consume, is connected to finding other sources of identity and satisfaction and a more ecological society.

Work is bound up in norms and expectations, so a society based on less work requires cultural change. With potentially less income and lower production, we would need to have more non-material values. We would need to have attractive alternative sources of identity to counter the very strong source of identity work gives many people. When asked what they 'do', most people give their job as the answer. We would need to attach more value to uncommodified work – things we do for each other outside the market and state for free, such as care, exchange, gifting, and providing skills – in a society where less of this is supplied through paid work. Ivan Illich, as will be discussed in the next chapter, says we are encouraged in many spheres to think that we must consume from institutions when we could just provide directly to each other. A non-work society requires success and achievement to be measured through criteria like well-being, autonomy, and creativity rather than productivity (for example, the gross domestic product measure many governments use as a sign of success). We would need to value idleness and free time and see doing nothing as a positive thing, not as a loss, waste, or stigma.

What do alternatives to paid work involve? The New Economics Foundation (2010) say that in the UK, the average number of hours people work, including the hours of part-time workers, is 21 a week. They propose this should be the norm rather than the average. Commodified work could be replaced by uncommodified work where we do things for each other just as part of life rather than as the separate category of work, like the street cleaning I mentioned previously. A non-work society would create more time for this. Non-work could provide time for greater well-being outside work, favouring alternative fulfilments and time for things like care, relationships, family, creative activities, political activities, community, and idleness. The website of the International Institute of Not Doing Much (slowdownnow. org) gives guidance. It is not updated very often. More time would allow us to grow and prepare our food – something that people found in COVID-19 lockdowns – with the personal and ecological benefits of this. Ironically, unemployment could be solved by less work because, as has been noted, people who work too much would labour less and their work could be redistributed to those who do not have it, nationally and globally. Retirement could be less of a sudden rupture. People often want to retire because of work stress, but retirement is a very big break involving loss of the benefits of work I have mentioned: income, structure, purpose, identity, social ties, recognition, and self-worth. In a society with lower working hours, people could labour less and redistribute work to the elderly, so everyone works part time but part-time work is extended later into life. This would also help lower pension costs, especially important in countries where the elderly as a proportion of the population is increasing.

A society with lower working hours can be good for the economy. It could decrease stress and increase productivity, a common view being that productivity decreases as the working day goes on. There have been many attempts at reducing work, including: three- or four-day weeks in times of economic crisis, such as after the financial crisis or during the oil crisis in the UK in the 1970s; a proposed four-day working week for post-COVID-19 economic recovery (Cowburn, 2020), trialled in the UK with 4 days' work for 5 days' pay (Kollewe, 2022); the reduction of the working week from 39 hours to 35 hours in the early 2000s in France; and several experiments in Sweden (Alderman, 2016; Savage, 2017) and Iceland (BBC, 2021), among other places. Not all of these have gone smoothly, but that provides a basis for learning from them to do it better.

A shorter working week could have implications for inequality and class. A society with less paid work could create greater equality between workers and non-workers if work is redistributed from those in work to the unemployed. It could give greater autonomy from the employer–employee relationship, a class-equalizing change. With work, and in turn consumption, cut back in the Global North, this could be redistributed to domestic companies in the Global South, boosting employment and consumption there, enhancing independence from rich-country consumer markets, and creating greater self-sufficiency and autonomy from rich-country producers aiming to exploit Global South workers. As we shall see later, some advocate Global South countries delinking from the Global North and from neoliberal globalization.

Turning to the impact on men and women, with decommodified work valued more, the care work carried out disproportionately by women could gain a greater value. Men working a short week would gain more time for childcare and domestic work, and women would get greater access to paid work vacated by men. Women have been quite successful at getting out of the private sphere and into the public sphere and paid work, although with great inequalities at work. But this has not been so reciprocated by men playing more of a role in the private and domestic sphere. However, in male–female relationships where women are paid less, they may consequently be the ones to work less in a low-work society, while better-paid men continue to work long hours, which would be a negative outcome. Furthermore, a study of people furloughed, and therefore off work temporarily, during a UK COVID-19 lockdown shows that gender equality in domestic work and childcare increased but the balance was generally still quite unequal, with women doing more, especially more domestic work (Zamberlan et al, 2021).

So, a 'less work' society has to go hand in hand with other structural changes, such as ending the gender pay gap. For both the Global South and gender inequality, there are no necessary outcomes, just potentialities that would have to be fought for to ensure a lower work and lower consumption Global North is not exploited for outcomes such as Global South sweatshops and increased gender disparity in work and non-work. Positive outcomes will not come without wider structural change to power relations and inequality (see the discussion on feminist utopias in Chapter 3).

How can we get to a low-work society? One much talked about means is a universal basic income (UBI; see Fitzpatrick, 1999). This is a popular idea across the political spectrum and has been making it from the margins of political debate to the mainstream. Under UBI, every adult would be paid a certain amount every week – not enough to live on but, in the context of this topic, enough to work less. This would be financed by tax (maybe on wealth and finance), redistribution, reductions in some welfare benefits and the bureaucracy to administer them (replaced by a simpler UBI system), and by cutting spending (such as military expenditure). A UBI would not be cheap but is perfectly affordable, as many studies have shown (see, for example, Lansley and Reed, 2019; Stirling and Arnold, 2019). Also, trials have not shown it to be an idea whose negatives rule it out. It would allow people to work fewer days if they wished.

UBI schemes have been trialled around the world – in Brazil, Canada, Finland, Iran, Kenya, Namibia, the US, and many other places. Where UBI schemes have been tried internationally, results have included greater happiness, health, school attendance, trust in social institutions, and reductions in crime (Samuel, 2020). In India, pilots of various types of UBI have been carried out at national and state levels. These often replaced subsidies with direct cash transfers, aimed at overcoming inefficiency and corruption in relation to the former. There have been positive results in terms of more trust in banking, improvements in housing and debt, more ability to spend on livestock, and opportunity for change of occupation from manual labour to farming or owning a small business. People have spent the income on farming, transport to school, health, education, and improved diet. The main focus here has not been on reducing work time, but the schemes seem to suggest that UBI can work and yield positive results (Mehta, 2019).

A decent living wage for work could have a similar effect to UBI. There can be tighter legal restrictions on maximum working hours. Jobs can be reduced by better opportunities for job-sharing, part-time work, and sabbaticals. In some areas, we could collectively self-provision – the street cleaning example again – so that paid work is not needed so much. We can encourage uncommodified labour and uncommodified free provision through means such as swapping, freecycling, and skills sharing. As mentioned, a big change in values will be needed, but utopian aims have been realized in practice before, as indicated previously. Those who could support this utopia include the excluded and precariat, people who already have only a partial involvement in the mainstream economy and can see the potential benefits, if underpinned by schemes such as a UBI, as well as the negatives of it.

There are possible problems with a low-work economy. Lower income may lead to increased poverty, although the unemployed may be better off if work is redistributed to them, and UBI, free collective self-provisioning, and a less materialistic society can offset the costs of lower income. Another potential problem is that people may just use the new free time to work overtime to earn more money. Also, restrictions on working hours may be seen as coercive. So, a cultural change to greater valuing of non-work and working hours limits will be important. Employers may resist because of the added costs – for instance, for doubled training where people job-share or work part time. And trade unions may be reluctant because of the loss of earnings for their members; though unions have fought for shorter working hours.

There are doubts too about the UBI. One concern is about the loss of incentive to do paid work, but that is less of a problem in this context, and the UBI will not pay enough to live off without paid work. Maybe the rich do not need to get a payment and the poor can get more to overcome some egalitarian doubts about the universal approach. Some say the benefits of the UBI are not clear, and the money could be spent better on social protection and universal basic services (Coote, 2019; Coote and Yazici, 2019). For some, the UBI is just a way of cutting welfare and replacing paid labour with unpaid work. Hogg (2022) says that the UBI can be used by the Right to undermine the welfare state and reduce workers' pay, this being topped up by the state. For him, the risk of this is too great, so the Left should instead pursue a better welfare state.

The UBI may increase dependency on the state and income within capitalism, whereas autonomous social reproduction provides autonomy (Dinerstein and Pitts, 2018 and 2021), although some argue that the UBI can also facilitate the latter. For the Global South, reduced demand from the Global North could impact economic development, but it also provides the opportunity to work less there, as everywhere else. Thompson (2022) sees positive possibilities in a UBI reducing poverty and providing a space for socially valuable activity beyond labour. But he argues it leaves in place basic structures of wealth and assets, and so of power and inequality, and therefore needs to be accompanied by democratization of ownership and control, something I discuss in Chapter 5. These are all genuine problems but not inherent ones. And many of the problems have potential solutions, so they should be treated as challenges rather than reasons to abandon the idea of UBI.

## Slow society

The idea of a society with less paid work relates to the concept of a slow society (for an advocacy of slow, see Honoré, 2004). With less paid work, we can take more time over non-work activity and pursue it with greater depth and at a more sedate pace, leading to a better quality of life. People go fast because technology allows us to. The pressure of work pushes us into speed. Capitalism does this in the pursuit of profit; consequently, going slow is one form of resistance used by workers. 'Slow' can even be a taboo or stigma. If you say someone is slow at work or as a person, it is usually a negative thing, as I have mentioned idleness is sometimes seen to be. Also, speed can be exciting. We may go fast because we want it all and we must do a lot quickly to get that. There may be a psychological aspect of fear of dwelling on things. So, there are personal and individual dimensions to speeding on.

There are different kinds of slow. It has its origins in the Italian slow food movement, which was a reaction to McDonaldization and fast food (Andrews, 2008; for a critique, see Simonetti, 2012). Rather than rushing into a McDonald's and getting a prepaid meal, eating it, and getting out within minutes, slow food involves taking time and being involved from the start of the process, even back to the point where the food is grown and picked in your garden or allotment, for example. We eat slowly and make the meal as a long process and an end, rather than as a means to an end and something to be got done. Often slow food is more natural and organic, rather than mass produced. If the food is grown and picked by the consumer, it can be local and regional rather than globalized food, with the environmental benefits of this (such as cutting the carbon emissions from food trade and transportation) and enabling the preservation of food diversity, as opposed to the global homogenization of food.

Slow has become generalized to other areas. Some people wish to spend more time parenting and with their children and family, doing it properly rather than rushing through the process (Honoré, 2008). They want a slower schedule for kids with fewer activities that must be done by them. This often involves what I have been talking about: less paid work to make time for it – and maybe fewer hours at school too. So, it may include fewer working hours, downshifting, and working more slowly, some of which can be regarded quizzically by our workplace colleagues if we choose to go down that road. One way to achieve slower work is by having more control over it, and a key concern of this book, democratic ownership and control over work (for instance, in co-ops), is a way of pursuing this.

There is slow transport, where people walk, get public transport, or cycle rather than take the car. The irony is that these slower means sometimes get you to places faster because of clogged-up traffic lanes used by cars. With slow transport, you see more, and it is often better for health and the environment. There can be slow cities. Big cities contain so many people that the volume and pace are rapid and people become blasé – they cannot respond intensely to everyone they meet – and stressed (Simmel, 1976). Crocodile Dundee, when visiting New York City, tried to greet residents this way, as if he was in his small Australian outback home. Slow fashion has parallels with slow food. It is against mass production and for local craft production, making clothes, and fixing and reusing them, rather than discarding items when worn or torn. So, there is a green dimension to slow.

There can be slow democracy (Clark and Teachout, 2012, 2013). What is sometimes called deliberative or dialogical democracy, where everyone is involved in deliberating and dialogue over decisions, takes time and is slower than nondemocratic means of making decisions. It sometimes involves close contact with others, and to really work, it may have to be small scale and localist. Real democracy is inherently slow, and so pursuing it leads to slow politics.

Information technology, social media, blogging, and the smartphone are important parts of fast society (Solnit, 2013; on digital deceleration, see Ranger, 2020). They allow (or require) a fast reaction to events and a quick response from the reader. The volume of information leaves less free time between outputs to go slow. There is constant availability of information which means we must be fast to keep up, and it is difficult to decrease speed, contemplate, and think in depth about what we are seeing. The internet, social media, and the smartphone mean that we are flooded with information, often in small, bite-sized chunks so we can cope with it, and we skim-read a lot, fast, rather than deep-reading a narrower range of things. But it is important not to focus just on the technology. What is just as significant is who controls it, how, and for what purpose. (See Kitchin and Fraser, 2020, on slow computing.)

Offline reading involves reading one thing at a time, slower, more deeply, not skimming (Kingsley, 2010). It may be more about finding yourself and self-development than the fast read, and what you read may last longer in your emotions and mind than what is read quickly. Some people join slow reading groups. There is slow media too. In Norway, slow TV is popular. Watching a log fire burning over time, all of a several-hours-long train journey or a long ferry trip – these have been the content of Norwegian TV programmes, and people find them restful and therapeutic. They allow stillness and deeper, calmer, and more contemplative watching than normal TV. There is also slow sport (*The Economist*, 2022).

Academia and scholarship are, in principle, especially slow (Pels, 2003). One of the specific things about academia is that scientists and academics are supposed to go into more depth, with greater testing and analysis, which takes time and slows things down. Yet universities are more and more oriented to quantification, money, and an impossible onslaught of multiple tasks. Because of this, some academics have been thinking about the possibilities and pitfalls of slow universities (see O'Neill, 2014; Vostal, 2016; Berg and Seeber, 2017). When I was first employed as a lecturer in the 1990s, my university's motto was 'be still and know'. It has long since become inapplicable and noticeable by its absence from the university's public face.

Some associate slow with better health and well-being, higher quality of life (over quantity), less stress, and so greater happiness. It has a time dimension: more time spent on things and depth. Some associate slow with connectedness to others to whom we devote more time. Phenomena like slow food and slow fashion bring environmental benefits. Localism – for instance, in food and democracy – is linked to slow. Processes like slow food are more holistic, seeing the whole process through rather than just being inserted at one moment in it.

But the fact that slow is linked to so many other issues raises the question of what it's really about. How much is it actually about slow? Sometimes it seems like slow may be a cypher for other things. One approach is to see slow for what it says it is: going slow. But looking more closely, it may be as much about the balance between slow and fast (Honoré, 2004: 14–15, 275–7). Even slow advocates do not propose that everyone goes slow all the time. Speed is often good. So, it is a case of having more chances to go slow in the balance between fast and slow. Slow is not about slow, but balance. But this raises a further question about how we get the balance we want. And then slow comes to be about an important theme of this book: control. It is about us getting control over the balance between fast and slow as much as the balance itself. This raises an issue I will come back to: where that control is exercised – is it at an individual or more collective or structural level? If the issue is one of control, then it is also about autonomy.

So, now we are moving on to issues connected with slow, but also quite different ones. A lot of slow is about work. But problems at work are quite varied; they can be about the nature or volume or hours of work, which are not the same as speed or pace, even if they are sometimes related. Is slow about, for instance, time spent at work as much as speed? Or maybe it is about multitasking, having to do lots of things at once – which may feel like a problem of speed but is not necessarily so. We are now drifting quite a bit away from the direct issue of slow. And slow can sometimes seem to be about other things that I have mentioned: holism, localism, connectedness, quality of life, ecology, DIY, and reuse. Slow might be about things quite other than slow, a placeholder for some other concerns.

But sticking with slow, how can we achieve it? From one perspective, slow is a matter of psychological change, about achieving a slower state of mind

(Honoré, 2004). More widely, this may mean cultural change: appreciating slow in culture and values. It might mean individual lifestyle change, a question of individual choice. This could be about reducing working hours or individual withdrawal from society, maybe to a co-op or commune, for example. Or it may be more about economic and social structural change, because what makes us have to go fast is in societal structures as much as in individual psychology or social culture. If going slow is about gaining control and autonomy in the economy, then it seems that collective ownership may be a prerequisite, necessary if not sufficient. To gain control over the balance between fast and slow in our lives, we need to regain control over the economy, and as we cannot fundamentally do that individually, it may require social ownership so we can determine pace and speed in economic life. This could be through wider public ownership, or it could be through smaller forms of social ownership in a free co-operative sector. As I have mentioned, these forms of collective ownership and democratic economic control, which is what I think defines socialism, are a key overall theme of this book, as is socialism.

Whether slow can be a personal choice or is driven by underlying economic and social structures raises the question of whether it is compatible with capitalism. Can we achieve slow within capitalism, or do we need to get rid of capitalism? Companies like Google and Amazon have slow training where employees receive help to go slower at work. Slow work, it is believed, leads to better work and better products. But this may well depend on the business and section of the workforce. So-called 'creative' workers may be encouraged to have slow moments and days where they step off the treadmill to reflect and do 'blue sky' thinking. But I doubt many companies encourage their cleaners or delivery drivers to do the same.

There are various ways capitalism can be made to go slow (Honoré, 2004: 278–9). It could be done by persuasion, or leadership. Economic growth could be reduced within capitalism, which would mean production does not have to be so driven. People could be allowed to work less in capitalism without loss of pay and be given more personal time away from work, and production could be done with less speed and lower quantity. However, it is difficult to see how, beyond some individual cases, these are possible on any significant scale within capitalism. Private ownership, profit, market pressures, and consumerism are defining features of capitalism, and all of these create enormous pressure towards speed. So, for slow to be achieved, these objectives would have to change. To do that, private ownership for profit would have to be removed, because that is what drives fast capitalism in pursuit of such objectives. This requires a change in ownership and control. To put collective human objectives of balance and slow above profit and consumerism requires collective interest and human well-being being put at the centre, above profit. And while collective ownership will not necessarily lead to such objectives, it is a necessary condition for doing so. Collective and human goals can only be achieved on a significant basis if humanity collectively, in a wide sense, is put in charge.

What criticisms or problems with slow are there? For one thing, it is not clear what it is about. As I have argued, it seems to be about so many things that are not directly slow, it is not clear slow is predominantly about slow at all. A lot has been lumped together under one theme that is not really, it turns out, the core issue. Some slow advocates are not even advocating slow so much as balance and autonomy, which are different things. And speed can be progressive (Mendick, 2014). Blogging and social media commentary are ways of quickly participating in public debate and trying to affect it. These kinds of fast information economy methods can be valuable and useful, especially for voices who otherwise – economically or politically – have no power. Information and the capacity to comment in the moment gives them sway where otherwise they do not have it. Some people do not have enough time, but that is not the same as saying fast is bad. What they may lack is time, not slowness. In fact, speed can be motivating, energizing, and exciting.

Who can afford to go slow? To go slow, some people would need servants, money, or power. You need to be able to afford to work shorter hours or be able to do so without retribution from your employer. Some academics advocate slowing down at work, to be more contemplative, and taking time out where you resist the call of bosses or students (Treanor, 2006). But well-established, secure professors can afford to do this. The academic precariat cannot. They cannot afford to take risks with their security, and they have an avalanche of tasks to complete to earn the poor amounts of money they are paid. Slow may well be a movement for the Global North or the global middle classes, where people have the luxury to be able to control their lives and decrease speed. A key issue is what is behind slow. Talking about slow sometimes distracts from the structures that are behind speed and the possibility of slow: capitalism, inequality, and power, as I have been discussing. When the focus is on slow, these structures can disappear from view, behind something that is presented sometimes as if it is a matter of individual choice: turning our phone off, not checking our messages, meditating, taking time out from our fast days, and such like. Describing slow as a state of mind individualizes it.

## Eco-localism, confederalism, and the Global South

Many green alternatives stress the importance of ecological localism in eco-villages or communities. These often involve degrowth, and so I combine the discussion of eco-localism here with degrowth. Eco-villages are found in the Global North but are also alternatives theorized and practised in the

Global South (for a sympathetic critique of ecological alternative economies in Catalonia, see Rasillo and Wirth, 2022). So, included in the discussion here are Global South alternatives, often seen as post-development, seeing the future for the Global South beyond just emulating western development and growth. (Schwab and Roysen, 2022, provide a brief summary of key issues to do with eco-villages and change; Koduvayur Venkitaraman and Joshi, 2022, discuss Auroville in India as an eco-village.)

Eco-localism varies in practice but shares general principles. Small communities try to produce what they consume. This detaches them from networks of trade and transport that create the carbon emissions behind climate change. So, it is an approach of local self-sufficiency and food sovereignty, rather than producing for surplus and distant exchange on a large scale and for profit – non- or post-capitalism rather than capitalism. It enhances local economies' immunity from wider dislocations, such as financial crises or the effects of war. Knowledge used to design local economies and agriculture (for instance, understanding of local ecological limits) comes from those on the ground who know the area, rather than from distant experts lacking local knowledge. As eco-communities produce what they consume locally, they are closer to the environmental effects of their production, so they are more sensitive and responsive to degradation, and hence more likely to avoid it. Being small in scale can lead to a stronger sense of community and so public-mindedness, for the good of the community over private individual gain. Consequently, this supports a greener approach that requires going beyond individualism. For environmental sensitivity and genuine community, the scale of such communities must be reasonably small.

Eco-localism does not occur purely at local levels, but can be connected upwards (vertically), ideally from the bottom, rather than top-down, and outwards (horizontally), in confederal arrangements. I discuss democratic confederalism in Chiapas, earlier in this chapter, and Rojava, next. Delegates from lower levels sit on higher-up decision-making bodies at larger regional level. These may involve accountable mandated delegates as much as representatives acting for us. Where transboundary government and planning are needed, communities join together, and this is also an answer to worries that localism can lead to parochialism. This may be done according to the principle of subsidiarity, where decisions are made at the lowest level possible but taken at higher levels where necessary. So, localism involves going smaller than nation-states but also taking localities into bigger and wider arrangements where relevant. This could go so far as international confederated organization, which I come back to in Chapter 6 on alternative globalization. None of this means that eco-localism is not localist because it is confederalist: it is both at the same time (see Kothari, 2014; Basu, 2020a, 2020b, 2020c).

One way localism can be connected up is in bioregions. Living, production, and consumption can be organized in areas that have sufficient resources and land to enable the community to produce a lot of what it needs for itself. Such regions can be small or larger, depending on the resources available in the area. They break with nation-state territories (but not necessarily completely with states) for territorial boundaries more suitable for ecological self-sufficiency. They can build on Indigenous knowledge of an area's ecology and affinity with ecological interdependency, instead of being managed from distant nation-states or international agencies (see Sale, 2000; Cato, 2018).

Kothari (2014) and others mention examples in India. For instance, the parliament in Rajasthan combines 72 villages to manage the river basin they are located in. There is a federation of water user associations in Maharashtra where a government project has been devolved to local people. In Central India, 90 villages have formed a federation of village assemblies with a common biocultural identity to make decisions about their region (Bajpai et al, 2022). Other examples of bioregional governance include the territorial self-determination won by the Indigenous Monkox people of Lomerio in Bolivia, and the Great Eastern Ranges project in Australia (Bajpai et al, 2022). The 'territories of life' initiative gives voice to Indigenous conservation of territories across Africa, the Americas, Asia, and Europe (ICCA Consortium, 2021). A prominent example is the grouping of communities to protect the biodiverse Amazon Sacred Headwaters in the Upper Amazon, home to nearly 600,000 Indigenous people from 30 nationalities (Pachamama Alliance, 2021). This initiative was formed by Indigenous confederations from Ecuador and Peru to protect the area from industrial extraction and large-scale infrastructure projects from outside, and to seek Indigenous self-determination of a diverse economy.

Eco-localist approaches emphasize harmony with the natural world – that is, living within what the local natural world can support and absorb without it being despoiled in ways that are damaging not only to humans but also to the rest of the environment and animals as well. This involves not only environmental anthropocentrism (much anthropocentrism is not green), adapting to the environment to protect human life, but also eco-centrism, where animals and the rest of nature are maintained and respected for their own sake and because of their intrinsic value, regardless of the benefits for humans. Eco-centrism, however, does not necessarily work by following laws of nature beyond humans, but can involve active human management to maintain the environment for its own value. A deep green approach that does not manage nature will not work. Eco-centrism must involve human intervention, but of a protective and environmentally informed sort.

Eco-localist communities often try to harness renewable energy using sun, wind, and tidal power rather than fossil fuels like oil, and they practise permaculture. Permaculture involves care of the environment so that it is preserved rather than eroded, agriculture that continues in a permanent way, with a culture appropriate to this. It uses agricultural practices designed for the ongoing survival of the environment, preserving enough for future generations, with the lower consumption this entails. Permaculture agriculture moves away from mechanization and pesticides to relationships between farming and the soil that aim to preserve fertility. There is active management, but this is to ensure diversity and the ongoing stability and resilience of agricultural land for sustainability. Measures include: cover to protect the soil and retain water, rather than irrigation or transportation of water, with the large-scale energy used for that; perennials and robust crops to maintain soils and reduce irrigation and chemical inputs; biodiversity and recycling of nutrients; alternatives to fossil fuels; and local proximity of production to consumption to cut down on carbon-emitting transport and refrigeration. Permaculture includes more than just agricultural techniques; it is also about culture, social organization, technology, and consumption that ensure sustainability over industrialism to make a surplus. (For a good, succinct outline of permaculture, see Leahy, 2019.)

Eco-localism is practised in the Global South as well as the Global North. It is an alternative to conventional development and growth approaches, industrial and capitalist, with the environmental damage, social and political dislocations, and threats to human life and the environment that involves. The approach is more one of producing for need and sensitivity to ecological effects, hence one of degrowth where economies operate at a stable state level. It is about subsistence and need more than surplus and sale for profit. It is a decolonial approach that avoids abstract western and Eurocentric ideas, instead favouring concrete bottom-up localist practices. I return to this theme in the discussion of concrete utopias in the next chapter. It is, as such, a post-development approach. Local approaches, while following broad general principles, can vary depending on local environmental, social, and cultural conditions. So, post-development involves a pluriverse (see Kothari et al, 2019; Kothari, 2021). Rather than economic growth and huge economic development, the approaches focus on stability and sustainability, to lift people out of poverty in an environmentally friendly and sustainable way. (See also D'Alisa et al, 2015, on degrowth.)

Another way eco-localism is pursued, in the rich world but also globally, is through transition towns and in the adoption of the transition approach beyond towns to other institutions and policy areas. Here, communities practise post-oil approaches geared to living that does not lead to climate change, trying to build positive post-carbon futures. In transition towns, prefigurative steps are pursued, bypassing or supplementing state and law, putting in place social and political arrangements that work for a greener, self-sufficient society. Such towns pursue low and alternative energy, and create provisional templates for transition, locally but also with wider connections and learning networks. Resilience to shocks is seen as important, as well as sustainability through diversity and modularity so that parts can fail without the whole failing. Good feedback in response to crises is emphasized. Transition towns create prefigurative hopes for the future, based on well-being measures and community ownership rather than wealth. Steps in transition town development include establishing bottom-up steering groups, awareness-raising, becoming embedded in existing groups, starting theme groups, maintaining open decision-making, having visible projects, ensuring resilience and adapting the community, and linking with government. (For useful outlines, see Ganesh and Zoller, 2018; Hopkins, 2019. See also Chatterton, 2018.)

## Rojava

One well-known experiment in the sort of initiatives discussed is in Kurdish regions and especially famously in Rojava in Syria. Rojava has a deliberative democratic system in which the main units are communes consisting of 30–200 families. The communes deal with local needs. Committees must have 50 per cent female membership and two elected presidents – one male, one female – and must mirror the ethnic composition of the area. Communes have co-ordinating boards. They represent communes in neighbourhood assemblies, which are represented on district assemblies. The pyramid goes further upwards to cantonal assemblies and the federal assembly. Representatives are elected with gender and ethnic quotas throughout, unpaid, and subject to recall. There are women's committees, councils, and assemblies at all levels. Economic committees in Rojava fix prices and make decisions on production. Health is free, and education in the region's philosophy is prioritized. This system is one of democratic confederalism (nicely summarized by Raekstad and Gradin, 2020: Chapter 6) and links with the PB projects in Barcelona, Fatsa, and Chiapas, discussed earlier.

Rojava bases its practices on the social ecology ideas of Murray Bookchin and those of thinkers like Abdulla Öcalan. Bookchin saw ecological progress as being based on overcoming inequalities and domination within humanity that affect dominating relations between humans and nature. Bookchin saw hierarchies, as well as just capitalism, as being behind ecological and other problems. This has the merit of showing that capitalism is not the sole cause of all such problems. But it runs the risk of excluding hierarchy as part of the solution to some critical issues, especially urgent ones like climate change, which need fast and radical action. Also Rojava's structures have hierarchical elements.

So social ecology is against inequality, including gender inequality, and for overcoming it as part of the process of overcoming human destruction of nature. This leads to a preference for participatory democracy over hierarchy. With popular democratic control – for instance, through bottom-up councils – decisions can be made to ensure sustainability in use of resources, agriculture, production, consumption, and processing of waste. This can allow us to treat nature in a way that is not about exploitation and commodification, as is the case under capitalism. Bookchin says nature should be protected and preserved sustainably, rather than treated destructively. This is pursued through a decentralized deliberative method, in place of state hierarchy and domination.

In practice, the approach in Rojava has favoured diversity and more organic agriculture, protecting soil nutrients and water, in place of monoculture and pesticides and the transportation of water. Production is more for local consumption, so reducing long-distance transport and the environmental effects of this and providing greater food security. Agroforestry is practised, which helps with water and nutrients, and wastewater is managed to make it useable for agriculture and less harmful than when discharged into the water supply. Much energy is hydroelectric. More is possible with Rojava's ecological, co-operative, and decentralized democratic self-sufficiency approach, which fits agriculture and production to community needs on a less inegalitarian basis (see Internationalist Commune of Rojava, 2018; Aslan and Akbulut, 2019).

However, the problems we face environmentally in terms of climate change and the hugely threatening social, political, and conflictual effects it is bringing very fast are on a vast scale and urgent. As such, plural eco-localism is not enough by itself and must be supplemented with grander state-led macro-change, including states collaborating internationally (something I come back to in Chapter 6). I am not arguing in this book that prefigurative localism should be abandoned because it is not enough, in favour of macro state change (Schwab and Roysen, 2022, make the case for keeping up eco-localism in this context). That each approach has deficiencies is a reason for allying them, not putting them into a false dichotomy of either/or. But for transformations that will have to be massive and fast, state-led change is required (Malm, 2020, says we can learn lessons from statist approaches to tackling COVID-19 and argues for 'war communism' to deal with climate change). This will not be environmentally and socially friendly, though, unless taken from state and private hands, where there are interests in not pursuing radical ecological approaches. State macro-change must be brought under the democratic control of collectivities whose interests it is in to pursue environmental change. So eco-localism requires allying with democratic ownership of production on a macro state scale through a democratized state with inclusive collective ownership. The state can also ensure equality and redistribution across communities, and provision – for example, in health and technology – that cannot be supplied in small local communities alone. This approach is one I return to in later parts of the book, especially, but not only, Chapter 5. (See Frankel, 2018, 2020, on rethinking politics in response to environmental crisis.)

## Alternatives to surveillance capitalism

Despite the explosion of the internet since the 1990s, and the growth of smartphones and big tech corporations more recently, there is not much discussion in the mainstream alternatives literature of digital alternatives ensuing from surveillance concerns. The digital commons, open-access, and peer-to-peer sharing as an alternative to enclosures and copyrighting digitally are important and have been analysed well (Berry, 2008). Free and open-source software has been important in projects in the Global South (see Pearce, 2018). Also discussed has been the use of social media in uprisings and protests, like the Arab Spring and the #MeToo movement. There are discussions on anxiety when people are not connected, which raises questions about the right to be connected or, on the other hand, the benefits of digital detox. Later, I will touch on the use of information technology in digital socialism, making democratic planning for need possible, in place of a market-driven economy. There are many other important analyses in the digital politics literature on issues such as expression, access, equality, the digital divide, power, openness, and innovation (for a good overview and analysis of the area, see Issin and Ruppert, 2020; see also Bigo et al, 2019).

I will focus here on alternatives in the light of surveillance and privacy concerns that have come to the fore since the Snowden affair in 2013, the Cambridge Analytica scandal in 2018 (Véliz, 2021a: 77–83; although Cambridge Analytica may have exaggerated what they did or were able to do), and the Pegasus spyware revelations in 2021. There have been numerous other hacks and mega-leaks of individual and company data. For Zuboff (2019), there is a new era of surveillance capitalism. New or not (I agree with Sadowski, 2020, that it is a variation of old capitalism rather than a new form), it raises age-old issues, among them ownership (private or social), private profit and the public good, capitalism and socialism, liberalism and libertarianism, individual rights and social responsibility, democracy and markets, collectivism and individualism, among others. To take examples of two authors on this area raising quite traditional questions: Véliz (2021a) argues for a legislative and regulatory approach to big tech, within existing structures, aimed at individual privacy but also about what society should be like, essentially within a liberal framework but with public-mindedness. Sadowski (2020) argues that regulation will alleviate the pain but will not address the root causes. From his political economy perspective, he argues for change to different structures, beyond liberalism, for public ownership based on the public good (with some Luddism or 'unmaking' too, especially of anything that involves surveillance), based on the perspective that at the bottom of it is private ownership for profits (see also Tarnoff, 2022; Tarnoff, 2019b, like Sadowski, sees dismantling the technology in some cases as important, as well as changing its ownership). Old inequalities of class, racism, and gender are also reproduced in digital capitalism. (See, for example, Browne, 2015, on surveillance and Blackness; Hicks, 2017, on gender inequality in computing; Eubanks, 2018, on tech and policing of the poor; Noble, 2018, on racism and sexism in online searching; and Benjamin, 2019, on tech and racism. More positively, see McIlwain, 2020, on Black software and Brock, 2020, on the Black internet.)

Big tech corporations like GAFAM – Google (Alphabet), Amazon, Facebook (Meta), Apple, and Microsoft – have come to dominate and often create oligopolies in the digital and tech worlds. With their country origins, they create a kind of digital colonialism (although, more internationally, systems like WeChat, LINE, and QQ have also become prevalent). They have an extensive hold over sectors such that we are constrained inside their systems to get the online services we want or have come to rely on. Google is a prominent example of this, with the company's early motto, 'don't be evil', not to be seen these days. These companies' oligopolies over tech and the digital are of concern because they limit our ability to choose and be free, and so is their invasion of personal spaces with surveillance and the capturing of personal information.

Many of these corporations gather information about our digital activities, including web browsing, searches, IP (internet protocol) addresses, purchasing activity, movements, communications, and contacts, through tracking in web browsers, other apps, and emails. (Other data gathering I am not directly discussing here include camera surveillance and facial recognition, tracking in wearable devices, smart TVs and speakers, and medical records: see Véliz, 2021a, on these and less known methods such as audio beacons and IMSI (international mobile subscriber identity) catchers, or 'stingrays'. These collect our information, often invisibly and unknown to us, in many cases without real consent, and sometimes pass it on. Information is aggregated, anonymized, or encrypted. But before that, it is not, and it can be disaggregated, de-anonymized, and decrypted. From this information, it is possible to infer where we live and work, our relationships and friendships, political views and activities, interests, and more. Conclusions about us can be hypothesized by authorities, and evidence for speculations about people can be fished for. Some of this information is not just about ourselves but also others (for instance, via contacts, messaging, and photos we upload, while combining information about people's movements shows who we and they mix with). Véliz (2019a, 2019b) argues that because our data provides information about others, we have a duty to them to protect our data; it is a collective issue and not just about individual privacy. Money is made from surveillance and data collection, and its use for advertising and 'nudging' (although how far the advertising works is open to debate; see Hwang, 2020). In this system, the user is the commodity who is sold. Aggregated information about us is used by big corporations to shape us. (Sadowski, 2020, and Véliz, 2021a, provide good outlines of digital data surveillance from, as I have suggested, more Marxist and liberal perspectives, respectively.)

If someone turned up at our front door asking to go through our computers and phones and collect information about where we have been on the internet and our searches, then requesting a full record of our address books, our post and its contents, our diaries, our hobbies and all the TV programmes and music we have been consuming, and the news sources we use, then wanting to look through our homes so they could compile a list of the books we have been reading, asking for a record of our movements, electronically tagging us to monitor this, who we hang out with and where and when, and wanting to retain an ongoing log of these for many years, we would turn them away without hesitation, whether we had something to hide or not. This would be before they said they were going to aggregate this information and sell it so people could shape our interests and make it available to the state on demand. But this is what tech corporations and our internet service providers collect routinely and on myriad occasions through each day. This is not to mention the surveillance and data gathering they subject their (highly unequal and often precarious and exploited) workforce to. Some who are critical of big corporations and governments, including in liberal democracies, become strangely optimistic about this kind of data not being misused currently or in the future.

We are often so reliant on digital providers that it is difficult to avoid this information being collected; plus it is done in a way that is complex and opaque, so hard for us to see and respond to. It is often in principle carried out with our consent, but withdrawing consent is so complicated and the practices so obscure and normalized for many that in effect we are giving information without especially wanting to. As such, Sadowski (2020) describes the data collection as theft. As well as being available to digital providers, the information gathered is available on request, to varying degrees in different contexts, to governments and police. Sometimes, states use corporate databases through companies like Palantir, avoiding legal restrictions on government use of citizen data, especially in the US, to monitor some of the most mainstream, benign, and harmless groups and individuals. There is a 'chilling effect' for some, where people are hesitant about saying things or using online resources like web searches in a way they feel could attract unjustified government attention (Penney, 2016; 2022; Marthews and Tucker, 2017; Büchi et al, 2022).

Questioning approaches to this situation have focused on critique, action in the form of boycotts – for example, of platforms like Facebook – and more general protection, disconnection, and unplugging. There is a degoogling movement of people who wish to go online and use the internet, computers, and smartphones in ways that avoid organizations like Google. For many, degoogling (or de-GAFAMing) is a complex process, technically and in the amount of work and time involved. Privacy concerns are also followed through by the avoidance of nonessential cookies and by using system-wide tracking blockers (like NextDNS and TrackerControl), anti-tracking browser extensions (like uBlock Origin), encryption, virtual private networks that conceal our IP address and, to some extent, internet use (like Mullvad or IVPN – the latter a bit more politically oriented than Mullvad), privacy-conscious apps (like the email clients Thunderbird and FairEmail), and alternative search engines that avoid tracking (like DuckDuckGo). Apple builds anti-tracking into its products; this has had a big impact on Facebook, which uses tracking for its advertising-led approach. Firefox (with uBlock Origin added) and Brave (and versions of Firefox like LibreWolf and Mull) have also taken a lead in providing privacy in web browsers and beyond. Brunton and Nissenbaum (2016) provide a user guide on obfuscation, which is the use of ambiguous, confusing, or misleading information or noise by users to interfere with data surveillance. Sadowski (2020) argues for Luddism or unmaking in the approach to surveillance capitalism and data gathering, and the blocking and breaking methods I have mentioned fit with that. Of course, there have been criticisms – for example, over deals with big tech. Anti-tracking DuckDuckGo quietly allowed Microsoft to track users of their browser. Firefox (owned by not-for-profit Mozilla) have been paid a lot by data gathering pioneers Google to make them the default (though changeable) search engine.

As well as blocking, there can be banning – for instance, of facial recognition, stingrays, predictive policing algorithms, and algorithmic welfare methods (see Tarnoff, 2019a). These are dangerous and often discriminatory. At state level, responses have been oriented to attempting to limit monopolization and ensure competition, although these have not stopped oligopolies in digital information and tech. There is variation internationally in anti-monopoly attempts by states or the supranational European Union (EU). States have varying privacy laws limiting access to personal information digitally, with governments like Switzerland's being more rigorous and outside the 'eyes' states that share intelligence, while states like the Netherlands' have moved from stronger to weaker privacy laws. The EU's General Data Protection Regulation is important in this context. Véliz (2021a) proposes measures such as banning personalized advertising, banning trade in personal data and default personal data collection, placing restrictions on the making of sensitive inferences from personal data, introducing fiduciary duties by data owners to users (like the duties financial advisers, doctors, and lawyers have to their customers), the facilitation of personal tracking of our own data, putting curbs on government surveillance, banning surveillance equipment, introducing digital regulatory agencies, and bringing in stronger antitrust laws, among other things.

The Occupy and anti-austerity movements and the radical politics of alternatives in the Arab Spring have often relied on social media, such as Twitter, to organize and act. Many in such movements believe in independence and autonomy, including in conventional media, but do not go much beyond critique to suggest digital alternatives, which tend to remain the preserve of the tech-minded and committed. The latter sometimes have a political critique and approach, but often their concerns are just to do with privacy, within an effectively liberal or libertarian approach. The emphasis of activists on openness and transparency can be given as reasons for not using existing means, such as encryption and others mentioned previously, for greater privacy and anonymity in information and communication (although there is training for activists on countering surveillance; see Coughlan, 2012).

Beyond critique, boycotting, and evasion of privacy incursions, there is less focus on alternatives. However, alternatives there are. Some involve decentralized federated digital spaces where individuals and groups can access internet resources for communication and media from means that are alternative to GAFAM and plural, so we are not reliant on single or few major corporations. Some of these alternatives promise a greater emphasis on privacy, not collecting or supplying our information to commerce or the state, and, to different degrees, encryption of communication or information in transit or 'at rest' on servers. In some cases, encryption by alternatives is not much more extensive than through mainstream providers, but we are assured on trust that our data will not be shared, sold, or read. Some build free and open-source software, provided not for profit or gain and sometimes, but not always, by volunteers. Code is open source rather than proprietary, so we can see and access it and assess how it and the alternatives operate, and we can use and adapt the code. Many provide alternatives (such as Mastodon) to social media platforms (like Twitter, Facebook, and Reddit) and to mainstream cloud storage, messaging, and email providers, although some of the alternatives have low levels of users and activity, and many critical and alternatives-oriented activists are still pushed to use big corporate suppliers because of the volume of their content and number of users. In a more plural media, one thing that is important is interoperability – for instance, so users can use one more alternative messaging platform to communicate with people on another more mainstream one.

Groups like Disroot, a collective of volunteers, provide alternative email which limits the collection, storage, and sharing of personal details. Disroot gives links to many platforms alternative to the big corporations for email, messaging, chatting, social media, and cloud hosting. Groups like Riseup, for Leftist activists, provide invite-only email, data storage on their own servers, and other means for digital activity beyond big corporations and prying eyes from whom they intend to protect information; they also limit the collection of information, although this is sometimes constrained by levels of encryption and the laws of the states where they are sited. Email providers like Proton and Tutanota promise not to collect information about users and to encrypt our communication more rigorously so we can avoid both GAFAM and surveillance (on email surveillance, see O'Flaherty, 2021). Some of these are still capitalist corporations, although semi-alternative companies like Runbox are (majority) worker owned, and Autistici, like Disroot (but more explicitly political), is volunteer run on non-capitalist lines, monetary aspects limited mostly to voluntary donation. Some alternative providers (like Runbox, Tutanota, and Posteo) use renewable energy to reduce carbon emissions. Others go beyond a corporate form and have more of a social movement identity. There are campaigning organizations, like the Electronic Frontier Foundation in the US and IT for Change in India, that focus on digital rights and freedom, and cryptoparties that help people adopt privacy and anonymity means in their digital activity.

Some alternative privacy-oriented providers gained more attention and users after the Snowden affair, but many otherwise alternatives-oriented people continue to use providers like Google because they do not know about the alternatives or switching to them is, sometimes justifiably, seen as a big job. Others feel that email and other online activity can never be private, and some take alternative measures to block tracking while continuing to use mainstream resources to, for example, send email. For some users, there is much to be gained by what data harvesting allows – for instance, personalization of content and making connections with others across platforms like Facebook and Instagram – or they feel that most of the data collected is trivial for them and so lack of privacy is accepted. In such cases, the dangers and morality of data harvesting and selling are not worrying enough to resist or avoid it. There may also be less individualistic benefits for social research and improvement of tech and the digital that, for some, mean that some of the data gathering outweighs privacy incursions.

Many of the alternatives are at the levels of software and online providers, but this leaves the sphere of hardware and connectedness, where states can stop resistance and rebellion by turning the internet off or censoring it, as has happened in China, Egypt, and Iran, among other cases. There are alternatives for connectedness, though – for instance, in the open-source hardware movement, through devices linked independently in infrastructure or mesh networks. Interest in these lags behind that in software alternatives, and their effectiveness depends on how many join such networks (see the discussion by Lopez and Bush, 2020, on the Global Tapestry of Alternatives network).

So, the alternatives are around a politics of privacy, independence, and autonomy, with anti-monopoly and sometimes non-capitalist and green elements. It has been argued that the online world as it is requires the insertion of concepts of anonymity (Rossiter and Zehle, 2018) alongside concerns such as equality, liberty, democracy, and community in the lexicon of political ideas and concerns, and anonymity rather than the oft-advocated ideas of openness and transparency (a key actor in digital alternatives has been the network Anonymous). And, as mentioned, it is proposed that the structure of alternatives digitally should be federated and decentralized.

While online anonymity is desirable, just as it may be in the offline world, it has limits in the face of what has been called 'surveillance capitalism' (Zuboff, 2019). This is because, as offline, online anonymity and privacy are difficult to achieve if faced with a determined high-level authority like a government, as the Snowden and Pegasus affairs showed. Also, seeking anonymity is a reactive and evasive approach. For Sadowski (2019), privacy is as much about power as obscurity. For a better world, what is needed is resistance and an alternative. Resistance involves tackling the power of big tech and the capturing of data they are allowed. Via social movements and states, this needs to be challenged and turned back. And in the context of alternatives, alternative tech and an alternative digital world need to be expanded. So, implied is a regulated and hauled-back big tech and its replacement by a more plural tech and digital world, decentralized and federated. One advocate of this is Tim Berners-Lee, the founder of the World Wide Web. Anonymity may be desirable individually and for groups, but collectively what is required is overturning of big intrusive tech now by state power, through regulation, anti-monopoly activity, and public ownership. But state power can be a problem as well as a tool, so the alternative of decentralized, collectivist, democratic tech is needed too in a pluralist digital world.

So, to clarify key issues: Oligopoly and the harvesting and selling of our digital lives have become a norm and an economic sector of capitalism. State responses, to very different degrees, have been to resist too much monopolization and ensure modest privacy protections or awareness. Individual responses and those of some organizations have been to use software that blocks tracking and aims to maintain privacy and anonymity. But positive as these approaches are, they are in part defensive and limited in what they can achieve against high-level attempts at intrusion, and some of these individualize action. Alongside state and individual processes, we need a more proactive and collective approach. This involves stronger regulation and breaking up tech and taking it into collective ownership. In the sphere of alternatives, it means expanding and strengthening a parallel sphere that is decentralized and federated, and not for profit so there is less economic incentive for data harvesting. And alternatives require putting control in the hands of those affected, so collective democracy with inclusive participation. Then oligopolies are challenged and regulated, and there is a link between those affected and those in control. As I discuss elsewhere in this book, this has a worth in itself as an alternative, parallel sphere. But it must be made accessible and more easily understandable to the non-techy and beyond the expert, and it does not just have to be an alternative on the side, but can be a prefigurative basis for spreading to the way the digital and tech world is more widely. It involves supplementing liberal individual privacy and rights approaches, often defensive within the status quo, with collective democracy and control approaches, more proactive and constructive of alternatives (see Liu, 2020). If there is an erosion of capitalism out of such an approach, so there will be an erosion of capitalist profit incentives in surveillance capitalism. With an extension of collective control that is not for profit, then motivations for surveillance and data capture are reduced. But this must be done through inclusive democratic control as much as possible, rather than the state, as the latter has its own reasons for surveillance. So, what is implied is democratic socialism as well as liberalism, and rather than capitalism or authoritarian socialism. A democratized approach that is inclusive globally is also best suited to dealing with differences and divides digitally – for example, those to do with class or those across the Global North and Global South.

## A democratic public media

Some have proposed the nationalization of Facebook (or Meta) or collective ownership of the company by its users (Raddi, 2018; Muldoon, 2020; Staal, 2020). It is argued that social networks have become critical infrastructure for the public globally, akin to public utilities. Yet they take our data and use it to shape our behaviour, narrow our experiences, and undermine shared unity through personalization and narrowcasting; they reinforce biases and in doing so, polarize politics, allow hate speech, and undermine democracy, or at least try to (see Sadowski, 2021, on Facebook). As such the issue is not just one of individual privacy, but collective and about power, as Véliz (2019b, 2021a) argues. Targeted advertising and the use of personal information for commercial gain could be banned, which would undermine Facebook. But it is argued that alternatives at the margins, self-regulation, government regulation, or breaking Facebook up are not enough. For some, the only solution to allow Facebook to be harnessed for the public good is to put it under public control, turning it into an independent democratic public entity (see Malmgren, 2018, and Tarnoff, 2018, for suggestions on how this approach could work). Tarnoff (2022) says the root of the problems with the internet is that it is privatized and run for profit, despite being built on public initiative and funding. So, it needs to be made publicly owned for the public good, and he outlines how this has been done or could be.

On similar grounds, the requisition of Google for an independent non-profit foundation has been advocated (Muldoon, 2022), and, including also concerns for workers and the environment, the nationalization of Amazon has been suggested (Marx, 2020; see also Srnicek, 2019, and Davis, 2020). There is a precedent in state public tech platforms in Argentina, Brazil, and Indonesia, allowing the possibility of wider motivations around the public good, worker, consumer, and merchant welfare, and the environment, and more ethical and democratic use of data, over private profit (Rikap, 2020). But public ownership need not be state ownership. This has its own dangers, especially when it comes to control over information and communication, and ownership of personal data. It can include more diverse and democratic forms of public control, such as independent public organizations, trusts, and public ownership or control at levels from municipal to international, with diverse stakeholders, not just the state, empowered in democratic governance (Muldoon, 2020; Sadowski, 2020. Tarnoff, 2022, gives concrete examples of types of collective ownership of the internet in the US).

For the media more generally, there have been proposals for a more democratic approach, in line with the economic democracy approach of this book, that I will return to. Some of the proposals discussed here have been made for a specific context (the UK) but have more general applicability. Hind and Mills (2018) argue for media democracy and decentralization, and new modes of public ownership of the media – to ensure public participation in, and oversight of, editorial decisions – and the development of media technologies in the public interest (see also Corbyn, 2018; Stuart and White, 2019; Basu, 2020a; Fenton et al, 2020; Fuchs, 2020b; Fuchs and Unterberger, 2021). Hind and Mills propose a national digital corporation, publicly owned, to provide public digital technologies and infrastructure to democratic bodies (Muldoon, 2020 and 2022, suggests a global version of this).

This could provide technology for social networking and social media, for decision-making and audience commissioning of programmes, entertainment to rival giants like Netflix and Amazon, and a data commons or data trusts. The latter involve democratic control of data collection with privacy protections and opt-outs, and is used for the collective good rather than to extract value; this is something that has been experimented with under Barcelona en Comú, discussed earlier (Bria, 2018; Muldoon, 2022: 108–12). The Solid project (solidproject.org; see Verdegem, 2021) sets up pods where we keep our own data, and organizations can apply for access to it in return for services and without being able to pass it on. (Hicks, 2022, outlines literature and themes on data commons, arguing, among other things, for more non-western perspectives.)

Hind and Mills advocate a national broadcaster under common ownership and devolved plural independent and co-operative news media to counteract any metropolitan domination of news and ensure plurality. Public media can be made available to all, democratic rather than top-down, run by elected representatives of audiences and staff who are also representative of audience composition, and independent of government and market. A public media regulator would oversee such media.

Media plurality should be ensured by limitations on private media companies, to prevent concentrated ownership. The large private companies could be required to include elected worker and consumer representatives in editorial positions and on the board. Another option is to redirect control from multinational media corporations to co-ops. Each locality could have one democratically owned media co-operative with the editor in chief regularly elected. Audience panels could have oversight on behalf of the co-operative's owning body. All this could be funded in many ways, including regular public taxation. One way could be a hypothecated tax on the huge excess profits of big tech companies, starting with a windfall tax to kick-start the alternative structures outlined previously.

There could also be voluntary and alternative media, such as a Left-wing newspaper (Peat, 2020), and the sort of alternative digital platforms discussed previously. But Hind and Mills say this is not enough. Democratization and pluralization of stable mainstream media are needed. Many of these proposals are for reforms, albeit significant ones, but they can be non-reformist reforms, scaled up and showing what an alternative media in an alternative society could look like.

I have outlined a number of approaches in this section. They are on a continuum from unmaking, avoidance, or undermining at one end through to acceptance, even celebration, but remaking at the other. The former end seeks privacy and anonymity and is about blocking and breaking surveillance. The latter end accepts the world of big data but wants to remake it and bring it under public control for the public good. Of course, most approaches are somewhere along the continuum or even mix both ends of it. I have outlined four approaches. One is individual and is about preserving privacy and anonymity on a personal level. A second is one of alternative tech and includes actors from anarchist collectives to capitalist corporations. These provide the alternative tech that individuals in the first approach use. These two avenues lean to the unmaking end of the continuum. The next two approaches lean to the remaking end. The third approach I have discussed is a liberal regulation and legislative path to constraining big tech and trying to roll back its oligarchic reach. This may also include the unmaking tool of banning some tech, a modern political Luddism. Fourth, there are some that, while they endorse liberal regulation, see the problem as more structural and about private companies pursuing profit. This way, therefore, seeks structural change rather than just regulation within a liberal or social democratic framework. It is more democratic socialist and about bringing tech under social ownership so that it and data can be used for the public good.

## Conclusions

This discussion has brought us back to where we started this chapter: structural and collective control over our lives, especially the economy and work. This requires collective ownership of the sort called for under communism and practised in co-ops, discussed at the start of this chapter. And I take democratic collective control of the economy as what defines socialism as distinct from other ideologies and politics. I have been discussing utopias, and they have brought me to economic democracy and socialism. Later chapters of this book are devoted to a more in-depth look at these areas. But first I will move from alternative economies to social alternatives that people pursue within existing society to find a different way of living.

### Further reading

J.K. Gibson-Graham and Kelly Dombroski's (2020) *The Handbook of Diverse Economies* is a large edited collection covering the area very widely. Ashish Kothari et al's (2019) *Pluriverse: A Post-development Dictionary* is a great edited dictionary-style collection covering economic and social alternatives from a Global South post-development perspective, including eco-localism and confederalism, discussed in this chapter. Also see Kothari's (2021) article 'These alternative economies are inspirations for a sustainable world', in *Scientific American*, about Global South alternative economies and see the Global Tapestry of Alternatives website.

On Marx's idea of communism, Michael Evans' (1975) *Karl Marx* has good sections on revolution, transition, and the communist society (Part III, sections 3, 4 and 5, pp 136–64). In Michael Levin's (1989) *Marx, Engels and Liberal Democracy*, Chapter 6 on democracy in the transition to communist society and in communist society itself is helpful; see also pp 156–68 on actual communism and its relationship to Marx's thinking. Levin's is a more critical interpretation of Marx's ideas than Evans'. In Matt Dawson's (2016) *Social Theory for Alternative Societies*, Chapter 2 on Marx and Engels is an accessible introduction, and in Kieran Allen's (2011) *Marx and the Alternative to Capitalism*, Chapters 9–12 give a particularly accessible and concrete outline of Marx's communism. Also, in David Held's (2006) *Models of Democracy*, Chapter 4 covers direct democracy and the end of politics in communist society. Unlike Levin, Held interprets Marx's vision as involving direct democracy. Peter Hudis' (2012) *Marx's Concept of the Alternative to Capitalism* is an excellent more advanced discussion of Marx's idea of communism, drawing this out in part from what is implied in his writings on capitalism. See also Shlomo Avineri's (1968) *The Social and Political Thought of Karl Marx*, Chapter 8 on 'the new society'. Marx's (and Marxists') works are available freely online – for instance, at marxists.org.

**Table 1.1:** Alternative economies

This table outlines alternative economies and should be seen in relation also to social alternatives discussed in the next chapter and set out in Table 2.1. The meaning of these approaches is contested, so not everyone will agree with the characterizations, but I think mostly they will be generally shared. Furthermore, as argued in this book, many of these alternatives overlap and are not as dichotomous as they seem. Individuals are often involved in more than one of these and may support several them as complementary rather than opposed approaches.

| Alternative | Alternative to | Scale | Institutions and actors | Method of change | Agent of change | Relation to other alternatives | Political ideology |
|---|---|---|---|---|---|---|---|
| Traditional political communism (as opposed to co-operative communism) | Capitalism | Society wide National but ideally international | State withers away, so there is collective economic ownership and determination by councils of workers and consumers | Revolution, insurrection, or maybe revolutionary reforms Via workers party taking control of state and private ownership, with state eventually withering away | Usually primarily the working class but in alliance with other groups Workers party | Clean society-wide break from one system to another, rather than non-capitalism within capitalism | Communism |
| Co-ops | Capitalist ownership Not necessarily a society-wide alternative to capitalism, but the aim can be to erode the latter gradually | Company wide, but can be networks between co-ops | Social ownership – for example, by workers, consumers, or community | Transfer of ownership from private owners or creation of new co-ops Can be bottom-up or politically engineered by government | Workers, consumers, or community setting up co-ops Change can be facilitated by government or shelter organizations | Company-wide rather than geographical, although can be embedded in regional networks or supported by national or local government | Co-operative ownership, so communism or socialism of a more micro kind Left co-operative anarchism |

**Table 1.1:** Alternative economies (continued)

| Alternative | Alternative to | Scale | Institutions and actors | Method of change | Agent of change | Relation to other alternatives | Political ideology |
|---|---|---|---|---|---|---|---|
| Parecon | Capitalism | Companies, but also local or national economies | Self-management by those affected Remuneration according to incentivizing and moral criteria, planning by worker and consumer councils, mixed job tasks | Mainly political – for example, via government Or economic, by setting up new companies | Workers, consumers, social movements and unions, Left political parties, and government | Within as well as beyond capitalism Company-wide but with society-wide structures | Socialism with elements of revised communism |
| Participatory and communal initiatives at local/city level | Capitalism, the central state | Often local, urban, city wide | Local participatory and communal democracy, assemblies, neighbourhood councils | Devolution of decision-making to citizens | City and urban political leaders, citizens in common | Urban, localist, combination of leadership with devolution | Radical democracy, communalism |
| Less paid work | Paid work Favours abolition of work as a separate category | From individual to society wide | Diverse proposals, but can include UBI and collective ownership Compatible with liberal democratic institutions but changed by policy within them | Individual choice, company policies, social ownership, government policies like UBI, cultural change | Can be anyone, but likely to be precariat, socially excluded, or privileged middle class | Focused on work rather than primarily wider structures of society, but can be reached via changes to the latter Abolition rather than democratization of work | Tends to be advocated by anarchists and greens, but also part of some communist and socialist ideas |

(continued)

**Table 1.1:** Alternative economies (continued)

| Alternative | Alternative to | Scale | Institutions and actors | Method of change | Agent of change | Relation to other alternatives | Political ideology |
|---|---|---|---|---|---|---|---|
| Slow society | Fast society, with a fast, rushed pace of life | From individual to company or workplace to society wide | Can be individual or cultural or policy change rather than delivered through specific institutions, but institutional means include social ownership and politics | Individual choice, cultural change, political legislation, collective ownership | All kinds of groups, from different classes Bottom-up politics Without structural change likely to be mostly a middle-class possibility | More about pace of life than structure and in theory compatible with different sorts of society and structure, although I am arguing collective ownership is important | Varies, from conservative to anarchist and ecological |
| Eco-localism – for example, in the Global South | Global South and western development approaches Top-down supranational or national plans | Local communities, in confederal arrangements, agricultural social reproduction | Bottom-up local agriculture and grassroots ecological knowledge | Bottom-up localism and local knowledge, and local infrastructures Permaculture and sometimes bioregionalism | Local on-the-ground actors engaged in social reproduction and ecological alternatives Non-party, non-state | Alternative to state, western, Global North alternatives, and to top-down alternative models Post-development | Bottom-up local autonomy Indigenous ecological Decolonial, post-development |
| Digital and tech alternatives to surveillance and public media | Global capitalist and state surveillance | Diverse, dispersed, federated National and international | Decentralized networks and federated alternative tech Democratic public control | Blocking, alternative tech fora, alternative diverse non-centralized, anti-monopolistic Political parties and electoral politics | Autonomous tech actors and tech users Political parties, labour movement, the state | Focused on online tech world, anti-state and anti-corporate, decentralized federated approach Democratic public control | Libertarian, liberal, anarchist, decentralized collectivism Privacy, anonymity Democratic socialist |

For biographical insiders' accounts of life in so-called communist Romania and Albania, see Carmen Bugan's (2012) *Burying the Typewriter* and Lea Ypi's (2021) *Free*. George Orwell's (1987b) *Animal Farm* and *1984* (1987a) are well-known fictional accounts. There are several films about life in societies labelled as communist, such as *Barbara, Goodbye Lenin*, and *The Lives of Others*.

On co-ops, Chris Cornforth's (1995) 'Patterns of co-operative management: beyond the degeneration thesis', in *Economic and Industrial Democracy*, looks at the degeneration thesis about co-ops. Cornforth (1983) looks at 'Some factors affecting the success or failure of worker co-operatives', in *Economic and Industrial Democracy*. Neil Carter's (2006) 'Political participation and the workplace: the spillover thesis revisited', in *The British Journal of Politics and International Relations*, looks at participation in co-op democracy and whether this leads to wider participatory democracy. Neil Bate and Paul Carter's (1986) 'The future for producers' co-operatives' in *Industrial Relations Journal* is useful.

On parecon, see the ZCommunications website at zcomm.org/category/topic/parecon/, Michael Albert's (2012) 'Summarizing participatory economics', on the same website, and the debate between Mark Evans and Joseph Kay (2009) in 'Parecon or libertarian communism' at libcom.org. There are many books on parecon – see, for example, Michael Albert's (2006) *Realizing Hope: Life beyond Capitalism* (Chapter 1 is especially useful but other chapters are relevant too). A collection edited by Chris Spannos (2008), *Real Utopia*, goes into more detail. See also the Foundation for a Participatory Society's website: realutopia.org. Brian Wampler et al (2017a, 2017b, 2017c) provide a good concise outline of PB.

On working less, the New Economics Foundation's (2010) *21 Hours: Why a Shorter Working Week Can Help us All to Flourish in the 21st Century* is a clear accessible policy pamphlet arguing for a 21-hour working week. David Spencer's (2014) 'The case for working less', on the *British Policy and Politics at LSE* blog, is a good short summary of key points. André Gorz is a classic writer on the area – see *Farewell to the Working Class: An Essay on Post-industrial Socialism* (1982), but many other of his books too. More recently, see Nick Srnicek and Alex Williams' (2015) *Inventing the Future: Postcapitalism and a World without Work*.

On slow society, Carl Honoré's (2004) *In Praise of Slowness: Challenging the Cult of Speed*, a free e-book, is an advocacy of slow in a non-academic way by a slow guru (see especially the introduction and conclusion, but other parts too). I do not agree with all he says, but it helps to get the idea. For a critical view on slow academia and slow in general, see Heather Mendick's

(2014) 'Social class, gender and the pace of academic life: what kind of solution is slow?', in *Forum: Qualitative Social Research*. From a feminist and critical point of view on academic slow, see Alison Mountz et al's (2015) 'For slow scholarship: a feminist politics of resistance through collective action in the neoliberal university', in *ACME*.

Carissa Véliz provides a detailed yet concise, accessible, and powerful assessment of data and privacy concerns and what we can do about them politically and personally in *Privacy is Power* (2021a) and shorter pieces (2019a, 2019b, 2021b); these focus on doing things more within existing than alternative frameworks. On digital alternatives around surveillance and more broadly, see Engin Issin and Evelyn Ruppert's (2020) *Being Digital Citizens* and Didier Bigo et al's (2019) *Data Politics*. See Jeremy Corbyn's (2018) Alternative MacTaggart Lecture and Dan Hind and Tom Mills' (2018) 'Media democracy: a reform agenda for democratic communications', in Macfarlane's New Thinking for the British Economy, on democratic public media. James Muldoon's (2022) *Platform Socialism*, especially Chapters 6, 7, and 8, is a useful outline of key issues on its topic. Paris Marx's 'Tech Won't Save Us' podcast is a good resource. Ethical.net gives ethical alternatives to big tech, especially more green and privacy-oriented options. Privacyguides. org suggests alternatives with a focus on privacy and has a Reddit forum with community discussions.

# 2

# Social Alternatives

In Chapter 1, I looked at alternative economies, with social dimensions coming more to the fore towards the end. In this chapter, I will turn to social alternatives in education, communes, food counterculture, social centres, criminal justice, and welfare. The cases discussed are chosen for the following reasons: they provide alternatives to dominant important social institutions of capitalism, the market, education, the family, punishment, individualism, and globalization; they are prevalent and important alternatives that can be found widely in practice; they have theoretical substance that explain their meaning and aims; there are literatures about them. I have differentiated these from the economic alternatives in Chapter 1 to break up the book and because, while having economic dimensions, they are situated primarily in social institutions of society. This, along with themes they share, are what links them. These links should become clear as the chapter progresses.

## Alternative education

Free universities are one type of co-op (Gander, 2016). A developed example was the Social Sciences Centre in Lincoln in the UK (Bonnett, 2013; Class War University, 2013), and they can be found all over the world. They are, in part, a response to marketized higher education, which is expensive. Students must pay high fees in many places in the world. So, some free universities provide education free of cost, taught by unpaid volunteers. They are open to tutors and students regardless of their income or qualifications. Students do not need qualifications to study, and tutors do not have to have certificates in their area to teach, just knowledge and a willingness and enthusiasm to share it. They are a reaction to the managerialism of universities, where responsiveness to citizens of the university, students, and staff has been reduced and institutions are governed more like corporations under managerial power. So free universities are run by their members, with co-operative control. They are also an alternative to universities being operated like businesses to make money, rather than with goals of education and the public good. Free co-operative universities *are* about education and the public good again. In my town, there is the Free University Brighton. Their motto is 'education for love not money', which summarizes well what free universities are about.

In this section, I will discuss some other perspectives on alternative education that may not use the word 'co-operative' to describe what they do but which I would put in the category of co-operation. I will look at three examples: the first proposed by A.S. Neill, who valued happiness above academic achievement and ran a school called Summerhill; the second put forward by Paulo Freire, an educationalist who was for a more dialogical education; and the third based on the suggestions of Ivan Illich, who was for education outside school.

## Neill and Summerhill

A.S. Neill's school Summerhill still exists and is run by his daughter (see Hart, 1970, Vaughan, 2006, Goodsman, 1991, and Neustatter, 2011, for good accounts). Most of what I outline about the school here is relevant to when Neill was head of Summerhill, but the school continues in much the same spirit and many of the points still apply. Neill lived from 1883 to 1973. He was a Scot who wrote prolifically about alternative education (most famously in Neill, 1962). Initially, he worked in conventional education, where he took an unconventional approach, as outlined in his Dominie books (for example, Neill, 1986). Disillusioned with mainstream schooling, he set up his own school, Summerhill, which, after some relocations, settled in Suffolk, England, where it remains to this day. It takes children up to 16, mostly boarders. At first, it focused on children who had problems fitting into the normal education system, but increasingly pupils were sent there by parents attracted by Neill's philosophy of education. The school charges fees – unavoidably, as it would be unlikely to get state funding because of its unorthodox approach. At the same time, not all children who have attended have come from rich backgrounds. Neill was influenced in part by Freudian psychology but mostly by the practical experience of education.

Neill believed that discipline and authority are harmful and lead to fear, guilt, hostility, and self-hate. He was critical of parental authority, and parents during Neill's headship were encouraged to stay out of things at Summerhill. Neill felt it is important for authority to be lifted, and for the school to fit the child rather than vice versa. He believed happiness comes before education as academic achievement, and that self-development is very important and can be learned through experience and feeling as much as through academic education, feeling being as important as intellect. Learning, he felt, is not good for everyone, and education often has too much emphasis on work and not enough on play. A happy childhood, he argued, is the basis for a happy adulthood. Classes at Summerhill are conventional. Neill said alternative methods of teaching were not important, because he did not consider teaching itself to be important. Lessons are voluntary and kids are encouraged to play, and to learn through play. Learning is seen as being as much about emotional development as academic knowledge, and about self-expression and creativity over conformism. Learning, for Neill, is also about big life questions as much as school subjects, and practical as much as academic skills.

Summerhill is best known for the fact that pupils do not have to attend lessons. In addition, rules of the school are set by weekly meetings of teachers and pupils, who all have an equal vote. Neill felt children could be trusted to be good, wise, and realistic, which is what allows voluntary attendance and school democracy to work. Trust in students and resistance to treating them as passive recipients is a common theme in alternative education. Making decisions at the school meetings was, for Neill, as much about learning as democracy. In the meetings, pupils develop as people, learning to practice rational discussion rather than subordination to power and to think about justice by practice. Some Summerhill graduates report being seen as problems in the later life of work because they are used to seeing policies and practices as things to be discussed, not just accepted (see Goodsman, 1991).

External inspections report that Summerhill children have high levels of emotional maturity and self-development, and graduates of the school feel that in wider society, compared to others, this is the case (Bernstein, 1968; Shepherd, 2007; Lucas, 2011). Summerhill kids and graduates seem to be questioning and confident. Despite attendance being voluntary, many Summerhill pupils get qualifications and enter conventional life successfully. Other free schools, like Sands in Devon in the UK, are in practice less free about non-attendance. However, Sands extends democracy over a wider area than is the case at Summerhill, where meetings are mostly about rules and less about areas such as appointing teachers, finance, curriculum, boarding arrangements, food, and the overall school philosophy. Schools like Sudbury Valley in the US have been freer about lessons. There have been no lessons set up in advance at Sudbury Valley but rather they have been provided at the request of pupils, a sort of unschooling where education follows children's curiosity and interests (see Griffith, 2010). In Sudbury Valley, parents are more involved in school democracy than Neill would have countenanced.

Of course, there have been problems at Summerhill. Faced with voluntary attendance, some children have left without learning enough, although the same happens in conventional schools where attendance is compulsory. Democracy is extended to a limited range of issues. Members beyond teachers and pupils – cleaners and cooks, for example – have not been included, even if they are long-standing employees. The classroom education is conventional, for good or ill. Yet Summerhill has been very influential and takes its place among many other alternative schools internationally. Gribble (1998) discusses free schools like Neel Bagh, Sumavanam, and Mirambika in India, the Pestalozzi school in Ecuador, Tokyo Shure, Nonami Children's Village, the Global Free School, and Kinokuni in Japan, as well as other alternative schools in Israel, New Zealand, Switzerland, the UK, and the US. There have been many others in, for example, Australia, Austria, Belgium, Denmark, France, Germany, Palestine, and Thailand.

## Freire and dialogical education

Another advocate of alternative education is the Brazilian educationalist Paolo Freire, author of *Pedagogy of the Oppressed* (1970), his perspective informed by writing from a post-colonial context. Freire lived from 1921 to 1997 and was an advocate of democratic dialogical education. His principles for the relationship between tutor and student were those he believed should also characterize the relationship between revolutionary leaders and the oppressed. Freire believed in education where students set the themes and the job of teachers is to problematize those themes. So, the curriculum is student led, and the role of the teacher is to respond to that. Freire was against certainty and fatalism, where the truth is decided in advance. What is needed is a dialogue with, not for, the student or, in the case of politics, between the revolutionary and the oppressed, rather than a relation of the former explaining to the latter. This requires confidence in pupils and the oppressed, in the way that Neill's alternative education rests on confidence in the pupil. Freire was against monologues, slogans, and communiqués, coming from one and pushed on to the other.

Freire opposed what he called the 'banking' concept of education, something he observed as also evident in vanguard revolutionary leaders' approach to oppressed people. This involves narration with a telling subject and listening objects or passive students. In this approach, the teacher chooses the content and students adapt to it without consultation. Students are receptacles or containers to be filled. Their role in the education process is to receive knowledge and file, store, and deposit it: like banking. In this process, students do not have any creativity or power to transform or create knowledge. This undermines critical consciousness and inhibits creative power.

Freire's alternative is dialogical education. This involves cognition, thinking about, not transferral of knowledge. Objects of cognition are not the property of the teacher. The teacher and student are jointly responsible for them, the teacher being taught as well in a mutual process. This process is based in the world and comes from issues in the student's objective life, rather than being predetermined in an academic curriculum. Freire believed in reconciling the teacher–student contradiction, so the teacher becomes a student and the student is a teacher. The process between them is one of becoming, not finalizing, and education is always unfinished; people are always incomplete and undergoing change to become human. This is very different from the banking process where education is decided and concluded.

The dialogical process is against the self-depreciation of the student and deference to the teacher. It is an encounter between both parties to understand and define the world. There should not be a situation where some define on behalf of others – that is, a depositing form of education. As it was for Neill, the dialogue involves love, commitment, and humility towards others, not a sense of being apart from them. It involves faith, trust, and hope in them, as a basis for allowing a horizontal relationship rather than a top-down one. This happens in a critical process and is about process and action rather than normalizing the present, so fixing it or ending interpretation and change.

The way Freire's alternative education works is through generative themes. Students decide what they want to know more about, and in the dialogue with the teacher, the latter represents this to students and poses problems about it. Education starts from the objective situation of people and people's awareness of it, and develops a thematic universe or generative themes from that. Students find their own themes, and the teacher's job is to re-present these to students, not as a lecture with pre-decided knowledge, but as a problem to be worked through. Teachers put themes into the totality and context, and emphasize causality, so they can be made sense of in this wider view, students being asked to see the issue in terms of what might be behind it or what could explain it. So, the teacher has a distinctive role, not identical to that of the student, but in a dialogical process.

Some teachers and lecturers are quite critical of power and complain about lack of consultation and lack of accountability in their lives at work and in other areas. But some academics, if this involves giving students power and giving away their own authority, are against that. There is an inconsistency there. Academics use discourses of consumerism to reject accountability to students. They say they should not ask students about their courses because that involves the operation of the market and consumerism. But rather than rejecting accountability to students for these reasons, they could be using ideas of democracy to embrace it. An interesting development concerning student say has been the fight by economics students at Manchester University in the UK, and in many other places internationally, to challenge the one-dimensional neoclassical curriculum they are taught. But in rejecting that curriculum they are also challenging something else, which is the power and authority of their teachers to control what they are taught. Freire was all about the role of students in determining the curriculum.

For some, a problem with Freire's approach is that there is still a relation of the academic superiority of the teacher, who effectively has a role in leading the student in particular directions. Relatedly, some complain that he has a too passive and negative view of the oppressed as being at the mercy of banking education and in need of the educator to help them see the light. One particularly tough interpretation is that this makes the anti-imperialist Freire a colonizer rather than an agent in the liberation from colonization (Esteva et al, 2008). For some, he places too much hope in education itself as an agent of transformation. As far as the student goes, a query may be about whether the onerous role they have in Freire's approach will work as well for schools as adult education. In addition, Freire is accused of not paying enough attention to social divisions like gender and race, something he accepted and tried to remedy. (For a survey of criticisms, see Schugurensky, 1998.)

Nevertheless, Freire has been influential. Many educational processes over the years have grown to give a greater role to students in active learning and consultation, and Freire has been part of the shift in this direction. At the same time, student-led education is often not true to the details or critical radicalism of what was envisaged by Freire, including in Brazil where teachers have tried to directly follow Freire's approach (see Bartlett, 2005). Another alternative point of view is that the whole way we see education in terms of institutions and teachers is all wrong. We need to abolish the system and see education as best placed outside educational institutions. Free universities, mentioned previously, sometimes adopt elements of this approach in combination with Freire's dialogical perspective.

## Illich and deschooling

Ivan Illich is the author of *Deschooling Society* (1971a; see also Illich, 1971b). Illich lived from 1926 to 2002 and wrote this book while working in Mexico, after other writings on education in Latin America. There is a libertarian or anarchist angle to Illich's work and, like Freire, he was writing in the context of the radical late 1960s and early 1970s anti-establishment counterculture, the civil rights movement, anti-war protests, anti-colonial independence struggles, student movements, and gender and sexual liberation movements. Illich talks about education in networks outside institutions like schools and universities, and taught by those who are not certificated as teachers. So, it is not necessarily done by people like me and many others who have lots of letters after our names, but by anyone who has the knowledge to teach, even if they have no qualifications (see also Lister, 1974).

Illich was an advocate of deinstitutionalization in general. He argued that we cannot hope for educational change as a result of wider economic and social change. School as an institution is the same whatever the teachers or ideology. He said that alternative education is no more feasible in alternative institutions than in mainstream ones, and he was sceptical about reforming schools and 'free schools', the positions of Freire and Neill, respectively

(Illich, 1971b). He argued that we need channels for education beyond institutions. For him, the institutionalization of education shapes us into consumers, and we learn to value institutional commodities – including education – over the non-professional help of those outside institutions, such as a neighbour. Education, he said, is designed for consumer society and creates a dependence on institutions.

Illich criticized the compulsory nature of schooling and said it compels and confines people. He advocated deschooling and said this means abolishing the compulsion to attend. Illich believed states should have a constitutional guarantee that citizens should not be forced to submit to compulsory education. They should also not be discriminated against based on certification – in other words, excluded from educating on the basis they do not have educational certificates to do so. And we should not be compelled to fund institutional education through taxation.

For Illich, pupils conflate learning with being taught. School monopolizes education and discourages other institutions from assuming educational tasks. Yet, most of us acquire lots of knowledge outside of school. Education happens in the family, work, leisure, politics, and the city. Compulsory schooling divides society into two realms: one academic and pedagogic, and the other not. Education becomes unworldly, siphoned off into schools and separated from the world as a whole. The world, on the other hand, becomes noneducational, as education is taken away from most of its spheres and confined exclusively to institutions.

Furthermore, educators package instruction with certification. Industries create artefacts whose inner workings only specialists are allowed to understand. The human-made environment is made inscrutable. Educational material is monopolized by the school, and teachers are given the role of making the inscrutable products understandable. For Illich, both educational products and the school should be made accessible.

The means for doing this are edu-credit cards or vouchers. People are given educational vouchers and can spend them where they like, beyond institutional and certified education if they wish. This has been advocated by those who wish to have a more marketized and less statist educational system. Many people are better than schoolteachers at introducing peers to knowledge and skills. Illich thought that we should open the market to them and that there should be free and competing education.

The starting point for Illich is not what we need to learn, but what kind of people we need to be in touch with to learn. We need information on this and a critical appraisal of the sources for learning. So Illich advocates reference services to educational objects. In public places, there could be stores of things we need for formal learning, and professionals would be less teachers and more librarians who make reference services available and provide access to people who can educate. These could be financed by governments redirecting money that would have been spent on education or advertising. There could be exchanges where people list skills, and we would seek them out. We demand people are certificated pedagogues, and certification makes their skills scarce. But we could channel educational funds to non-certificated teachers and to funds for people to spend on education from such sources. People would be tested as educators based not on certificates but on learner feedback. And we could have peer-matching networks where we describe what we want so that peers can offer themselves to us. There could be directories of educators at large, chosen based on polling of their learners. Illich wrote about this in the 1970s, but the internet and online user feedback makes all this very possible, and such systems do now exist online, in horizontal learning exchange networks as well as corporate form, although unequally (Hart, 2001, and Kahn and Keller, 2007, discuss Illich in relation to the development of the internet).

Of course, not everyone agrees with Illich. His work is not always consistent and can be obscure. He is accused of proposing an overly speculative idea and not explaining how the radical change he proposes would come about. In a deschooled society, people may just be exposed to those with the same biases as their own and lack the broader social and ideological exposure they get in mainstream schools. What Illich advocates sounds like a market, where people become more oriented towards competition and profit than the public good in offering educational services. Education could become geared to what sells rather than what is needed or educationally beneficial. There will be winners and losers, and some educators could start to monopolize the sector. Public education could be replaced by corporate education (Illich, 1971b, himself warns against marketized and corporate outcomes of deschooling). Maybe Illich underestimates what progressives, like Freire, can achieve within the institutional system. Perhaps change in wider society is needed for a more free and equal education, and this is as much a precondition for these objectives as shifting purely away from institutionalized education.

Illich later expressed reservations about his proposals, saying he had been 'barking up the wrong tree' in his deschooling book (Illich, 2008). The title of the book, chosen by the publisher, was misleading, he said. He was advocating not the abolition of schools but their disestablishment. Illich said that, on reflection, he did not intend to criticize schooling so much as discourses of education and learning of the sort mentioned previously, and of modernity more generally. He was concerned about these spreading through society well beyond institutional education (Illich, 1971b). This perspective opens up a space for schools outside mainstream discourses of education, such as grassroots, Indigenous, or degrowth anti-capitalist schools with a different approach, potentially like those in Chiapas and Rojava, which I mention in Chapter 1 (see Prakash and Esteva, 2008, on grassroots education). (Critiques of Illich, including his self-critique, are discussed in Zaldívar, 2011, Bruno-Jofré and Zaldívar, 2012, and Snider, nd.)

In COVID-19 lockdowns, confinement to the home was a danger and disadvantage for many, and educational inequalities grew, highlighting the progressive and safeguarding possibilities public schools offer for many (see Breslin, 2021; Buckingham, 2021). Bartlett and Schugurensky (2020) discuss learning at home under COVID-19 in relation to Illich's approach. One thing to note is that this remote learning was just that – an extension of schooling to the home, with school still at the centre rather than independence from the school or its disestablishment. Yet, it did bring to the fore alternatives such as home schooling, microschooling, and unschooling. In home schooling, education is located outside the school and parents have more flexibility. But it is often still restricted by the need to fulfil curricular requirements. It, as deschooling could be, is affected by the infrastructure at home so can accentuate inequalities that school can, to some extent, compensate for. Bartlett and Schugurensky say home education can narrow the child's exposure to the myriad of cultures and beliefs, and restrict socialization – things public education can at least in part correct. It should be noted, though, that home schooling can address these limitations. One way of doing so is through microschooling in larger networks. This can correct some of the potential limitations of home schooling, but may probably often still reproduce them to some extent. Unschooling, closest to Illich's proposals, where education follows children's curiosity, was followed to some extent by necessity or choice under COVID-19 lockdowns, but again subject to the same potential problems. For Bartlett and Schugurensky, these forms of schooling provide creative alternatives for autonomous education if pursued with an egalitarian rather than neoliberal ethos and in co-operative webs rather than in isolation. But they see an inclusive and democratic public education system as still important for pursuing democratic and egalitarian goals in education – less easy, as mentioned, to pursue in a deschooled environment.

## Intentional communities and communes

In the previous chapter and this one, I have mostly discussed alternatives to capitalism, work, and institutional life. Another alternative is to conventional modes of living and residence, like the family, and to mainstream approaches to coupling and child-rearing. This comes in intentional communities or communes. Intentional communities are deliberately set up with specific objectives, rather than communities that have developed more organically. I use 'communes' to refer specifically to instances where the priority of communal living over the family is a strong element. This term used to be more widely used; recently, people tend to use the phrase 'intentional community' more frequently. I will mostly be talking about communes and will use that word on the whole, even though for some it may be old-fashioned. My focus is as much on older communes. These generally provided more of an alternative to conventional forms than current intentional communities, which tend not to be so radical in their attempt to replace the family and coupling. This does not mean the earlier, more radical communes are better, but for a book with this one's concerns, they challenge more as an alternative. The focus on intentional communities here has deliberately been on those that pose more radical alternatives to the family and child-rearing, but many intentional communities do not have that character and have different projects – for example, ecological ones.

An important scholar of communes I am drawing on is Rosabeth Moss Kanter (1972; see also Ben-Rafael et al, 2013). Communes are historical as well as modern, and eastern as well as western. One of the most well known modern intentional communities is Auroville in India (see Clarence-Smith and Monticelli, 2022; for a critical appraisal, see Bhatia, 2015). Communes usually involve a living arrangement that goes beyond the family and blood, adoptive, marriage, or coupling relations. They typically try to remain as self-sufficient as possible away from the wider community and its values. They have elements from among common interests, values, property, possessions, resources, and maybe common work and income. Members join partly for their commitment to the idea of living in a wider community, but sometimes also for the specific utopian projects being pursued in some communities.

Communes may have religious critiques of society as sinful and evil, or political critiques of society as, for example, materialist, industrialist, based on private ownership, bureaucratic, and unequal. Some have a focus on the psychology of self-actualization, personal growth, and personal liberation, and these see modern life as 'sick' in psychological terms. They are attempts at utopias in the here and now, trying to create an ideal mini-society based on escape, refuge, harmony, and perfectability. They also have an element of change built in, as they are experimental, exemplary, and prefigurative; alternatives are tested and then, if successful, the idea can be copied. They may hope to have influence beyond their small numbers and offer models others can follow.

Typically, communes practise non-hierarchical group decision-making. They often have systemic rules and are quite organized. Sometimes they involve an economic union, maybe non-profit and a co-op. Work, living, and education can be combined, so one thing specific to communes is a combination of functions. Some have an ethos of returning to the land, rural and agricultural, and getting closer to nature, with ecological concerns. Some are quite ideological, committed to a religious, political, or psychological ideology. But many are pragmatic, based on more general principles, within which they work out what they are about more particularly and positively.

Some have been based around a charismatic leader. Physical and social boundaries and an inside/outside distinction can be important. A key concern is to maintain commitment and internal solidarity, and relations with or separation from the outside world are a significant element in this.

There have been many well-known communes: the Shakers, the Twin Oaks Community, and some Israeli kibbutzim, for example. A classic example is the mid-19th-century Oneida Community. This was a religious community that had some common elements of communes. Oneida involved economic communism with money and possessions transferred to the community. There was communal living, with the family being the community. Exclusiveness was abolished, and special relations were discouraged. Wider complex marriage and free love or celibacy were seen as alternatives. There was communal child-rearing, with attachments to parents discouraged. They practised mutual criticism in encounter group-type activities.

Adapting Kanter, communes can be separated into two types: retreat communes and mission communes. Retreat communes moved away from the political approach of the libertarian social movement New Left of the 1960s and 1970s, to more of a separation from politics, dropping out of society more than trying to change it. Personal growth is put above sociopolitical change, and they tend to start more with the psychological and personal. The aim is to retreat to renew, without an alternative to mainstream society and no decided answer, but trying to find one outside the mainstream. Their boundaries can be affirmative – what they are about – as well as negative – what they are not about – though the emphasis is on the negative. Having an affirmative identity is better for commitment, says Kanter, so retreat communes may be weaker and dissolve more easily than mission communes. These types of communes have been mainly rural, anti-technology, simple, retreating from the achievement culture, oriented around personal growth, and anarchistic. They are quite open to all comers, with a high turnover in membership. They try to be self-sufficient and withdraw from society, but sometimes benefit from external welfare and windfalls. Sometimes they are more libertarian than collective. They have permissiveness internally that allows for diversity and conflict and reduces commitment. The Ranch commune studied by Bennett Berger is an example of a retreat commune, and I will come back to this case shortly.

Mission communes have more affirmative boundaries – for instance, based on religion – and commitment in the commune is as much about the affirmation of what it is for as it is about rejection. They renounce the external world and two-person intimacy, and have a sense of superiority to wider society. But membership is more regulated and restrictive than in retreat communes, because having a positive identity is more exclusive than just a negative one based on what you are against. Mission communes have longevity and order because of their affirmative identity. They have strong boundaries and control the flow of information across them, underpinning the strong commitment. They are often based on communal living and homogeneity, whereas retreat communes may combine private housing with communal spaces. They can have their own education and schools, and sometimes there is a charismatic leader. They feature mutual self-criticism confessional meetings, mentioned earlier.

The distinction between retreat communes and mission communes is, of course, not hard and fast. These are models, and some communes have some features, but not all, of one kind, and some have aspects of both. Kanter suggests that communes face three kinds of problem. First, they can be short-lived or, if they survive, become sterile and lose their vitality and striving for perfectionism. Second, they may be a reaction to wider society but without being relevant to it. They escape from that society rather than tackling its wider problems, such as inequality and exploitation. They do not, on the whole, promote political change and can be introspective and isolationist. At the same time, prefiguration is one method for promoting change and communes can be prefigurative. Third, they feature group pressure and control. This can have a cost to the individual and intimate relations and be anti-individualistic. Sometimes communes say they are about freedom but promote another model that must be conformed to, so they are free from wider society but at the cost of freedom within their own.

## The Ranch

I want to focus now on one example of a retreat commune: The Ranch in 1970s rural California. We can see a bit more what such a commune is about from a study of this one. Bennett Berger (1981) studied The Ranch (not its real name) in the 1970s. It had one or two dozen members plus children, owned its land, had communal and private houses, and lasted for about 20 years before losing its communal character. It was an alternative, counterculture hippie commune. It was thin on rules, organization, and hierarchy compared to some other communes. The members of The Ranch saw themselves as a common family, and living as that was what they were about more than any strong identity in terms of politics, religion, or psychology. They had no creed or leaders, and no single income-generating centre.

The Ranch contained the ideas of the surrounding hippie counterculture. They were for peace, freedom, love, spontaneity, spiritual quest, drugs, nature, health, intimacy, brotherhood and sisterhood, eastern ideas, and psychology. They were against urbanism and suburbia, middle-class life, bureaucracy, impersonality, war, competition, consumerism, careerism, technology, alienated work, money worship, repression, hierarchy, corporate capitalism, sexual possessiveness, and the isolated nuclear family. They departed from the politics of the New Left of the time, being more about revolution by example in microcosm than political revolution. They had distinctive ideas about children, child-rearing, and coupling, and I will say a bit more about these areas.

Conventional views of children see them as in a distinctive social category, with socializing done in age-homogeneous groups and kids raised according to often quite set developmental principles of child-rearing. As with A.S. Neill, The Ranch saw themselves as respecting the wisdom and virtue of children and rejected age grading or the differential allocation of behaviour according to age. The Ranch was questioning what it is to be a child and the way children are categorized and brought up.

They argued that egalitarianism from other areas should be extended to children. Criteria for role allocation and the ascriptive inequality of race and sex had been rejected, and so they should also be for children, an issue of children's rights. Ideas about groups, they believed, should not be ascribed by those who are not members of those groups. Children were seen as communal, not the property of the family or the state. Childcare was communal, at birth and in terms of where children slept. Care was in the hands of parents generally, not just the children's own parents. Over the age of 4 or 5, supervision of children was reduced and they were treated more like other members of the communal family. Children, it was believed, should be allowed to grow naturally and be autonomous, to come and go, to decide when to eat, and to express views on communal affairs. However, while the decline of age grading was reduced, it did not disappear. Children were not treated as fully autonomous or equals. They had more equal rights than other children, but only to the extent that adults supported this.

'Joints', as they were called then, were passed to children. It was seen that kids should only be excluded from harmful things, and cannabis was seen as not harmful. But children were not allowed to use stronger drugs like psychedelics. They were left to settle disputes and disagreements without adult intervention. It was seen that they should work things out for themselves. Adults only tended to intervene where they got annoyed by a dispute or thought there was a risk of injury. This was viewed as being about people learning to live communally and with hassles. Victimization by larger or stronger kids was seen as a lesson in learning to respect size and strength. Larger children in this situation were treated by adults as troublemaking peers rather than constrained as children. Seeing children as less distinct from adults opens them up to the possibility of sexual abuse in the name also of free love, although Berger was not aware of this happening at The Ranch.

The dyadic withdrawal of coupling was seen in communes like The Ranch as a threat to group solidarity. For Freud (1985), energy drawn into the family is pulled away from communal bonding and can undermine broader bonds in wider society. The solutions in communes have been: celibacy, so the couple does not draw energy from the community – sometimes the choice in 19th-century communes; or promiscuity, wider love – a more common alternative in modern communes with exclusive coupling disavowed. The Ranch had a permissive approach, not advocating celibacy, group marriage, or coupling. It did not have an in-commune taboo against sex with other members of the commune, in other words, for celibacy. It did not prescribe group marriage, but was like an extended family composed of nuclear subunits. It disavowed sexual possessiveness, but did not ban self-selected coupling. It had neither stable coupling nor group marriage.

There were tensions in relationships because of membership turnover and the complexities of communal living. Couples were often not commonly resident. Coupling was not seen as giving exclusive rights over the other person, and all members of the community were expected to 'love' each other. Single members of the commune were a problem because they could find partners outside the group. Some couples left the commune when commitment to the couple they were in became greater than commitment to the commune. Relationships beyond the couple and jealousy that followed from this threatened the group. People were supposed to subordinate feelings like jealousy to the welfare of the group. There was quite a bit of coupling and recoupling, and Berger did not see any relationships survive. Uncoupling went on in full view of the community and involved lots of suffering, though maybe less than in conventional nuclear families.

Berger talks about some examples of coupling at The Ranch. Colleen, who was in a relationship with George in the group, got together with a musician from outside and was not supported because it was seen she had gone beyond the group and weakened it. Patricia, who was not in a couple, got involved with someone outside the commune. He came to The Ranch to visit, which was not seen as weakening the group and so was not negatively sanctioned. Paul, who was with Vickie, became involved with someone else at The Ranch and Vickie was jealous and upset. She got little support as her feelings of property in Paul were seen as inappropriate. However, she did get some degree of sympathy, and the feelings of commune members overcame their beliefs to some extent. It was seen that if Vickie could 'burn out' her jealousy, she would get support, but if she continued with possessiveness, she would not.

Self-isolation and social distancing under COVID-19 drew attention to confinement to the private home, a happy place for some, but for others, a site where coupledom and kinship are romanticized, which is unsafe, violent, and patriarchal. For some, the private home and family are places where there are inequalities of labour and power. Women, queer, and trans people may feel the family an unwelcoming place. Some who find the private home desirable have great trouble accessing one, leading in some cases (like

Moms 4 Housing in Oakland, California) to squatting and occupation. For those who make it, there can be the angst of renting and mortgage debt. One response to these problems is living outside the private home or family – for instance, in self-managed communal arrangements. Alternatives can be community kitchens, community child-raising, collective housing, communal living, and extended families of kinship or more chosen types. These are not about ending values of family life such as love, care, mutual aid and commitment, safety, and comfort, but seeing these as not confined to the family and there being other spaces for them. Mutual support and nurturing need not be dependent on what we are born into and where. These can be found in different communal living arrangements, more suitable for some (see O'Brien, 2019a, 2019b; Basu, 2020a; Lewis, 2020; Silverstein, 2020).

I have discussed the way an alternative to mainstream culture, family, and coupling has been experimented with in communes, and I have focused on earlier types of commune where the alternative was more radical than in many intentional communities today. I will look now at more contemporary counterculture, developed in alternative food subcultures and alternative social centres. Here, different values and forms of community alternative to the mainstream are experimented with and practised materially.

## Food counterculture

### Punk cuisine

Dylan Clark (2004) has written about the Black Cat Cafe in Seattle, US, which practised what he calls 'punk cuisine'. This was a mini alternative society, with a separate subcultural identity, a safe space and haven for those who did not feel part of mainstream society. It contested the status quo in food, but also more widely politically. For the café, food worked as ideology. Some food, Clark says, was code for alienation. And the café involved a critique of corporate capitalism, patriarchy, environmental destruction, and consumerism. Drawing on the anthropologist Claude Lévi-Strauss, Clark separates the food meanings and practices of the Black Cat Cafe into 'raw', 'cooked', and 'rotten'. The punks were against processing food, more broadly a rejection of how the world works: the cooked. They sought out the wild, organic, and unprocessed: the raw and the rotten. Punk cuisine acted as a code for wider values beyond the food.

Their critique of the cooked was to do with the caging of animals; processing and chemicals; branding and commodification; and the homogenization of food. They were against the domination and exclusion of nature, locality, and diversity in food practices. In mainstream food, animal parts behind the meat are hidden; images of food in its selling are of consumption and divert from the production of the meat, its origins concealed. As mentioned concerning slow food in Chapter 1, there is seen to be a monoculture of food, like the homogenization of culture generally, and consumerism. This leads to the erosion of specificity – culturally, ecologically, and regionally (although see Watson, 2006). The punks' raw food was a resistance to this monoculture, with initiatives such as organic and home-grown food. Food was seen as colonialism, through the destruction of rainforests and the use of pesticides by agribusiness destroying ecosystems. The café resisted colonialism and agribusiness by making food produced through different routes, providing alternative practices and a counterculture in the realm of food.

The Black Cat Cafe offered an alternative to food as a commodity, instead providing organic and unmodified food. Punks bought food brandless and direct, or they grew or stole it. In doing so, they tried to decommodify it, removing from it the status of consumer product, and restoring it from an item of exchange value to one of use value. Clark also saw the café as rejecting hygiene, which was associated with chemicals and suburbia. Sterility was seen as a form of marketing and a way of hiding the human input into food. There was a less antiseptic environment at the café; it was messy, cramped, and not especially clean, and so avoided presenting the food as if purified from the process it had come through to get to the table.

There is a gender aspect to punk cuisine, food being seen as a site of repression of women. Food and pharmaceuticals are part of the world of dieting and beauty, idealized femininity, and commodification of the body. It is associated with control over women and anorexia, bulimia, pressure to do with body shape, and women managing food and their bodies in ways defined by patriarchy. Meat is associated with masculinity, prestige, and violence; vegetarianism is seen as feminist. Punk veganism was seen as an animal rights and environmental issue, and against corporations and the bad treatment of animals. This anti-meat and vegan approach is separate from the mainstream, an act of otherness and alternative society.

Upmarket natural food retailers are seen from the perspective of punk cuisine as about the ego and identity of the consumer, not food. These are commodified places, and purity and health are sold. People buy from them as much to practise and present an identity as to consume the more healthy and ethical food itself. Health and organic food are closer to the raw food punks prefer, but they want it cleansed of commodification to make it suitable for punk cuisine. One way this can be done is by theft, which decommodifies food and makes the food the preferred 'rotten'.

Clark also talks about dumpster, or skip, diving. Dumped food is commercialized, nonorganic, and processed, but when passed through the skip, it is made rotten. Food is made redundant, showing gluttony, and it is protected by security, with those who eat it seen as untouchables. Eating the skip-dived food is a statement on gluttony and inconsistency, favouring the rotten over the clean and unspoiled.

The Black Cat Cafe offered an anti-corporate environment, for alternative organizations to use, outside the mainstream, providing solidarity and family, operating as non-profit and political, as well as just being about food. So, it was a sort of alternative social centre, something I will come back to shortly. It was also about freeganism and skip diving, as mentioned, and I will turn to this by looking at a study by Edwards and Mercer (2007).

## Freeganism and counterculture

Food may seem a strange example to use when talking about alternative societies, but around it there are countercultures with values and ways of life beyond just the food, alternative societies, as we saw in the case of the Black Cat Cafe. This is the case for freeganism, which involves the practice of skip diving, where people go into supermarket skips and take the food that is thrown away there. This is food that is past its use-by or sell-by date but still perfectly edible. But freeganism is about more than just getting good food that has been thrown away. It is also a counterculture with important meanings that signal what an alternative society could be about.

Freeganism is anti-waste, so it has an ecological meaning. It is against the gluttony of the rich in capitalism, where we are well off and produce more than we need while there is not enough for the poor. Skip divers do not just eat the food themselves; they give it to the poor. So there's a poverty and equality agenda as well as a waste and green one. Skip divers often target bigger corporate supermarkets, those with the worst environmental and labour rights records; hence, there is an ethical agenda. They take food distribution and consumption out of the market. They decommodify food and are about distribution based on need, not through the market or for profit. As such, freeganism is a basis for countercultural values and ethics for an alternative society. And it is about more than ideas for an alternative society, but also practices now which are the foundation for a different society in the future.

For Edwards and Mercer (2007), freeganism raises issues of waste, greenhouse emissions, the global food divide, and food deserts in rich countries, and it involves political gleaning. It combines food, urban social movements, post-capitalist politics, and alternative subcultures and identities. Freegans have links to the DIY punk movement, squatting, zines, free sharing informal economies, and alternative lifestyles. They are composed of subgroups of purist food co-op hippies, anarcho-punks, autonomistas who are a combination of activist and intellectual, and more anti-intellectual forest ferals. The freeganism Edwards and Mercer studied was composed of people in their twenties, educated, middle class, ideological with an ethical lifestyle, often male and activist, although it can be more diverse than this.

(For a discussion of food activism from a Black feminist perspective, see Chennault, 2021.)

Skip-diving gleaners construct themselves as other, with alternative identities, opposing the mainstream. They run an informal as opposed to a capitalist economy, with free rather than commodified food, without hierarchies, and with self-regulation as opposed to external control by government or corporations. They work with dumped rather than supermarket food, the raw and rotten as opposed to the cooked, and the dirty over the clean. They distribute food in collective areas rather than practising individualized food collection as consumers do normally, eating in public rather than in commodified and regulated spaces.

In terms of time, they have links to the slow movement I discussed in Chapter 1. It takes a while to collect the food and they practise slow preparation of it. They often work a shorter duration, and they may value less skilled work, increased free time, downshifting, and happiness through creativity. In terms of space, they occupy alternative economic locations on the fringe or edge of society, sometimes appearing on streets or in community spaces giving out food, as with The Real Junk Food Project, sending a message publicly to the mainstream about capitalist waste and morality.

Favouring public as opposed to private spaces, there are also countercultures in squats (ADILKNO, 1994) and community gardens. They create public places for community need and resist those spaces being turned into private spheres for profit. These often occupy areas targeted by private property developers, to make them for the local community rather than for profit or gentrification. The Occupy movement has been about this kind of thing. (See Arcilla, 2022, on subaltern anti-gentrification practices in the Philippines.)

## Alternative social centres

Paul Chatterton (2010) has written on alternative societies of the sort discussed in this book, based on his research on the area. Here, I will look at his findings on alternative social centres. These can be found in many cities and towns; in my city, Brighton, there is the Cowley Club. They are like community centres, but with an alternative identity. Chatterton outlines them as often semi-permanent, self-governing, not for profit, space bounded, political, about grassroots activism, and run by volunteers. They are anti, post, or despite capitalism, against it, hoping for after it, or for non-capitalism within it, often at the same time, an antithesis to capitalism through their everyday practices. As I will discuss in Chapter 6, alternative social centres have things in common with the anti-globalization movement but are different in that they are less on and off, less mobile, more localist, and more about outreach to the local community than about conflict. They combine elements from early 1990s squatting and the late 1990s anti-globalization movement, moving to the use of more permanent bases in the 2000s. Their origins are, as with slow food, in Italy. They link with other urban alternatives, movements to occupy where capital is encroaching, and right to the city and anti-gentrification movements (see Harvey, 2012). They try to be more professional than squats. These alternative social centres have meeting spaces and host talks, films, libraries, cafés, bars, gigs, art, computing and language classes for refugees, and education and classes more broadly. Some are co-ops.

Chatterton looks at alternative social centres in terms of space, political identities, social relationships, organization, political strategies, and external outreach. In terms of place, they move away from anti-capitalist and anti-globalization movements that were global, mobile, confrontational, transient, and critical. Instead, the centres are more territorial, deglobalized in form if not ideology, semipermanent, in local spaces of anti-capitalism, and constructive. They are grounded, but less organizations than convergence spaces, with safe spaces, acting as bases with anchoring characteristics. They occupy urban sites, sometimes renting or buying them, while another path is squatted social centres (see Finchett-Maddock, 2017, on the differences between these types). There are links to movements against gentrification, property speculation, privatization, and loss of public services, and for the commons, occupying spaces where some of these private movements are invading, to try to protect the commons for the public sphere. Social centres occupy the space that has in the past been that of the workplace, church, and working men's clubs (see also Bauman, 1998). They can be part of a defensive localization, responding to crises, privatization, and welfare cuts, and helping victims of these, including refugees and the homeless. They host political groups, and their space is a base for organization. Despite being localized and situated in local spaces, they have transnational links and knowledge.

In terms of political identity, Chatterton argues, those of social centres are messy, complex, and with multiple identities, open and incomplete, and fluid and changeable, rather than pure and fixed. They are less overtly politicized than some other anti-capitalisms. Their identity involves indeterminacy, a process not always with a fixed aim, and prefiguration, moving from the blueprints of futurist utopianism to experimentation, showing alternatives and possibility. Identity is constituted in the everyday practice of the centre, in slow time, on small scales of change, in conflict and mediation. In this way, alternative social centres are different to political revolutionary forms of change, being more micro, based in current time and place, more pluralist and less predetermined. At the same time, it would be wrong to draw too strong boundaries, as many of those involved will see what they do in the centres as compatible with politically focused, future-oriented anarchist or socialist change too. A key focus of this book is on multilevel political change and how different approaches to change can overlap and be combined, and how participants may be involved in more than one approach, these not being mutually exclusive.

There is an emphasis on social as well as political relationships in the daily activity of alternative social centres, in the form of collective working, building social relations, and self-development. This involves solidarity, trust, shared practices, and emotions – a psychological aspect to politics. So, in the everyday running of social centres, they are as much about social relations as about political identities. These are bases for further social links beyond the physical space of the centre. But centres include activists who are not just negotiating social relations as a means and an end but see that as linked to political change too. The centres host, for instance, political organizing meetings.

Social centres, Chatterton outlines, are based on autonomy and self-regulation, and organized via self-management, direct democracy, horizontal consensus, and equal relationships. The centres use assemblies, working groups, and facilitators, all with changing participants. They accept mistakes and learn by trial and error, and they practice the slow democracy discussed in Chapter 1. But they face the danger of being taken over by external neoliberal governance when seeking grants, and in replacing state support potentially undermine the public sector.

Political strategy is about revolution now in experiments more than a future large rupture, which is not to say some members are against big political transformation or do not also support that; this is a key point I am making in this book about the compatibility of different modes of change. They move away from grand anti-globalization mobilizations at summits, and from occasional actions to ongoing ones. They cover many things rather than concentrating on a single break and shift from hegemonic politics and state power to acts, spaces, and cracks. Again, some participants favour the combination of such modes with political and state change. Social centres are about ordinary people as much as a vanguard party, and about change through examples of material acting and living as much as more ideologically through propaganda for change. The danger, though, is that they slip into forms like consumer cafés, about lifestyle as much as activism and political change. Alliance with political change can help with this, and there is nothing to say social centres cannot be part of change that involves politics too. They often are.

Finally, alternative social centres, according to Chatterton, have an external outreach approach. They reach beyond activists and are sometimes keener on engaging with the wider public than some more conflictual Left groups; from confrontational global movements to public engagement. The broader community maybe more conservative though, so there is a possibility of tension in such relations.

## Alternatives to prison and punishment

This section looks at alternatives to prison and, to some extent, other forms of punishment and also the police. It draws on prison abolitionists such as Angela Davis, Dylan Rodriguez, Ruth Wilson Gilmore, and Mariame Kaba, and contributions from people of colour, Black feminists, and Marxist feminists (see Level, 2020; see also Carrier and Piché, 2015). The section draws links with Black Lives Matter, the Defund the Police movement, and prison abolitionist groups like Critical Resistance. Racism and anti-racism are a key part of the discussion.

The basis for alternatives is, of course, criticism of how things are, and prisons are criticized for being inhumane, responding to crime with harm, keeping people in cages, encouraging reoffending, failing in deterrence, and more. They are also seen as criminalizing survival and associated with problematic policing and institutionalized racism. Critics see alternatives as providing more humane and more effective ways of dealing with crime and offending, and protecting security and safety. If so flawed, why has incarceration proliferated? Ruth Wilson Gilmore, focusing on California, suggests that prison expansion is based in the wider political economy (Gilmore, 2007). For her, in California, prison building provided a way of using surpluses of capital, land, labour, and state funds. Plenty of profit-making corporate actors are ready to step in to make money out of incarceration, building prisons, providing prison security, and so on. If carceration is based in political economy, then solutions require different social, political, and economic structures beyond capitalism. (For an overview on prison abolitionism that goes beyond the US more internationally, see Coyle and Scott, 2021.)

As well as anti-racism being key in discussions of alternatives to prison, there are important perspectives relating to gender. Penal (or carceral) feminists see issues affecting women, such as sexual and domestic violence, as ones where the police are reluctant to intervene and prosecute, and prison sentences are rare and too lenient. Therefore, what is required is a more serious and punitive attitude by the police and courts to issues that predominantly affect women. This may also involve criminalizing areas where women are exploited, such as sex work, to protect them. So, the police and the courts need to be tougher and maybe more expansive. But for prison abolitionists, the police and the courts are part of the problem. They are racist and sexist and sometimes agents of the crimes penal feminists are asking them to clamp down on. In addition, penal and punitive approaches do not deal with the root causes of the problems, and so allow them to continue. A better approach is to tackle the bases in society for such crimes. This involves alternatives to punishment rather than more power for the police and courts system. And it raises the issue of alternative societies. (For queer and trans perspectives, see Stanley and Smith, 2011.)

One approach is to look at reformist proposals for alternative forms of punishment and reforms beyond punishment. Options include: intense surveillance of offenders who are a risk to the community outside prison, for example, community corrections and e-surveillance; treatment orders for alcohol, drug, mental health, or adverse childhood experience issues leading to crime – this places less emphasis on what's wrong with you and more on what happened to you; shorter sentences and exemptions from jailing for certain offences, especially victimless and non-violent crimes; and bail, probation, and parole reform. Here, incarceration is the last resort and only used when other approaches would compromise safety. Alongside such changes, there needs to be police reform.

For a book on alternative societies, however, the focus is less on reforms to the penal regime and more on the abolition of prison, defunding the police, and restorative and transformative justice. In restorative justice, important features are the role of the victim and community, compensation or restitution, healing, and rehabilitation, instead of incarceration and retribution. Restorative justice puts it in the hands of those involved to define how wrong the offender was and what outcome is relevant to the offence, rather than taking this away from the individuals involved and assigning it to state agencies, like the courts and judges. This provides an answer to questions about what we would do if we relieved the courts and police of responsibilities. The courts do not resolve the problems behind offences they are faced with. But these alternative means give people the chance to do so. This approach stops crime from being perceived as badness on the part of the individual offender, instead making it something to be discussed, defined, and decided on by the offender, victim, and community. They decide on liability and repair. It leads us to explain the crime rather than just take it as something to be punished. And it redistributes responsibility and resources from institutions to society.

Transformative justice addresses causes of crime and situates solutions not in prison or policing but in wider society, in prevention rather than punishment. While this is more about transformation than restoration, it often includes restorative justice. The argument from this perspective is not that we need to change the prison system specifically but that we need to, as Gilmore (2022) says, 'change everything'. The emphasis is as much constructive and on building, making, and change as on stopping, shrinking, and dismantling. Proposals start with policies such as community control over a much smaller police force, decriminalization, legalization, and decarceration. More radically, what is proposed are alternative kinds of society that address root causes and the wider ecology, and lead to problem-solving and prevention rather than punishment. This involves challenging punishment and exclusion in everyday life throughout society, in education and other spheres as well as in criminal justice (see Lamble, 2021).

Transformative justice proposals focus on health, including mental health, education, housing, rewarding employment and job skills, the eradication of racism and racist power relations, poverty, art and music, and recreation. The focus is on care rather than criminalizing survival. Davis (2003) says that enslavement was abolished without such structures and opportunities being made available equally. So current crime and policing are a legacy of enslavement being abolished without putting in place replacement structures for people of colour. Racist structures carried on after freedom from enslavement. Measures to counteract this can be pursued through state and electoral politics as well as bottom-up through community institutions and networks, as with Cooperation Jackson discussed in Chapter 1. Transformative justice measures can be resourced by defunding the police and redirecting resources, possibly decided through participatory budgeting, discussed in Chapter 1. And they benefit the poor and people of colour, who are over-represented in prison.

This perspective raises the question: what are the police for? If they are there to control crime, then a better solution is to save them unnecessary work and address the causes of crime. And the police have a long-running history of racism within a system that especially penalizes and imprisons people of colour, so they are said to be about systemic racist control. A lot of police work is not law enforcement and tackling crime, but activities that are not what the police are trained for and could be done by others. It could be cut so there is more focus on direct engagement with crime. In terms of tackling crime, police officers could be replaced by community safety officers, conflict resolution staff without arms and powers to arrest. Their training and roles could be in trauma and mental health management, incident management, and basic security. They could have positive community help roles to integrate them into the community and be localized, so part of and sensitive to the community. If we can envisage this sort of approach as possible, we can see we do not need to rely so much on the police and criminal justice system. (For concise accessible discussions about police abolition, see Duff, 2021.)

A common question related to abolitionism is about the 'dangerous few', such as murderers. What do we do about them in a society where prisons have been abolished (McLeod, 2015)? One response is that these are 'few'. And many who commit crimes of violence do so in situations of poverty, illegal economies, mental health problems, and lack of support, not to mention that these crimes get focused on often at the expense of other forms of violence, like military or economic. The former would be less prevalent and less serious in alternative social conditions. But few as these people are, and even fewer in an alternative society, prison abolition does not rule out keeping people who are a threat to others separately, though not in a punitive context; this is as an act of protection rather than of penal justice, and in tandem with restorative justice and societal transformation.

For some, the reformist approach outlined earlier stands in stark opposition to the transformative approaches I have been outlining. In fact, from this view, reformism is regressive and reactionary, because it brings people into tinkering with the status quo and a belief this can be the basis of change when the status quo itself is a structure underlying key problems or racism and failure to deal with crime and justice. But while some radicals see reforms as setting things back, others see them as compatible with transformative justice (see contributions in Level, 2020, and Coyle and Scott, 2021). They can be non-reformist reforms. Transformative justice is a process, and steps towards its ultimate demands are moves forward and can be partial victories. For instance, reforms can amend the system and at the same time show its deficiencies and draw attention to its failings. Non-reformist reforms are worth it if they are seen as part of a path to something more ultimate rather than just ends or a success in themselves. If the latter, then you settle for that. With non-reformist reforms, you can take the partial advance rather than rejecting it as just reformist, but move it forward as part of a process. It is possible to make some advances within the system but also continue to try to transcend it entirely.

The transformative justice approach, with restorative justice and a shift from policing to community safety systems, situates safety and security in social relations rather than policing and prison, and approaches harm systemically and in terms of social conditions rather than at the level of the individual (see McLeod, 2015). The aim is not to disappear people but to disappear problems, based on social well-being rather than social control, systemic change rather than individual punishment. These involve the redirection of funding from prisons and policing to alternative areas which address the roots of crime. They also imply economic justice and a different kind of society – socialist or communist – and this links to arguments for socialism in later parts of the book.

## Restorative justice and community internationally

Van Ness (2005) of Prison Fellowship International estimates that restorative justice has been, or is, practised in up to 100 countries in all parts of the world. Many are based in Indigenous approaches – for instance, Maori, First Nations, and, as we shall see, precolonial approaches in Africa. Van Ness also highlights Bangladesh, Colombia, and the Philippines, among other places. There is great variation in form and scope, from local to national levels. There are too many examples to discuss individually, but Van Ness' survey brings out key themes from across the world.

He defines restorative justice as about repairing the harm caused by criminal behaviour, accomplished through inclusive and co-operative processes. He distinguishes: restorative processes that include victim–offender mediation, conducted in conferencing and circles, sometimes incorporating wider community members; restorative outcomes that include agreed apologies and amends to the victim and community; and restorative interventions used by police, prosecutors, judges, prison officials, and probation and parole authorities. Research suggests higher satisfaction among victims and offenders from restorative justice than court processes, and victims feeling more secure than after a court process. Offenders get a greater understanding of harm and have more empathy with victims, and they are less likely to reoffend. Restorative justice is used beyond criminal justice in, for instance, education and post-conflict reconciliation, such as in South Africa and Rwanda. In response to concerns about human rights, the United Nations (UN) has endorsed a declaration of basic principles for restorative justice for practitioners to follow.

Restorative justice often has an Indigenous basis, in the Global North and the Global South. I discussed the Zapatista justice and police system in Chapter 1, and Gabagambi (2018) outlines restorative justice in post-colonial Africa, focusing on Ghana, Kenya, Nigeria, Rwanda, South Africa, and Uganda (see also Omale, 2006). It was used in Africa before colonization, but replaced by adversarial, punitive, state-based court justice under colonialism, or a mixture of this with customary laws of Indigenous Africans. In Africa's post-colonial era, restorative justice has started to come back, and Gabagambi argues for it to be developed further in Africa. Restorative justice from the precolonial period, she says, is based on identification of the truth and root causes, acknowledgement, reconciliation, compensation, reintegration of the offender, and repair to relationships and restoration of them after crime or conflict, so better at healing and maintaining community. It is more likely to end trouble and recidivism. It is based in the community, which is better suited to such objectives, including the main stakeholders in the process. The colonial system is less suited to such objectives because of its adversarial approach, based more in the state and on individuals contesting guilt or innocence, and retribution and punishment. The restorative approach lets communities develop their own systems of dispute and conflict resolution, rather than these being imposed from outside, with greater respect and less denigration of Indigenous practices.

In her case studies, Gabagambi outlines how restorative justice has been re-adopted in criminal justice and post-conflict reconciliation. People are encouraged to accept responsibility and seek forgiveness in cases like post-genocide Rwanda, where a court-based system is unsuited to healing. Similarly, customary law has been reintroduced post apartheid in South Africa, with the aim of restoring community (see also Mutisi and Sansculotte-Greenidge, 2012). Blagg (2017) warns that restorative justice can be different to Indigenous justice and merely a reform to western-style systems. It is important to retain Indigenous justice in restorative initiatives, he argues, so that they are decolonizing and transform relations between settler colonialism and Indigenous people.

## Community policing

Restorative justice is accompanied internationally by community policing. This covers a range of practices from those that are more radical to the mainstream. Nalla and Newman (2013) cover 34 examples from countries in Africa and the Middle East, the Americas, Asia and Oceania, and Europe. Common themes are policing being part of the community, more representative of it and decentralized, focused on building community and police–community links in a consultative approach with local civil society. Police and the community interact outside the context of distress or arrest to build trust and head off problems arising in the first place in pre-crime spaces. Community policing can focus on proactively building community institutions that guide people away from crime, and neighbourhood problem-solving or mediating to stop crimes from occurring, rather than reactive crime-fighting. It may involve integration with other services – for instance, mental health. The aim is crime prevention rather than punishment, and greater feelings of safety and security among the community. At its most radical, it may involve community self-policing. for instance originating in and by Indigenous communities, bottom-up in decolonial form rather than top-down, with non-uniformed and unarmed mediators replacing crime-fighting police and involved in conflict resolution, community building, trust, and mutual respect. Societally, these principles lead logically to the idea of transformative change, to alternative societies where there is greater opportunity and trust, so crime is less likely.

## Politics and social democracy

I have outlined extra-political change as a route to alternatives, aside from political or state routes. In this book, by 'extra-political', 'non-political', and 'anti-political' I mean being outside mainstream political institutions, or even counter to them. Such anti-politics remain political in broader terms of having political thought, ideas, values, involvement in action, and relating to power. But I have also suggested that extra-political and political paths do not have to be exclusive or opposed – a key point of this book. They can be complementary and combined as much as alternatives to one another. In this section, I will mention one further area where there are possibilities for alternative societies within capitalism, and this is in politics. Some who have agreed with me so far may disagree with what I will say next, which is that social democratic reformism has a place in building alternative societies.

Social democracy built institutions for human well-being and the public good, such as the welfare state, public housing, free health services, and free education. Tony Judt (2011) wrote about this in *Ill Fares the Land*. He says the welfare state is one of the great achievements of human history. Yet in western Europe, the welfare state was built in the 1950s and 1960s, but was being dismantled as soon as the 1970s and 1980s. This is despite the great benefits it had for my generation and my parents' generation, which my grandparents never had, and it looks like my children won't either.

The welfare state provides non-capitalist alternatives within capitalism. I do not think it is only about countering the worst of capitalism and keeping capitalism going, which is a common Left criticism of it, although it can be in part about those things (but see Calnitsky, 2022, who says social spending and welfare is associated with greater political participation and worker power). It can also be about building non-commodified institutions, so that the balance of society is more socialist, and introducing alternative non-capitalist social arrangements within capitalism. These involve planning for need by the public sector – in education and health, for example – as opposed to private ownership for profit. There is an element, especially in Scandinavia, of social democracy introducing non-capitalist social arrangements within capitalism gradually until the balance of society is more socialist overall and we reach an alternative society (see Tilton, 1991). Unfortunately, social democrats became complicit in the neoliberal dismantling of social democracy. They became not social democratic. More recently, a resurgence of democratic socialism in the mainstream of politics revived the building of non-capitalism from within capitalism, especially in economic democracy. Here, the institutional changes proposed can lead to greater democratic socialism. I have merely introduced political social democracy and democratic socialism at this point, and I will come back to these in more detail, especially in Chapters 4 and 5.

## Concrete utopias and decolonial alternatives

In this chapter and the previous one, I outlined concrete alternatives, economic and social. I will finish this chapter by discussing the concept and practice of concrete utopias. This will be a bridge between the alternatives discussed so far and utopia, discussed in the next chapter. Dinerstein (2017) introduces the idea of concrete utopias built on Ernst Bloch's perspective, outlined in the next chapter. Dinerstein's work brings in important perspectives of decoloniality and feminism, alternatives that depart from Eurocentrism, and abstract utopias and state approaches like socialism, discussed in this book. Concrete utopias link to post-development and pluriversality, outlined in Chapter 1 in relation to eco-localism and the Global South. Concrete utopia activities do not adhere to western ideas of development. Other plural means are pursued for the reproduction of life in the Global South, and so exemplify a post-development approach. So, the discussion of concrete utopias involves a critique of western, state, and socialist approaches. The emphasis is not on wage labour, but on socially reproducing the means of life, and this links with Marxist feminist perspectives that emphasize the latter as being as important as the former in capitalism (see, for example, Bhattacharya, 2015). (I come back to feminist utopias in Chapter 3 and feminist criticism of socialism in Chapter 4.)

For Dinerstein, the world faces a crisis of social reproduction, of the reproduction of life. This is caused by crises of waged employment and welfare, which are the basis for people reproducing their lives. There has been a proliferation of work situations. In the Global South, there has been organized class action – for instance, large-scale strikes in countries such as China, India, and South Africa. New forms of social reproduction of life have emerged internationally. In a mostly theoretical contribution, Dinerstein herself highlights waste picking, rural work (which covers a lot), and community gardening. Action has moved from work as conventionally seen to social reproduction, with collective activities in housing, food, land, education, and health. Much of this has been through co-operative action, self-management, and communal projects in the vein of the concrete alternatives I have been discussing in this chapter and the previous one (and which, to avoid repetition, I will not list again here). This goes beyond representational politics to the politics of reproduction, and beyond imposed pedagogies to bottom-up education and learning. In such ways, these are alternatives to state and party politics of the sort practised and advocated by socialists among others, so also alternatives to Eurocentric and colonialist ideas of politics and socialism.

For Dinerstein, these alternatives, many in the Global South, are not just defensive and resilient, trying to cope. They also set up new collective arrangements to ensure people can secure the means for their survival, so they are positive, proactive, and seeking alternative collective societies. At the same time, the practices do not line up with an abstract political utopia, like socialism, to be put in place by a party. They work on their own initiative, inventing independent ways for social reproduction, in a world where a wage, earning money, and welfare are getting harder to come by. They put together alternative means of social production, beyond wage labour and capital. The alternatives are based on practical experience on the ground, in everyday life, critical and stepping aside from patriarchal and colonial systems. They are also prefigurative in constructing operations that can be part of an alternative society not yet existing. So, their utopia is not of a distant dream or of an abstract utopian ideology, but comes out of practical everyday experience and knowledge, which is anticipatory of an alternative. Unlike defensive, survival, and resilience practices, concrete utopias are innovative; unlike abstract utopias, they are embedded in the historically specific economic and social experiences of particular realities. (See also Kothari et al, 2019.)

Dinerstein emphasizes the potential in initiatives themselves, rather than in surrounding objective circumstances that allow utopias to be viable. She sees possibility in initiatives that surrounding objective circumstances may make seem unlikely. Her barrier of possibility is less whether the objective conditions of society make alternatives seem possible and more whether the initiatives themselves can be anticipatory of something different. In this sense, there is a move away from more orthodox Marxist socialism to one based on agency, and this increases what we may see as possible to a wider range. The anticipatory possibility of hope can expand, and start to cause problems for capital, moving towards something not yet existing. The hope comes not just from rational reasoning, but also from what is emerging as concretely possible. So, there is a greater emphasis on Indigenous action and less on Marxist (or capitalist) reasoning.

Dinerstein provides an antidote to colonial and Eurocentric party- or state-oriented change from above and outside. The decolonial perspective emphasizes people's own initiatives and hope residing in them. Yet, for me, this need not be a polarization. Local initiatives can, and often should, stay independent and appropriate to their historical and social specificity, rather than products of abstract reasoning insensitive to local experience and knowledge. But they can also imply or be supported by wider party or state approaches, which exist across and over them, to more scaled up and redistributive structures that support such initiatives. I argue through this book that socialism can be socialism with pluralism, allowing independent initiatives from the bottom up. Different approaches can complement each other and be mutually supporting; they should not be put into dichotomies and polarizations which make them opposed. At the same time, Dinerstein is right to warn about colonial oppression, subsumption in money and law, and the circumscription and exclusion of the experiential approach of subaltern collectivities that may not feature in abstract ideologies of the colonializing and the state. And she provides a valuable emphasis on the possibilities and struggles of concrete utopias in the Global South and elsewhere.

So, Dinerstein adds a decolonial perspective, anti-Eurocentrism, feminism, post-development, and Global South bottom-up material initiatives to alternatives and utopianism. There are many other debates about utopianism and its possibilities and dangers, and I discuss these in the next chapter.

### The practice of concrete utopias

Concrete utopias for social reproduction are discussed throughout this book and I do not want to list those again here. Further examples can include the mutual aid groups that sprung up globally under COVID-19, as well as ones that pre-existed this period, throughout the world. Sitrin and Colectiva Sembrar (2020) collect examples from Argentina, Brazil, India, Iraq, Mozambique, South Africa, South Korea, Syria, Taiwan, Turkey, and Zimbabwe, as well as Europe and North America. In the slums of the world, people raise animals on rooves and grow vegetables on windowsills. Urban squatters internationally are self-provisioning. In Africa, landless women have migrated to towns and appropriated vacant lots of land. Accra community gardens supply the city with up to 90 per cent of its vegetables. In the Democratic Republic of Congo, manioc is grown across the city and goats graze on green areas of streets. In Southern Nigeria, crops are grown and cows graze on university campuses. In Athens, the Exarchia neighbourhood hosts squats and social centres that provide solidary housing, healthcare, social and cultural spaces, and food to refugees, migrants, and others (Karlin, 2022). In the Taita Hills in Kenya, following the failure of colonial irrigation systems, locals have returned to precolonial systems based on complex common property, with households responsible for the sections close to them and repairs and decisions about the allocation of water policed locally (Brand, 2010; Federici, 2019; Basu, 2020b). Kothari (2014) highlights thousands of initiatives in India for decentralized water provision, biodiversity conservation, education, governance, the production of food, materials and energy, and waste management rurally and in urban areas. In the Mexican Oaxaca Commune of 2016, women organized collective reproduction, appropriating and redistributing resources such as food, water, fuel, and medical supplies.

## Conclusions

I have been outlining in this chapter and the last one a mix of Marxism, anarchism, social democracy, and democratic socialism. These perspectives can all be the bases of alternative societies within capitalism. I have talked about transformations away from capitalism, the Marxist part. I have outlined autonomous initiatives from below, an anarchist element. I have introduced reformism via the state, the social democratic aspect. Economic democracy, which came up in Chapter 1 and that I will return to, especially in Chapter 5, is the democratic socialist component. These perspectives are often seen as opposed, and they can be. But they can all be part of alternative societies within capitalism and beyond it. In this book, I think the points made imply pluralist democratic socialism, incorporating these diverse tendencies, as an overarching framework.

Some of the themes and alternatives I have discussed in this chapter and the previous one, but not all, I will take up in the rest of the book in more depth. I have talked about: communism, co-operation, participatory economics, less work, a slow society, eco-localism, and online alternatives; alternative education, communes, food counterculture, alternative social centres, alternatives to prison, and social democracy. I have outlined forms of alternative society based less on money and corporate and managerial power, and more on human needs and self-determination. The examples I have used have been about these goals. They have often involved communist or socialist and utopian principles but within capitalism, here and now, as well as breaking with capitalism and going beyond it.

I will finish this chapter with a contribution made by John Holloway. I do not agree with everything Holloway says. For instance, he is against using state power, and a key point for me in this book is that I see non-political initiatives and state politics as compatible and mutual, if not without tensions. However, Holloway wrote an interesting book called *Crack Capitalism* (2010). He uses the word 'crack' as both a noun and a verb. So, he says you can find cracks in capitalism where non-capitalist things go on, like some of the examples I have mentioned – co-ops, freeganism, squats, Occupy, and so on. But you can also crack capitalism (crack as a verb) – you can create cracks like these. Holloway talks about alternative societies being built in the present and not in the distant future, and he discusses alternative societies or cracks being made by ordinary people, not leaders. He discusses them as prefigurative. So, types of alternative society are experimented with now and if they work out well, they can be a basis for a bigger alternative society in the future. I mentioned this approach in Chapter 1 when outlining Mill's proposals for co-operative experimental socialism. Holloway discusses crack capitalism as a politics of misfitting. People who do not want to devote themselves to making profits for private actors do not fit in, so they must find new, alternative places for themselves. This misfitting becomes the basis for alternative societies within capitalism. He talks about dignity and says lots of us lack dignity because we do not have much self-determination in our lives. This is what I have been looking at: alternative societies which are about putting humans first and where we can have the dignity of self-determination.

In the rest of the book, I want to focus more narrowly on key themes that have come up in this chapter and the previous one. I have discussed utopias – post-capitalist, society-wide, future utopias like communism, but also micro, prefigurative ones in the here and now. Many of these feature attempts at collective self-management and co-operative control. In being anti-, alter- or post-capitalist, they have implicitly socialist aspects. In Chapters 3, 4, and 5, I will look more analytically and in greater depth at these areas: utopianism, the democratic economy, and socialism.

**Table 2.1:** Social alternatives

| Alternative | Alternative to | Scale | Institutions and actors | Method of change | Agent of change | Relation to other alternatives | Political ideology |
|---|---|---|---|---|---|---|---|
| Alternative education | Academic, didactic, or institutional forms of education Sometimes managerialist, commodified, instrumental, certificated education | School/ university or education sector Does not necessarily imply society-wide change | Educational institutions – change within them, abolition of them, or alternative to them | Educationalists' decisions Political change | Educationalists, politicians, bottom-up alternative education practitioners No specific class or social group | Specifically about education rather than broader or society-wide change, but can have implications for wider change | Can be compatible with various ideologies, but perhaps fits best with more anarchist, radical, democratic, and libertarian approaches |
| Communes | Family and conventional views of coupling, childcare, and childhood | Residential community | Community Not especially political or social movements | Opting out from mainstream society But may change wider society through experimental, prefigurative, demonstrative means | Individuals and communal groups | Alternative to wider society, rather than attempt to change wider society directly But in theory can lead to change prefiguratively by example and demonstration | No specific ideology A kind of anarchist and libertarian approach as stepping aside from society, but also can have communal or communist aspects Sometimes mission is of a religious or ideological kind |

**Table 2.1:** Social alternatives (continued)

| Alternative | Alternative to | Scale | Institutions and actors | Method of change | Agent of change | Relation to other alternatives | Political ideology |
|---|---|---|---|---|---|---|---|
| Food counterculture | Usually capitalist and industrialist approaches | Often localist – for example, at café level or in local community – but with society-wide and global connections and consciousness | Café, community, grassroots | Experimental, demonstrative, prefigurative social movement Less emphasis on change through politics | Diverse Often middle-class, educated activists but by no means exclusively so – also includes the working class, people who are excluded, and the precariat | Focused on food sector but with this having broader social and political meaning | Primarily Left, community oriented, anarchist, and ecological, but with socialist and communist elements |
| Alternative social centres | Capitalism, the state, anti-immigration | Local community social centre with outreach to local community Post-globalist localism but with global consciousness and networks | Local community social centres, grassroots | Change via the social centre and community outreach Exemplary, prefigurative, and demonstrative, but sometimes the centre is the end and the change itself as well as the means for change | Local community social centres and groups reached via outreach Political groups are hosted there | Based on local social centre Not primarily political or social movement, or directly about society-wide change, although potentially prefigurative An end in itself as much as a means to another end, but can serve the purpose of the latter | Variety, but maybe predominantly Left community anarchist |

(continued)

**Table 2.1:** Social alternatives (continued)

| Alternative | Alternative to | Scale | Institutions and actors | Method of change | Agent of change | Relation to other alternatives | Political ideology |
|---|---|---|---|---|---|---|---|
| Alternatives to prison | Punishment, carceration, police | Society-wide restorative justice and social transformation | Decarceration replaced by society-based justice and social change Social movements | Political change arising out of social movement action | Abolitionist social movements and intellectuals Anti-racist movements | Critique of carceration and prison Deinstitutionalizaton Social change | Socialist Communist Anti-racist |
| Social democratic welfare | Private and commodified institutions of capitalism, but not necessarily capitalism itself | National and society wide primarily | The state | Politics and the state, but sometimes originates from community self-help which prefigures wider state and society change, and from social movements and trade unions | State politicians, primarily centre-Left, so linked to social democracy-supporting sections of the electorate, Left-collectivist working class, and liberal, educated middle class | Change primarily via the state, although with bottom-up elements Not anti-capitalist | Social democratic Socialist, non-market, non-capitalist institutions, but within capitalism Mixed economy |

## Further reading

On alternative education, for A.S. Neill and Summerhill, see Neill's (1962) *Summerhill*, especially the foreword by Fromm and the introduction and first chapter by Neill. Danë Goodsman's (1991) PhD thesis, *Summerhill: Theory and Practice*, available online via the British Library, is a nice account by an insider. See also Harold Hart's (1970) edited *Summerhill: For and Against*, a collection of commentaries on Summerhill. Mark Vaughan's (2006) *Summerhill and A.S. Neill* includes updates by Neill's daughter Zoe Redhead and on government inspections. David Gribble's (1998) *Real Education: Varieties of Freedom* covers alternative schools globally, North and South.

For Paolo Freire, see his *Pedagogy of the Oppressed* (1970), especially Chapter 2 and the first half of Chapter 3. An accessible, concise summary of Freire's approach, with criticism of him and his replies to his critics, is Daniel Schugurensky's (1998) 'The legacy of Paulo Freire', in *Convergence*. For Ivan Illich, see his *Deschooling Society* (1971a); Chapter 6 on learning webs is the most relevant, but other parts are useful too. See also Matt Hern's edited volume *Everywhere All the Time: A New Deschooling Reader* (2008), which covers alternative education internationally, including in India, Israel, Mali, Mexico, Thailand, Turkey, and others.

On communes, see Bennett M. Berger's (1981) *The Survival of a Counterculture: Ideological Work and Everyday Life among Rural Communards*, especially Chapters 3, 4 (in particular, the sections on ideological work), and 5. This is a study of The Ranch commune I looked at in this chapter, examined from the perspective of a sociologist of knowledge. Rosabeth Kanter's (1972) *Commitment and Community: Communes and Utopias in Sociological Perspective* (especially parts I and III) looks at how commitment is maintained in communes.

On food counterculture, see Dylan Clark's (2004) 'The raw and the rotten: punk cuisine', in *Ethnology*, and Ferne Edwards and David Mercer's (2007) 'Gleaning from gluttony: an Australian youth subculture confronts the ethics of waste', in *Australian Geographer*, discussed in this chapter. See also Josée Johnston's (2008) 'Counter-hegemony or bourgeois piggery? Food politics and the case of FoodShare', in Wright and Middenhorf's *The Fight Over Food: Producers, Consumers, and Activists Challenge the Global Food System*; and Alex Barnard's (2011) ' "Waving the banana" at capitalism: political theater and social movement strategy among New York's "freegan" dumpster divers', in *Ethnography*.

Paul Chatterton (2010) reports on alternative social centres in 'So what does it mean to be anti-capitalist? Conversations with activists from urban social centres', in *Urban Studies*, discussed in this chapter. See also Stuart Hodkinson and Paul Chatterton's (2006) 'Autonomy in the city? Reflections on the social centres movement in the UK', in *City*.

Many key prison abolitionist writers contribute short accessible pieces to Level (2020) 'Abolition for the people', available online. A good broad edited collection on abolitionism internationally is Michael Coyle and David Scott's (2021) *The Routledge International Handbook of Penal Abolition*. Nicolas Carrier and Justin Piché's (2015) 'The state of abolitionism', in *Champ Pénal*, provides a careful dissection of the academic literature on abolitionism in broad scope, including older non-American literature. Daniel Van Ness' (2005) *An Overview of Restorative Justice Around the World* and Julena Gabagambi's (2018) 'A comparative analysis of restorative justice practices in Africa', on the Hauser Global Law School Program website, outline restorative justice internationally and especially in Africa and the Global South.

On social democracy and welfare, see Tony Judt's (2011) *Ill Fares the Land: A Treatise on Our Present Discontents*, but also see the sources and reading for Chapter 5 on economic democracy and democratic socialism.

# 3

# Utopianism and Its Critics

In the first two chapters of this book, I outlined utopias, future whole-society ones like communism and current, more micro within-society ones, economic and social. These utopias have socialist dimensions and involve collective ownership or control. In this chapter and the next two, I will concentrate on, and investigate in more detail, key themes from that discussion: utopianism, socialism, and economic democracy. In this chapter, I will focus on utopianism, especially on criticisms of it from Marxist and liberal points of view. Utopianism aims for somewhere better. Getting there, to the alternative society, requires change. This chapter focuses on limits to utopianism's capacity for social change, according to its critics.

From one Marxist point of view, but not all as we shall see, utopianism is idealist and steps aside from material and conflictual dimensions of society and so undermines change. Utopia avoids or undermines engagement with material reality and conflicts that lead to change. But I think utopias *can* be material and conflictual and contribute to change. Materialist and conflict criticisms of utopianism can be answered from a materialist and conflict perspective.

I will also look at liberal and pluralist criticisms that utopianism is totalitarian, endist, and terminates diversity and change. Where utopia has been achieved, it seems totalitarian and against freedom and pluralism, because it implies that something different from the utopia is not possible or desirable. Furthermore, if the perfect society has been reached, then it is against change, because change is no longer required. But in my view, utopianism can be free, plural, and dynamic rather than static. Utopias do not have to be final ends. They can involve criticism and diversity, which lead to change and make utopias processes and not ends. So, utopianism can be defended against liberal and pluralist criticisms, with freedom and pluralist points of view rather than by rejecting such perspectives.

## Utopias and change

Thomas More (1892) is credited with inventing the word 'utopia', the title of his 16th-century novel. It refers to components from ancient Greek that mean something good (*eu*) but not (*ou*) a place (*topos*). So, it means a good place that is no place. It is a better society that does not exist yet. Utopia is what is wished for; wishing for it is utopianism. Utopianism occurs when we think about a future happy life not individually as a private aspiration, but on a public, societal scale. A utopia can be a prescription or blueprint for an ideal society in the future or in a different place. It can also be in the past, in a time we are nostalgic for that does not exist anymore, and maybe never did if we have romanticized the past. Utopianism is also related to the present because concern about how things are makes us think about a better future (see Bauman, 1976; Levitas, 2011).

Ernst Bloch (1970) saw utopianism in a variety of often everyday things – literature, theatre, art, architecture, music, and religion – as well as in social and revolutionary thought. These contain wishes but, in addition, an aspiration to fulfil hopes, so are also about social change. Utopianism is about the anticipation of something better, it becoming possible, and is in visions of the future and practices of the present.

There are two ways in which utopias and utopianism may be about social change (see Bauman, 1976; Levitas, 2011; Sargisson, 2012). First, utopianism is a basis for critical assessment of the present. An idea of an ideal society is something we can evaluate the present against. We can see where the present does not match up to what we think society should be like. This is a footing for critique and change. Goodwin and Taylor (2009) say that critical utopianism is a foundation for constructive utopianism. Second, utopianism is an ideal for the future that involves a wish for the future. This helps drive change away from the present to something different. Something that supports idealism and a wish for a better world can help social change. While some emphasize the critical role of utopias (see Moylan, 1986; Levitas, 2011; Sargisson, 2012), utopianism cannot just be about criticism or even change, as this fails to distinguish it from other critical or political projects. Being about the goals or the alternative, their design – not just an aspiration for something different – is what makes utopia distinct.

Utopianism involves planning for what a future society could be like. As mentioned, when discussing criticisms of communism, the danger of not having enough of a plan is that we overturn existing society without a good idea of what the alternative might be and how it would work (see Mill, 1989; Leopold, 2016). Too detailed or rigid a plan may not allow us to adapt to unforeseen circumstances or permit collective democratic determination of how society should be organized. But if we are to change to a better society, it is important to have some idea of what that would be like and how it would operate in a way that would make it better than current society. Otherwise, large-scale change is a big risk. Having a plan also stops people from misusing a political idea in the future because the society we are striving for has not been set out, as could be said happened in so-called communist societies. One way we can develop a plan is by testing the main features of a model in small-scale experiments in current societies. These also show people that an alternative is possible and so can encourage change. They are experiments but also demonstrations (as A.S. Neill said about Summerhill school: see Neill, 1962: 4; Hemmings, 1972: 71). So, both future and current utopias are important for making sure that change to a better society works out well.

I wish to look at future utopias, ideas of an ideal society in the future. These are often speculative and on a macro scale. I also want to discuss current utopias, projects now that can be seen as utopian because they are very different to mainstream society and attempt a utopian alternative. Current utopias are actual and often micro (see Cooper, 2014). They include, as we have seen, co-ops, sharing economies, intentional communities, alternative education, urban social centres, alternative food cultures like freeganism, and ecological communities (on the last, see Pepper, 1991; Ergas, 2010; Chatterton, 2013, Fischer, 2017; Schwab and Roysen, 2022; on green utopianism, see Bradley and Hedrén, 2015; Garforth, 2018). Current utopias can be in reclaimed land – like the private land claimed for common use by Marinaleda, the communist village in Spain discussed in Chapter 1 (see Hancox, 2013) – built architecture – like new towns or estates – squats, occupations, and gardens – including community gardens and landscaping (see Harvey, 2000; Miles, 2008; Crossan et al, 2016; see also Kirwan et al, 2016, on spaces for alternative commons). They are found in a localist turn in the anti-austerity and alter-globalization movements that I will come back to in Chapter 6 (Chatterton, 2010; Pleyers, 2010; della Porta, 2015).

These aim to make an ideal or better place not just through conventional future-oriented means of change, such as political parties and protest, but also via countercultures and alternative communities in existing society (Firth, 2012, looks at such alternatives in the context of utopianism, citizenship, participation, and politics). Current alternatives can be attempts to build utopias bit by bit here and now. They are endeavours at a better society in practice and can be prefigurative. By practising a society now, they create a basis for that society being implemented more widely in the future. In this sense, they address the mechanisms of transition to a better world, which future utopias tend not to. Current alternatives combine traditionally counterposed approaches of gradual change, revolution, and more anarchist initiatives alongside party politics and social movements. Current utopias have been tried in the past, and I include historical attempts in this category.

Small alternatives within existing society can be a reaction against large-scale total utopias that everyone must conform to. They maintain utopian ideals alongside wider society, avoiding the dystopian total way utopia has been envisaged. I will return to the issue of utopias existing in a pluralist way alongside other forms. By occurring within or aside from current society, present alternatives are in another place. If utopianism is about a better world that does not exist, then projects that try to create this and get micro institutions of it in place are utopianism, experiments in utopia, or even utopias, in that they are putting into practice structures of an alternative ideal society (Goodwin and Taylor, 2009, and Levitas, 2013, among others, see within-society initiatives in present or past time as utopias).

The Mayor of Marinaleda, Sánchez Gordillo, says:

> We have learned that it is not enough to define utopia, nor is it enough to fight against the reactionary forces. One must build it here and now, brick by brick, patiently but steadily, until we can make the old dreams a reality: that there will be bread for all, freedom among citizens, and culture; and to be able to read with respect the word 'peace'. We sincerely believe that there is no future that is not built in the present. (Quoted in Hancox, 2013: 3)

For him, utopia should be a positive practice rather than merely oppositional, and be built now rather than something just for the future. Pursuing utopia is partly about utopia now as a form of social change.

## Left utopias

There are many sites of utopianism – in literature, for example (see Kumar, 1987; Jameson, 2007), and in feminist and anti-racist utopias (discussed later in the chapter). There are capitalist, Right-wing, and libertarian utopias (advocated by Nozick, 1974, and Stirner, 2010, and discussed by Mannheim, 1979, Gray, 2008, and Featherstone, 2017; although some may say these are less imagining an ideal society than justifying capitalism) and conservative utopias (see Goodwin and Taylor, 2009). Utopias have come from the East as well as the West and from both modernity and premodern societies (see Longxi, 2002; Sargent, 2010). In the final section of this chapter, I will discuss liberal and pluralist utopianism. In the next sections, I will focus on Left-wing, feminist, and anti-racist utopias.

Left-wing utopias have waned in popularity since the decline of communism and social democracy, but not completely (see Devine, 1988, and Albert, 2003, for designs for alternative economies; and as we shall see in Chapter 5, there has been a rise in confidence in communist and socialist ideas – see, for example, Bastani, 2020). Attempts at communism were repressive. For some critics, as we have seen, this resulted in part from trying to create a novel total society that had not been tested before. Communism as a utopia became less attractive and associated more with dystopia (although views differ on whether Marx's communism was a utopia; see Paden, 2002; Lovell, 2004; Smith, 2009). It has also waned because of a problem of agency. The working class has not proved to be a collective actor for socialism, leading to a quest for alternative means of transition beyond a class or party one (for discussions of Left agency, see della Porta, 2015; Honneth, 2017; Masquelier, 2017b).

Social democracy is about reforms within capitalism, so less about a future, different society. The welfare state of social democracy has a different logic to capitalism, though – about collectivism and need rather than private ownership and demand. So, as suggested in Chapter 2, it points to alternative social relations. Critics who see the social democratic state as maintaining capitalism, or as too statist and centralist, defend it when under attack, for its alternative social principles within capitalism (see della Porta, 2015: 76, 86, 96–7; Masquelier, 2017b: 193). But social democracy declined from the 1980s onwards, as the economy and public sector were privatized and marketized in parts of the world. Democratic socialism has had an upsurge, and policy forms for this are discussed in Chapter 5.

Bauman (2003), who has written on socialism as utopia (Bauman, 1976), argues that there has been a loss of confidence in societal transformation – that it is possible or will turn out well. People no longer believe in models of perfection that cover all of society and leave no space for difference or change. Utopias are no longer, as communism was, about final ends in the future, settled, public, in state territories, and with people happy to conform. Bauman sees utopianism as more individualized, in private imaginations, sporadic in society, and current. This is a consequence of the experience of communism and the rise of postmodern and sceptical thought. It is also a result of globalization, which undermines the power of states to create alternative systems and which is so pervasive that it is difficult to have separate societies aside from it. (See also Kumar, 2010, on the end of utopia.)

However, Bauman's critique can prompt different conclusions. One I will come to at the end of this chapter is that utopianism does not have to be rejected because of a failure to allow difference and change. We can think of utopias that are plural and keep developing. The other is that a shift away from society-wide utopias need not lead only to ones in private, individual imaginations, but can yield others that are still social but at a more micro level within wider society. These, if they are to be generalized, even if not totally, are tested at the small scale first.

With the loss of confidence in future total communism and the erosion of social democracy within capitalism, some socialist utopias now are about other alternatives within current societies. They share communists' or democratic socialists' principles of collective control, the public good over private gain, need over profit, and egalitarian and non-market provision. They include, as discussed previously, alternative economies, social centres, free education experiments (like free universities), and food counterculture, anti-waste, and provision according to need. There is a precedent in 19th-century utopian socialism for pursuing non-capitalist utopias within capitalism (see Taylor, 1982; Geoghegan, 2008; Levitas, 2011). In recent sociology, writers like Holloway (2010) and Wright (2010, 2015, 2019) have outlined current utopias within capitalism that involve change in the direction of different future social forms. For Wright, alternatives include not just smashing capitalism but also, as discussed throughout this book, escaping, taming, and eroding it. There should not be a dichotomy between current micro-practices and future utopia. The former need not be an alternative to the latter.

## Feminist and anti-racist utopias

Feminist utopias (see Sargisson, 1996) are often found in fiction, sometimes science fiction – for instance, by authors like Charlotte Perkins Gilman, Marge Piercy, and Ursula K. Le Guin (see Bartkowski, 1989). Themes include: women living separately from men; biology, technology, and organization of childbirth and childcare that allow independence from men; and, because gender oppression is based in patriarchal ideology more than primarily economic structures, cultural change away from patriarchy. In *The Dialectic of Sex*, Firestone (2015) argues the disadvantages women have are biologically based, in pregnancy and childbearing. These link women to childcare, isolation, and dependence in the family. This can be overcome by contraception, artificial reproduction, state childcare, and a shift from the family to more communal childcare and relationships. Technology can also relieve women of domestic labour tasks. Gender inequality has a biological dimension but is imposed by patriarchy and can be overcome by technology and communal structures – what Firestone calls 'cybernetic communism'.

Proposals include a wage for housework, a caregivers' allowance, or a basic income for all, including domestic labourers and carers, making women in such roles paid workers. But this may reinforce women carrying out domestic roles, equalizing gender roles rather than overthrowing them. Fraser (1994) argues that both unpaid care and paid work should be generalized to all, not gender differentiated. In all jobs, it should be assumed that employees, whatever gender, may be caregivers, and there should be a shorter working week to allow for this. Care should be supported by social insurance and could be done by the state or in society. So, this is a feminist utopia based on an end to gender differentiation by the provision of social care and reduced working hours. (These themes are also discussed by Weeks, 2011.)

Robin Kelley (2002) outlines non-racist utopias from an African American perspective. Some of these are in spaces separate from White society, where people of colour own the land and share it equally. Kelley discusses visions of precolonial communal societies in Africa, separate from White people. In these, Africans have power and knowledge that are in advance of and educating the West. This was the case in premodern Asia also. Society in these utopias is seen as more ecological, holist, and communal, with a traditional, pre-capitalist life absent of western materialism and individualism. Needless to say, such societies in practice also had hierarchies and inequalities of power.

In modern times, there have been back-to-Africa utopias with freed enslaved people returning to Liberia and Sierra Leone, and those who escaped enslavement forming Maroon societies in the Americas and West Indies. For proponents of the back-to-Africa idea, like Marcus Garvey, this is not just about getting away from racism but also, in the spirit of utopianism, about building new societies with their own values and principles. Also anti-racist utopias have involved fighting for full rights, equality, and citizenship, integration on an equal basis in western societies, and self-determination within them in separate states or areas. Campaigns for reparation for enslavement are connected to utopias, because the funds can be used to set up new communities, institutions, enterprises, and media, or to purchase land (see Davidson, 2022, on Black utopias and the past of enslavement). An initiative coming out of Black Lives Matter protests, and following from the discussion of alternative education in Chapter 2, has been a free Black university (Swain, 2020).

Anti-racist utopianism has sometimes looked to communism. Racism is not caused by capitalism but is functional for it, linked to cheap labour and exploitation. So anti-racist utopias may involve going beyond capitalism, although anti-capitalism puts the onus for change on the proletariat as much as on people of colour. Chinese communism has had a focus in anti-racist utopias. One reason is that the Chinese are mostly not White. Another is that there was a cultural emphasis in Chinese communism, which fits with racism not being based primarily on economic structures like capitalism but on longer-running ideological and cultural structures of White domination. Culture is also a space where freedom can be lived or dreamt, so some anti-racist utopianism is in imagination, art, writing, and music.

Anti-racist utopianism has looked to the South and East, to Africa, Asia, and Latin America – to independence movements, Vietnamese resistance to the US, and liberation struggles in Africa and Latin America. These are seen as the vanguard of the international struggle for freedom that movements in the North can follow in the search for utopia.

# Materialism, conflict, and change

The utopias I have outlined involve changing to more ideal alternatives, current and future. But does utopia facilitate change or is it a hindrance? There have been many criticisms of utopianism, such as Marxist critiques of utopian socialism. Marx and Engels were positive about, and influenced by, utopian socialism, especially its critique of capitalism and in discussing what a communist society would look like (see Manuel and Manuel, 1979: Chapter 29; Paden, 2002; Levitas, 2011). But they were also critical, and in this section I will focus on two criticisms of utopianism that concern change, especially in relation to the material reality of mainstream current society (see Paden, 2002; Leopold, 2007; Geoghegan, 2008; Levitas, 2011). These suggest that utopianism and utopian projects are reactionary and regressive, and a hindrance to change. So, it is important to engage with them. Later in the chapter, I will discuss the criticism that endism and totalitarianism in utopias undermine change.

## Stepping aside, materialism, and change

The first criticism is that rather than facilitating change in mainstream society, utopianism encourages stepping aside from it to alternative current utopias, and this avoids and undermines transforming society. Or utopias may be dreams for the future that distract from making change in the present. (See Paden, 2002; Leopold, 2005; Geoghegan, 2008: Chapter 2; Pleyers, 2010; Allen, 2011.) A version of this point sees utopianism as having a compensatory function (see Levitas, 2011). When we imagine a rosier future, it helps us to cope with unhappiness about the present. This aids us in feeling happier now but may ignore the problems in current society and preserve the status quo rather than encouraging change away from it. From this critical point of view, engagement with current conflicts of capitalism is better than utopias that step away from them. The former involves changing society rather than avoiding its problems.

A related second criticism is that utopias separate the development of future societies from economic and social change by making plans for the future in an idealistic way, not based in material conflicts and developments. They are too much of a dream, not based in real processes. Utopias lack a political economy or analysis of present power or of current change and what possibilities for a future society this allows or facilitates. From this point of view, imagination alone is ineffective for social transformation, or even counterproductive and not the way to transform things. Historical materialism, in contrast, thinks about the future based on existing conflicts and tendencies, and where they may be going, and about material bases for change. (See Avineri, 1973; Paden, 2002; Geoghegan, 2008; Hudis, 2012; Dawson, 2016: Chapters 2 and 9; Leopold, 2016.)

There are answers to these criticisms. These need not defend stepping aside from society and pursuing idealistic dreams, but are on the basis that utopianism can be material and conflictual. They defend utopianism not against but from within a materialist, conflict, and Marxist framework. A first answer to the criticisms mentioned is that current utopian experiments do not step aside from society all that cleanly and are part of the conflicts and materialism of current society. One problem they face is that it is, in fact, difficult to disengage from society. Co-ops, intentional communities, or free universities, for instance, engage in meaningful and ongoing ways with surrounding society. This might be engagement with the customers of the co-op, the students of the free university, or the institutions and processes, state or capitalist, they interact with as part of their projects. Such initiatives engage with suppliers, retailers, the capitalist and market economy, funders, law, government, and local communities. Their members and users are part of wider society, in work, family, education, welfare, and other areas of their lives, and participate in it, as do the utopias they partake in.

Furthermore, the alternative ideologies and organization of current utopias create contradictions with existing society. They may, for instance, have non-market or non-capitalist principles that contradict those of the wider economy, society, and state. They are part of the contradictions and relations of current society, within and against it, economically, socially, and culturally, and do not avoid the conflicts of society. Forging a utopian experiment in the here and now is as much part of the material conflicts and development of current society, and the change that leads to, as it is apart from these. It contributes to conflicts and negations in society as much as evades them. (Moylan, 1986, discusses utopias in literature as critical, oppositional, and a negation of the present. See also Levitas, 2011, and Sargisson, 2012.)

A second answer to criticisms mentioned is that current utopias pursue change based on the material experience of alternatives as much as by propounding a theory or ideology for the future: they are not just conflictual, but also materialist rather than idealist. Existing small-scale experimental utopias ground change in current societies in their actions. They found future-oriented utopianism in current material practices of alternatives as much as in theoretical or ideological beliefs about future alternatives. In this sense, they can be more materialist than some revolutionary paths. Revolutionary perspectives base transformation in material changes to capitalism, but the alternative they propose can rely more on a theoretical and ideological case than the material experience of it. Current utopias, however, create material alternatives in current society as a basis for change to the future. They are about showing (more actual) as much as telling (more theoretical), or about 'deed instead of … argument', as Marx (1864) says when discussing co-ops as experiments that can be part of change to socialism. From a perspective that grounds change in material reality, future-oriented utopianism can be accused of speculative theory, but current utopias ground the future in current experiment and demonstration, rather than argument (see Goodwin and Taylor, 2009; for an advocacy of experimentalist socialism, see Honneth, 2017). Against them, a perspective that wants to build communism later and not also now can be seen to be working in the vein of speculative theory about the alternative. Raekstad and Gradin, 2020, argue that practice is as important as reading theory in developing the powers, drives, and consciousness for free, equal, and democratic organization, as is the case with the process of learning in all areas of life.

Utopianism is materialist in other ways. For Bauman (1976), utopian ideas, like others, develop from material experience and represent material interests, often dissenting ones, and they are based in the inventive elements of humanity. Similarly, Moylan (1986) says that utopias are rooted in class needs and wants, and the historical context. Mannheim (1979) saw ideology as of the dominant, looking back and maintaining society, while utopia is dreams of the future by the subordinate, part of transformation away from the present. Levitas (1979) and Goodwin and Taylor (2009) argue that utopias change with social forms of society, and so have a basis in material reality. Jameson (2007) contends that utopias develop out of material experience and are bound to it, so it is difficult to escape from this to imagine idealistic alternatives. In these senses, utopias are not ideas created out of the air, but have a material basis. Utopianism cannot be dismissed on the basis that future change will come out of material conditions rather than speculative plans, because utopia, as materialists point out about ideas in general, develops out of material conditions. The dichotomy between materialism and utopianism is false.

A third answer to the criticisms mentioned is that utopias are not just oppositional and conflictual within capitalism, but positive and creative, and this can be good for the morale of people involved in change and, so, good for change. Ongoing participation in oppositional and conflict politics can be disheartening, demoralizing, and even emotionally damaging. Creative utopianism can feel more progressive, with the focus in making and producing something. For some, creative change is easier and more uplifting to engage in than conflictual and oppositional change. The latter is important and necessary, but by also positively constructing, utopian alternatives contribute to social change as much as avoid it.

Both historical materialist and utopian perspectives can be revolutionary and about change. One issue is whether to start building utopian communities in the here and now as a basis for change or to leave it until after capitalism. I have mentioned materialist aspects of current utopianism, arguing that existing alternative forms provide a material basis for alternative forms in the future. Alternatives now can be part of change to alternatives in the future and do not need to be left until then. It is better to experiment with new social forms in current society than risk leaving them untested until after societal change.

## Utopianism and capitalism

An issue is whether the material bases for change are in fighting conflicts in and with capitalism, or also in experiments in utopia now. I have said that current utopias provide contradictions with wider society. So, they are not alternatives to conflicts now, but part of them. In terms of conflicts in capitalism beyond alternative forms, those trying utopias in the present day can take both routes: alternative societies now and participation in other conflicts of capitalism itself – for instance, in the capitalist workplace or in opposition to state policies. Many who pursue utopian experiments as a basis for future change are also often involved in material conflicts within capitalism and in relation to the state (see Pleyers, 2010, on the alter-globalization movement; see Raekstad and Gradin, 2020, and Monticelli, 2021, on prefigurative and in-and-against-the-state politics being combinable). The approaches are not mutually exclusive and do not have to substitute for one another. Current utopianism does not have to be an alternative to oppositional politics within capitalism; it can be part of and an accompaniment to it. The dichotomy between within-capitalism conflict politics and utopian politics is a false one.

One possibility is that pursuing alternative societies within capitalism will lead to them being dominated and co-opted by capitalism. In tension with the argument that utopias step aside from society, this view suggests they cannot do so. For example, as mentioned in Chapter 1, Greenberg (1981, 1983) argues that co-ops in market capitalist contexts can adopt wider possessive individualism rather than co-operative and egalitarian attitudes. Alternatives in current society must engage with and compromise with wider structures, which could reproduce those structures, absorb their ideologies, and undermine alternatives and their role in creating a different society in the future. Therefore, from this point of view, alternatives to capitalism should be pursued after capitalism. However, non-utopian oppositional politics aimed at the alternative after capitalism can also be co-opted or compromised when it engages in struggles against the state and with capitalism within a society where the economy, state, culture, and discourse are dominated by capitalism and power. Such politics has to relate to institutions like government and NGOs, such as trade unions, as well as capitalism and mainstream discourses and power.

There is a danger of co-option and domination by capitalism, as there is with all politics in capitalism. But, as I have argued, current utopias create contradictions with capitalism and conflict with it. Furthermore, alternatives are not monolithic or passive. There are variations among them. Some are more alternative and less likely to be co-opted than others. For example, co-ops set up to save jobs are more about economic survival than co-operative and democratic ideals, and may be more likely to succumb to co-option into capitalism. Alternative co-ops set up with co-operative and democratic ideals as their main aim are more likely to resist co-option (see Cornforth, 1983). Co-ops can and do react against incorporation, organizationally and ideologically, finding ways to counter co-option into capitalist and hierarchical forms and ideas (Bate and Carter, 1986, Cornforth, 1995, and Masquelier, 2017a, discuss how this can happen in co-ops; Kanter, 1972, discusses how intentional communities maintain their autonomy and values).

## Materialism, utopianism, and Marxism

Table 3.1 outlines views on social change from the point of view of materialist and utopian perspectives I have outlined. 1) Future utopia perspectives are oriented to an ideal society in the future. 2) Current utopia perspectives are oriented to utopian experiments in current society, for their own sake and also as the basis for wider social change in the future. 3) Materialist revolutionary perspectives envisage a different society in the future but are critical of perspectives that focus on future ideals or small-scale utopias now, aside from society, rather than present-day conflicts against capitalism and the state in trying to get to a future society. 4) Materialist utopian views see these different approaches as not mutually exclusive and as compatible.

Levitas (2011) discusses Marxist perspectives on utopia and change, and charts how some, such as Marx and Engels (although not with complete consistency), argue utopia prevents change (perspective 3 in the table), while other Marxists, such as Bloch, E.P. Thompson, William Morris, and sometimes Herbert Marcuse, argue that it facilitates change (more in tune with perspective 4). (Goodwin and Taylor, 2009, also include Rudolf Bahro as a Marxist utopian). This may reflect that Marx and Engels' criticisms are of aspects of utopianism that are contingent, not necessary (see Leopold, 2016), so it is possible for Marxists to also be positive about utopianism. While Marx and Engels criticize utopian socialists on materialist and conflict grounds, they are also, as I have mentioned, supportive, and Marxist defenders of utopianism appeal to statements of Marx and Engels to claim a Marxist heritage for their views. My reply to materialist and conflict criticism is a materialist and conflict one, consistent with Marxism. Monticelli (2018) discusses how critical and Marxist thinkers have been engaging positively with grassroots interstitial prefigurative initiatives, mentioning John Holloway,

**Table 3.1:** Utopianism, materialism, and change

| Perspective | Perspective on materialism | Perspective on utopianism |
|---|---|---|
| 1. Future utopia perspectives | It is important not just to focus on material conflicts with only basic principles for the alternative; there should be a plan for what a future society will look like | Future utopias can be a basis for criticism of the present, and an ideal, both of which can be catalysts for change and a plan for what we are aiming for |
| 2. Current utopia perspectives | Material experiments in utopian alternatives now, as well as theories and ideologies about alternatives, can be the basis for wider social change in the future | Utopian alternatives now are the basis for future alternatives; future utopian alternatives and present ones are aims |
| 3. Materialist revolutionary perspectives | Engaging in material conflicts in capitalism to overthrow it is the basis for change, not developing separate alternatives aside from or inside capitalism | Current utopian experiments step aside from and avoid conflicts within capitalism; future utopias are not based enough in current conflicts within capitalism |
| 4. Materialist utopian perspectives | There can be experiments in utopias now that are a material basis for alternative societies now and in the future; simultaneously, we can engage in material conflicts within and against capitalism | Positive utopias now can be pursued as part of and alongside conflicts within capitalism and as the basis for wider social change in the future |

Erik Olin Wright, and Ana C. Dinerstein as examples. She calls on younger critical and Marxist scholars to do the same. She argues that change can come through both political power and grassroots prefigurative initiatives, and these can be complementary and need not be seen as alternatives to one another. Relatedly, Raekstad (2018) argues that prefigurative politics is vital for revolutionary strategy and the development of revolutionary subjects towards a free and democratic socialist society, and that it is in Marxist theories of practice rather than in contradiction to these, as is often proposed, showing Marxism and anarchism to be closer than sometimes imagined (see also Raekstad and Gradin, 2020).

Marxists can stay Marxist in pursuing utopian change. But they need to incorporate liberal and pluralist concerns (if not liberalism and pluralism *in toto*) to keep utopia and change. This leads to the next section and is a concern of the next chapter too.

# Totalitarianism, utopianism, and change

My argument has been that utopias can be a material and conflictual basis for change within current society, rather than a retreat from transformation. Another criticism concerning utopianism and change contends that utopian societies are endist and totalitarian, so stop change once utopia has been achieved (see Dahrendorf, 1958). But this need not be the case. Self-determination and process can be utopian ideals, and these involve transformation. Utopia can have liberal and plural dimensions, which allow dissent, diversity, and criticism that lead to change. Experimental plural utopia can also be a counterweight to the rationalist constructivist utopianism that critics of utopia as totalitarian focus on. I will discuss liberal and pluralist criticisms and then come to the implications for change.

A key concern about utopias is that they are dangerous and potentially totalitarian. From this point of view, they are ideas of a good society that require conformity to the ideal. The ideal may be a particular one, of some, yet requires general adherence, from all. (See Butler, 1983, Gray, 2008, and Popper, 2011, for anti-constructivist, liberty, and conservative arguments, and Sargisson, 2012; although liberal critics of utopianism may propose their own utopias – for instance, Hayek, 1980.) Concern about the potential totalitarianism of utopias is reinforced by the experience of fascism and communism in the 20th century. They were ideologies with total visions of society, and in some cases envisioning the internationalization of their form of society, leaving not even global alternatives as a possibility.

Common conformity in a utopia can be justified on the basis that humanity has a potential nature that will be realized or expressed in such a society. Everyone will coincide with the utopia because it reflects their being. Or the society will lead to consciousness or human essence that matches it. If production or living are controlled and run collectively, for instance, we will all develop a collective consciousness. So, people will voluntarily accord with a total, society-wide form that fits with them.

This may be an unrealistic or too demanding idea of human nature or humans. In any society, there is likely to be plurality. Capitalism itself is hybrid and includes non-capitalist structures and values, despite the prevalence of the capitalist and market economy and culture. If there is plurality, then to achieve broad commitment to the utopia, people will have to be persuaded of its values. If people do not necessarily fit with a society because of their nature or its virtues, they will have to be convinced. If voluntary commitment or ideological persuasion do not work, then a utopia may have to use force or repression to ensure adherence. Furthermore, the passion for utopias by their supporters can be dangerous and involve a belief in their own rightness that is a threat to individuals who do not wish to fit into the model, non-conformity, and dissidence. In short, there are totalitarian dangers in utopian ideas of ideal societies. Furthermore, whether a total ideal is adopted voluntarily or by imposition, it will lead to an end to change, because the perfect society will have been achieved.

Liberalism is against totalistic ideas of a good society and in favour of individuals choosing their ends, within a framework of a state and law setting boundaries and maintaining order. Liberalism can be counterposed to utopianism because it permits individuals to decide their goals rather than being required to conform to those of society. This choice is undermined by the economic and power inequalities that liberalism allows to grow, as socialist criticisms show. But egalitarian or Left-wing liberals will argue this problem can be countered by redistribution of wealth, income, and power to underpin the realization of freedom that liberals value, redistribution being balanced with liberal institutions and principles. Socialists can be better than liberals at pursuing freedom, as long as they subject themselves to some liberal restraints. I will come back to this in the next chapter, and I emphasize I am not in this book advocating socialism adopting liberalism, but making sure it builds in liberal goals and values, yet within a socialist rather than liberal framework.

## Pluralism and change in utopia

One response to concerns about utopias as totalitarian is to contend that there should not be a dichotomy between utopia and liberalism. This involves acceptance of alternatives and plurality. A utopia can be an ideal society, but one that is tolerant of diversity. Belief in a utopia does not mean it must be imposed. So, we may decide that a society based on collective ownership of the economy and of work is our ideal. But we could also feel that such a society will not be for everyone and will never attract complete conformity and, therefore, that we accept plurality, including a minor role for private enterprise. To not do so would require imposition on those who wish to do something different. The utopia could be attractive enough to ensure that divergence from the dominant ideal is not widespread. Or there can be regulation to allow diversity but protect a strong role for collective ownership. This does not mean utopia is a variety of utopias, but a utopia in which alternatives are permitted (see Horowitz, 1989). This is relevant to what I argue about pluralist socialism in the next chapter, that it should include liberal protections and non-collectivist elements in a predominantly democratic economy.

We should not polarize liberal aims and utopia. One possibility is that liberalism is a utopia (for example, see Mannheim, 1979; Goodwin and Taylor, 2009). However, I wish to focus on the possibility of it being *part* of utopia. All societies are hybrids, and utopias can aspire to ideal arrangements combined with liberal tolerance of alternatives. Balances like this are difficult to maintain, and if the dominant drive is to an ideal rather than individuals pursuing all ends, it is right to highlight that the former is a threat to the latter. But it is also worth considering that people in society can try to make sure the two coexist. (Bobbio, 1988, 2009; Honneth, 2017; Sunkara, 2019, among others, argue that socialism should incorporate liberal concerns or institutions, if not liberalism as a framework, and I will come back to the relationship between socialism and liberalism in the next chapter.)

These points relate to the argument that utopianism rules out change because in a utopia the ideal society has been realized. There is no alternative left to strive for. This potentiality is raised by Marx's concept of communism as the final stage in history, and ideas like Fukuyama's (1989) liberal end of history. However, current or future utopianism can allow freedoms and plurality – in current utopianism by the utopia being within existing society and alongside other forms; in the future by allowing pluralism and alternatives in the utopia. In these versions, achieving a utopia does not end change. With pluralism, different forms and criticism continue, and so allow the possibility of change. If utopias now or in the future are not total but are combined with alternatives, this provides other and critical views that can stimulate change.

Utopian experimentation now and utopianism with pluralism in the future provide answers to criticism from writers like Hayek and Popper that utopianism places too much faith in humans' rational capacities to design and construct an ideal society (see Abensour, 2008). Such critics prefer trial and error, practical experiments, evolution, and conservatism. But utopian experimentation allows for material testing of utopia, for diversity in current and future utopias, and for alternatives should utopias fail. This gives utopia an empirical and testable dimension, not just a theoretical and speculative one. It allows modification or rejection and, so, change. This is a materialist approach that sees theory being proven or otherwise in practice or action.

But if utopia has been achieved, surely no change is needed. And if a change to something better is possible, that must mean we have not reached utopia. I think a utopian society is compatible with change. A utopian society will not be perfectly realized because of factors such as political and cultural blocks, complexity, and interpretation. So, it will always be the best that can be achieved in the circumstances, short of utopia, and so open to change and development. What is utopian now or at the time it is achieved may not continue to be ideal because of developments, intended or unforeseen, such as in technology or human nature, or unanticipated problems, and so will need change (see Leopold, 2016). If utopia develops from material experiments, these will lead to adjustments or changes to the utopia. In addition, utopian ideas are products of material circumstances. A utopian society will create new material circumstances that facilitate fresh utopian ideas, novel objectives, and change. A materialist perspective responds not just to materialist critics, as discussed previously, but also to liberal critics who see utopianism as totalitarian and final.

Ideals for a utopia can include criticism and pluralism, and these lead to change, which can also be a utopian ideal. It is possible to have criticism, pluralism, and change in utopia and utopia as a process, even when it is achieved (for a similar argument, see Drousioti, 2019, and Drousioti and Papastephanou, 2022). Sargisson (2012) sees utopia as engagement with and critique of the present and imagination of something better, but not a blueprint, perfect, total, realizable, and static. Levitas (2013) envisages utopia as an imagined totality but also as heuristic, provisional and reflective, and open to criticism and debate. For her, utopia, being about critical assessment of the present, holistic thinking about a better future, and trying to get there, is a method (of what she calls the 'imaginary reconstitution of society') rather than a goal or description. (See also Goodwin and Taylor, 2009: 111, 232–3, 241–3.) Marx's idea of communism may or may not have been utopian, depending on your perspective. But it was envisaged as an endpoint, yet one in which change was still possible. This is because communism, by definition, is about the collective self-determination of society, so it is open to society being changed by collective decisions. Also for Marx, communism allows human self-development so in theory allows people to change. A final society can be dynamic rather than static (see Paden, 2002; Geoghegan, 2008).

Goodwin and Taylor (2009) respond to liberal criticisms of utopia in part by questioning liberalism and justifying non-liberal utopianism. But rather than rejecting the liberal and pluralist framework of criticisms of utopia, I have argued that utopianism can be liberal and plural and is not necessarily in contradiction with the aims of such approaches, even if it is with their theory, means, and practice in total. The conflation of utopia with illiberalism, and the dichotomy between utopia and liberalism and pluralism, are false and not necessary. Liberal and pluralist critics can be answered with the goals they aim for, and not necessarily by rejecting them.

## Conclusions

Criticisms of utopianism make false conflations and dichotomies. Utopia is conflated with idealism, speculation, separation from society, the future, substitution for other forms of politics, rationalism, totality, endism, and totalitarianism. What is potential is made into necessity. Arguments against utopianism involve false dichotomies between utopia and materialism, conflict, liberalism, pluralism, oppositional and institutional politics, and trial and error. These conflations and dichotomies can be overcome while utopia maintains its distinctiveness.

I have discussed future and current utopianisms. I have discussed two possible perspectives from which utopias can be seen to undermine social change. One sees utopianism as idealist and stepping aside from material conflicts in society, rather than engaging with them to build change. I have not argued against the material, conflictual approach by defending ideal dreams or stepping aside as a basis for change, but rather for utopianism's potentiality for change on a materialist, conflictual basis. The second perspective sees utopias being endist and totalitarian, so stopping change. They envisage us having reached perfection, not allowing diversion from the utopian ideal. I have said that utopianism can be about process and pluralism. It does not have to be endist and totalitarian and, on those bases, end change. Rather than rejecting anti-endism and pluralism, I have said utopia encompasses these.

In terms of criticism from a materialist and conflict perspective, utopianism does not need to reject this approach but can have a materialist and conflict approach. I have given a materialist and conflict reply to a materialist and conflict criticism. On liberal and pluralist concerns about change in utopia, utopianism does not need to reject these but can encompass such concerns, if not liberalism and pluralism *in toto*. I have argued for liberal and plural dimensions to utopia in response to liberal and pluralist concerns. Criticism from materialist/conflict and liberal/pluralist perspectives have not been responded to by rejection of their concerns, but answered on their own terms. Utopianism is part of changing society, materially and now and in the future. In the next chapter, I will, among other things, look further at the relationship between liberalism and alternative societies.

## Further reading

Ruth Levitas' (2003) 'Introduction: the elusive idea of utopia', in *History of the Human Sciences*, discusses the different guises that utopia comes in. And Levitas' *The Concept of Utopia* (2011) is a good overview of sociological theories of utopia. In 'The ends of utopia', in *New Literary History*, Krishan Kumar (2010) discusses kinds of utopias in pessimistic mode. He has also written books on the topic: *Utopianism* (1991) and *Utopia and Anti-utopia in Modern Times* (1987).

Barbara Goodwin and Keith Taylor's (2009) *The Politics of Utopia* is very useful, and the journal *Utopian Studies* has, among many other useful articles, L.T. Sargent's (1994) 'Three faces of utopianism revisited', a good overview of many key areas.

Paul Raekstad and Sofa Gradin's (2020) *Prefigurative Politics* (along with Raekstad, 2018) gives an excellent outline and case for the approach (which combines here-and-now and future-oriented utopianisms) being combinable with Marxist anti-capitalism and politics oriented to the state, rather than counterposed to them as claimed by critics.

Robin Kelley's (2002) *Freedom Dreams* is great to read on non-racist utopias. Shulamith Firestone's (2015) *The Dialectic of Sex* is a radical feminist classic and brings out technological and communist elements found in many utopias. Readings on socialism are recommended in Chapters 1 and 4.

# 4

# Socialism and Its Critics

In Chapters 1 and 2, I discussed a range of social and economic alternative societies. Many of these are utopian, and in the last chapter I outlined utopianism and discussed criticisms of it. Many alternatives also have socialist elements, and in this chapter I will focus in more depth on socialism as an alternative society and how it may respond to criticisms. The chapter discusses the extent to which socialism must revise itself to respond to criticisms, or is so inherently vulnerable to their points that it must limit itself to meet their objections. I will be looking at green, feminist, liberal, and neoliberal criticisms. I have chosen these perspectives because I believe they address the core components of socialism and represent very important points of view in themselves.

I think that while socialism is vulnerable to green and feminist criticisms, it is not inherently contrary to green and feminist aims so can adapt its framework to meet them. In relation to liberal criticisms, while socialism has distinctive things to contribute to achieving liberal aims and so should be expanded to do so, I argue it is also structurally vulnerable to liberal criticisms and so adaptation to tackle their points is not enough and socialism must also be self-limiting to meet liberal concerns. The possibilities for responding to criticisms are expansion, adaptation, or self-limitation. Socialism needs to adapt and expand to meet green and feminist criticism, but must both expand and limit itself to meet liberal concerns.

Socialism is a much-criticized ideology, and its advocates have had to work hard to defend it. Attempts at socialism in practice have gone badly wrong (of course, capitalism has too), and capitalism has spread while socialism has not developed in recent decades in an ongoing way (though there has been a revival of support for socialism in recent years). Criticisms have been fierce, and responses from socialists are often very defensive. However, socialists need to be open to criticism, to see if it does expose problems and, if so, whether these are inherent and so require revisions to the ideology or more nonessential and require adjustment rather than more structural change. Socialists should also be open to the possibility that perspectives they disagree with more and are most resistant to could strike at the heart of their ideology, as well as ones they are more friendly to and more willing to take on.

Socialism's responses to its critics can involve:

1. Disagreement. The criticism is not valid.
2. Expansion. The alternative or critical perspective shows that more socialism rather than less is needed. Socialism actually provides a solution to the point or perspective that it is seen to fail on.
3. Acceptance and a need for extra dimensions to socialism. Socialism is not shown to be flawed fundamentally and so in need of rejection, but is shown to be limited and in need of adding to.
4. Adaptation. More than adding extra dimensions is needed; the changing of elements of the ideology is also required. There are flaws in socialism itself, so it needs to be adapted and changed, not just added to. However, socialism itself is not fundamentally flawed and so can continue in an adapted form rather than being rejected.
5. Self-limitation. Socialism cannot answer the problem. In fact, the problem strikes at inherent structural dimensions of socialism that need to be restricted to allow for counter structures that can answer the problem, in a more plural society rather than an entirely socialist one. So, socialism needs to limit itself and not cover all of society, but allow alternatives alongside or within it in a plural society.
6. Rejection of socialism. The criticism is so fundamentally penetrating that socialism must be abandoned.

Socialists are defensive towards attacks on them and critical of ideologies like liberalism. This is understandable and often correct, because they write in the context of capitalism and liberalism being dominant, and because criticism from such perspectives may be problematic and ideologies like liberalism flawed in themselves. In such circumstances, a critical attitude to liberalism and anti-socialism is important. However, I am writing from a perspective looking at the alternative of socialism. In this context, a critical attitude to questioning from liberalism combined with an openness to examining how telling it is should be pursued, rather than solely a defence against liberalism. Liberalism in a capitalist context rightly attracts a critical perspective from socialists. But I am discussing liberalism within a socialist context which should attract both critique and openness, albeit sceptical. Although this chapter is about criticisms of socialism and asking whether socialism is vulnerable to them, it is written from the point of view of exploring the possibilities of socialism. I am asking socialists to be open-minded about criticisms so that their ideology and practice can be improved, and not from an anti-socialist view.

This chapter includes communism, social democratic socialism, democratic socialism, and more anarchist versions of socialism in the remit of what is discussed (on the variety of socialisms, see Wright, 1996). My main focus is on socialism as a society or alternative rather than socialism as a critique or values, although the former and the latter cannot be separated. I am defining socialism in this chapter as the commitment to a society in which collective ownership is the dominant economic form and in which there is much greater economic equality than under capitalism, with distribution based more on need or work than power or the market. Of course, there are other ways of defining socialism, and some socialists would not agree with these definitions. However, I think these commitments mark socialism off from other political ideologies and are held by many socialists as defining their ideology.

For some, collective ownership is a means rather than an end and socialism should be defined by values like equality and community rather than instruments for achieving them (a view held by Tony Blair and Anthony Crosland, 2006). But I do not think socialist objectives can be achieved without collective ownership in the economy, because economic ownership gives the power to shape society. Ownership is essential for socialism as a constructivist doctrine. Collective ownership also distinguishes socialism from other ideologies, and collective control is a democratic end as well as a means. Democracy is incomplete and undermined if it does not include the economic sphere. Collective ownership can take different forms, from state ownership to co-operative and local forms, and government, community, worker, consumer, or more mutualist forms. This is one way it goes across communist, social democratic, and more anarchist approaches. I discuss economic democracy in more detail in the next chapter.

Economic egalitarianism also distinguishes socialism from other ideologies (Bobbio, 1996). Economic equality is distinct from social or political equality, which other ideologies are committed to. It does not need to mean complete economic equality, as distribution of income, goods, or services according to criteria such as need, effort, or the nature of work, as was discussed in Chapter 1, would lead to differing distributions. But while these would not lead to completely equal distributions, they would be much more egalitarian than distribution under capitalism. Communism and social democratic, democratic socialist, and anarchist socialism would all be more equal. Even though communism may be more committed to collective ownership than equal distributions, the former would lead to more of the latter. While collective ownership is a socialist commitment covering the production sphere, economic equality often covers the distributional sphere. However, some argue that economic inequality is based on wealth ownership and needs to be tackled there (see Piketty, 2021).

Other definitions of socialism could include co-operation, planning for need, or an end to alienation or exploitation. However, I think one thing that makes socialism distinctive is the pursuit of these via collective ownership and economic equality. So, these other principles are covered by the two definitional criteria I have set out.

## Communism, social democracy, and co-operative socialism

In this section, I will lay out some key elements of communist, social democratic, and more anarchist socialism, the latter of which I will discuss as co-operative socialism because of the forms it takes in practice. Chapter 5 will focus more on democratic socialism. Communism was outlined briefly in Chapter 1, so if you read about it there you could skim the discussion of it here, but I will develop aspects here relevant to this chapter.

### Communism

Communism takes different forms, but the main variant of it has been Marxist communism (see Avineri, 1968; Evans, 1975; Levin, 1989, Hudis, 2012; Dawson, 2016; also Marx's writings on communism discussed here can be found in, for instance, Marx and Engels, 1968; Marx, 1975, 1998, 2009). Other forms are part of the co-operative strand I will come back to. Marxist communism bases its principles in a critique of capitalism as much as in communism itself and has a historical materialist understanding of contradictions and developments in capitalism leading towards communism, as we saw in Chapter 3. The contradiction between the social nature of production on one hand and the private accumulation of the wealth it produces under capitalism on the other is seen to be unsustainable and only resolvable by social production being matched with the social appropriation of the wealth produced. This in turn requires social ownership of production. Capitalism creates a proletariat with a common interest and consciousness that will see their interests in conflict with capitalists and private ownership and so overthrow them and pursue social ownership.

This will lead to the end of people's alienation from the product, production, and other humans, because people collectively control production and the product, communally reap the rewards of their production rather than it being appropriated by others, and are united with fellow humans in one class of collective owners. It leads to the end of exploitation, because the wealth that workers produce is not taken by others but is collectively reaped. There are no longer two classes – capitalists and workers – because everyone collectively owns production so is in a common class. Without a division of classes, a state is no longer needed by one class to maintain control over other classes, so the state will wither away, as will fundamental ideological divisions, because there is no longer a divide between groups with contending material interests that generate diverging values. All that is needed is an administrative machinery to carry out the communally determined societal planning. Freedom should be increased, because people collectively control their destiny rather than being ruled by a capitalist class and state under conditions of great inequality.

In a communist society, production will be collectively owned and used to produce for social need rather than privately owned and done for private profit. As wealth will be collectively appropriated rather than creamed off by the rich, there will be greater resources for all in society. This, together with the productivity of new technology, can be used by the collective for the general good, to shorten the working week rather than increase production and profits. Consequently, people will have more free time, and there need not be such a rigid division of labour if the organization of labour is socially determined. While this system is about collective production rather than distribution, with distribution according to need rather than equality, you would still expect a collectively controlled distribution geared around need to be hugely more economically equal than under capitalism.

Societies that call or have called themselves communist have not achieved communism. State socialism is a better term for what materialized. Collective ownership stayed at a state level, theoretically on behalf of the people, rather than the economy being socially controlled by all, and a dominant political class took the place of the dominant economic class. The party and state, which was supposed to seize capitalist power and then disseminate it to collective ownership, did not let go of the economic power it had gained control of. Conformity to state socialism was maintained by propaganda and repression rather than voluntary will, and freedom was, as such, curtailed. However, making some generalizations, such societies did attempt forms of collective ownership and production according to a calculation of need, decided by the political class, rather than on the basis of profit for capitalists. In areas, there was greater economic equality than under capitalism. There was an attempt at socialist institutions but this got stuck at the statist transitional stage, went off track and stopped well short of and away from true communism (and state socialist societies generated their alternative societies within; see Fürst and McLellan, 2018). One question, however, is whether there is something in socialist ideas that leads to such consequences, however possibly unintended, and I will return to this.

## From communism to social democratic and co-operative socialism

Social democrats split with Marxism at the start of the 20th century (see Stephens, 1979; Esping-Andersen, 1985; Przeworski, 1986). They had a more optimistic view of capitalism. Rather than capitalism becoming polarized between the rich and poor, it seemed Marxist predictions were confounded, and social democrats saw a middle class emerging. These had a stake in capitalism, with the dynamism of capitalism not only enriching the bourgeoisie but also providing benefits to the middle class and poor, albeit in a situation of continuing inequality. This meant that the contradictions of capitalism, while real, became sustainable, because enough people had enough of an investment in the system to live with them, and capitalism was more robust and less crisis-ridden than had been predicted. Furthermore, writers following Weber felt that even if you accepted ownership-based depictions of the class system, people who had a common class location in terms of economic ownership had different chances based on advantages such as education, ethnicity, and gender, and so did not always develop anti-capitalist consciousness (see Parkin, 2002: Chapter 4). To appeal to the middle class and a better-off working class, who had more investment in capitalism, social democrats moderated their message, making it less anti-capitalist and more about reforms to capitalism.

So, socialism in a social democratic form became more about reform than revolution. But an accumulation of reforms over time could lead to a revolution in the sense of change to a socialist society, gradually and without violent insurrection. Where the latter happens, this is more a case of democratic socialism – for a democratic transition to socialism – than social democracy, the latter usually seen as about socialist gains within capitalism. One possibility for revolutionary reform is the taxation of excess profits of capitalist companies used to set up socially owned companies; another is requiring companies above a certain size to issue shares from profits to workers so that eventually they control the majority of the companies they work for, as in the Swedish Meidner Plan (Viktorsson and Gowan, 2017). This does not seize shares from capitalists, so reducing direct confrontation. It involves the gradual creation of social ownership step by step, diluting capitalism with more social ownership until it takes up such a proportion of the economy that it becomes predominantly socialist. Similarly, the expansion of public sector institutions based on need rather than profit involves, from this point of view, a gradual expansion of socialist principles in capitalism to the extent they become the dominant form in the economy. From another perspective, the revolutionary socialist Rosa Luxemburg (1973) argues that reforms can be part of the revolutionary process.

Social democrats tend to see the state as not so tied to the dictates of the capitalist economy and more useable for socialist achievements. So, with a more optimistic view of capitalism and the state, and a more stratified view of class, social democrats have a reformist and cross-class rather than revolutionary and proletarian view of change, within capitalism, maybe leading ultimately beyond capitalism but not necessarily so. As the 20th century went on, direct control through collective ownership became less central to social democratic policies, and intervention in the economy was channelled increasingly through more indirect levers like Keynesianism, which underpinned growth and the financing of welfare and public services via progressive taxation and public spending. Private ownership was left more intact in this approach, and the emphasis was more on distributional equality than on collective ownership of production.

Criticisms of communism led to greater support for social democracy and co-operative socialism. It was argued by some that private ownership and markets provide economic incentives for entrepreneurial and dynamic economic behaviour and can sometimes produce better information on what people want or need than planning does. So, socialists, it was perceived, should recognize the need for at least a mixed economy that includes private ownership and markets alongside public ownership and planning. More principled arguments that people should be allowed to earn money from entrepreneurial activity and maintain private property rights gave further support for such a system. Critics argued that a revolution to communism relied too much on collective altruism, which would not just appear but had to be developed over time, so supporting more gradualist routes. Another argument for such routes is that you should not try out a risky wholesale change to society unless it has been tried and tested to some extent; this supports co-operative experiments on a smaller scale before more wide-scale communism is built.

In Marxist conceptions, capitalism was supposed to develop collective class consciousness ready for communist consciousness after the revolution, but some have been sceptical about how far this theory will work out in practice. It has gone in part untested, because actual communism has been either imposed from outside or developed in pre-capitalist societies. Under capitalism, the development of collective consciousness is very mixed, which is not to say it is not there, especially considering how much pressure there is against it. The experience of dictatorial and inefficient central state ownership has also led to support for more small-scale, bottom-up collective ownership in the form of co-operative experiments. It supports the case for localist, co-operative, experimental, prefigurative, trial-and-error socialism, based on participatory democracy at a more appropriate scale (Schumacher, 1973), more in tune with the anarchist tradition of socialism. This involves a pluralist socialism as it comprises, at least at first, forms of socialism existing alongside private ownership and capitalism. If socialism is to be more all-encompassing, it would at least have to be on a voluntary, bottom-up basis, depending on the success of local socialism – rather than statist and top-down, forced and based on confidence that a relatively untested theory of communism will prove correct grounded on a theory of the failures of capitalism.

Of course, social democratic and co-operative socialism have their critics too. The pursuit of social democracy within capitalism and via electoral means and class alliances in a society with middle and embourgeoised working classes will lead to such compromises with capitalism, and even its more neoliberal forms, that socialism, it is argued, becomes lost. As long as capitalists are tolerated in a mixed economy, socialist ends will be undermined and changes that are achieved can be reversed. Socialism requires the revolutionary removal of capitalists. Co-operative socialism may also get swamped by capitalism, and its co-operative and democratic forms degenerate into more competitive and hierarchical forms in the pursuit of success in a market capitalist context, while also relying on example too much and state power too little to expand socialism more widely.

## Right-wing and neoliberal criticisms of socialism

In Chapter 1, I discussed criticisms of socialism by the liberal John Stuart Mill. In this chapter, I will outline criticism from more neoliberal and starkly capitalist perspectives, using the thought of the important thinkers Robert Nozick and Friedrich Hayek. Nozick (1974) argues that how economic assets are distributed in society should be based less on matching a pre-given pattern that society wants to achieve, like equality, and more to do with where property or income (his focus is on property) comes from – an issue of historical entitlement to what you have. The history of how you came upon things should guide what is just, not a pattern you want to achieve.

There are three key principles for Nozick. First, if property is gained through an initial acquisition of unowned land that leaves others no worse off materially, that is OK. So, if I stake a claim in some unowned land and employ you as a non-owner to work on that land for an income that does not make you poorer than you were before, that is fair. Second, if transfers of property are made freely and fairly from one person to another and this leads to inequality, there can be no legitimate complaints. If I decide to give my property or some of my income to my children and they benefit from that, and there was no force or coercion in the process, it is just. If I buy tickets to a football game and the proceeds go to highly paid players, that is alright. It may lead to huge riches for some football players, but no one made me buy the ticket. It is not right for socialists to coercively redistribute the property or income my children or well-paid footballers gained freely and without any coercion or fraud. Third, if property was unfairly or unfreely gained, redistribution back to the rightful owners or their descendants is right to rectify these injustices. So, this could be the case, for example, for land seized from Native Americans, Jews in the Nazi period, or middle-class families under communism. This was taken by force so should be given back. But redistribution is not acceptable on the basis resources are distributed unequally if that allocation came about freely and fairly and through legitimate historical means. This relates to Mill's point, albeit a different one, that it is wrong to take away property from those who have accumulated it under what they understood to be the rules of the old game of capitalism. Nozick's account defends unequal distributions of property gained historically freely and fairly against socialist redistribution done with a commitment to a pattern of distribution in society that is more equal.

Hayek's key criticism is that while socialists may be well intentioned, they overestimate human beings' rational capacity for understanding people's needs, and government's ability to deliver to those needs – an informational point (see Butler, 1983; Kukathis, 1989). Humans do not have enough capability epistemologically to build knowledge of needs and wants, and design a whole society according to key principles – what he calls 'constructivism'. Furthermore, if you try to decide democratically what people need, taking into account the plurality of groups and individuals in society and their views, people will not be able to agree except in small-scale homogeneous societies. Trying to do so on a larger scale will result in conflict and stalemate over what the good society should be. So, authorities will have to step in and decide for people what they need, and that is the beginning of a slide towards dictatorship or even totalitarianism, with government telling people what they need and imposing it rather than people deciding for themselves (Hayek, 1962).

Hayek believes the organic evolution of society is better than the conscious design of it, because under the former what works best survives in Darwinian fashion and is not imposed by specific groups. Markets, in particular, provide information more efficiently than plans. People's own consumer demand gives better information about what they want than government planners' calculations. Markets also provide, in the rewards that can be gained from designing and implementing successful projects, economic incentives for innovation and dynamism. If people can make money out of a good, creative, and popular project, they will have the motivation to pursue it. If, as under socialism, they get paid according to need or equality regardless of how hard they work or what inventive products they come up with, why should they try?

Without the information provided by markets, dictators will decide for people what is good for them. In the absence of monetary incentives for entrepreneurial behaviour and effort, people will have to be coerced to work; if they are not, there will be economic stagnation and lack of progress. Furthermore, according to Hayek, markets are freer and more just because there are no deliberate intentions designing the whole market economy, so no dictatorship, which there is under planned economies. The outcomes of markets are accidental rather than deliberate, so while they may lead to inequality, they are not imposed. Even if we do not like the outcomes, they are, in his view, more liberal and just.

There are many problems with Nozick's and Hayek's theories, too many to mention all here, but I will highlight some key ones. Nozick's theory is focused on individual entitlements to property and rules out required obligations to others as part of a balance in society. This is apart from the case of distributions that arise from unfree or fraudulent means, where he does agree with rectifications that give things back to the rightful owners. Voluntary charity to help others is fair for Nozick, but not forced obligations, as with obligatory government redistribution from rich to poor (except where that raises taxes to fund a minimal state, oriented mainly around the protection of property). But Nozick does not accept that while people have a right to what is gained freely and fairly, maybe they also have an obligation, that should be enforced, to help others much worse off, even if they are accidentally so. I argue that people have not just rights over themselves as individuals and what they own, but also rights – in what is a society and not just an assortment of individuals – to expect help from others. Furthermore, the inequality that would arise in a Nozickian society (albeit justly in his view) would lead to fewer chances of freedom and self-determination for some than others, often as a result of the luck of their birth. Those who inherit wealth from their parents freely and fairly in Nozick's estimation would have an advantage over those who do not, and the former would have greater self-determination and freedom as a result. In this sense, his preferred society would undermine the goal of self-ownership and autonomy he believes in so centrally. A society based on greater equality may increase freedom and self-determination for all, because it would even out and spread the resources you need to be free and shape your life.

The designed and planned society that Hayek fears may work better informationally in the internet era. In Hayek's day, collecting information about people's needs and planning provision for them could take so long that by the time you are ready to implement the plan, needs would have changed. As well, this would require an unwieldy bureaucracy. But online means make the collection of information about needs and wants much quicker and provision for them more possible. This may not iron out disagreements over the planning of society, but it allows greater input in the hands of ordinary individuals and permits planning to be more viable and efficient. Information technology makes constructivism more possible and potentially more democratic (see Saros, 2014, and Morozov, 2019, on 'digital socialism' and Tarnoff, 2018, on data and democratic planning; see also Fuchs', 2020a, special issue of *tripleC* on digital socialism, which includes criticism of Saros and Morozov). Hayek does not accept that outcomes not designed on a large scale – for instance, those resulting from markets – lead to a lack of freedom or injustice, because he says the resulting pattern must have intention behind it to be unjust. So, the accidental outcomes of markets are not unjust, but the deliberate outcomes determined by planners are. However, by most people's definitions of freedom, loss of life chances through market transactions would lead to a lack of freedom for those with negligible resources, intended or not. From this perspective, I may lose my job because of the vicissitudes of the market, but that no one planned that does not make it less unjust, especially if the market itself was favoured and there was knowledge of the sort of outcomes it may lead to. If you can foresee injustice arising accidentally from an unplanned market and do not change the situation to stop that, then injustice is committed even if the distribution itself is arguably unintentional. Redistribution, which Hayek is against, can underpin freedom as much as be a threat to it, as he sees it, because, as mentioned in relation to Nozick, it allows people to have the resources to express positive freedom. Freedom from coercion – the negative liberty that Hayek favours – prevents state infringement of liberties. But if people lack resources or opportunities to the extent that they cannot take advantage of their negative freedom, then redistribution and state planning may be needed to ensure they can; ensuring negative liberty – freedom from – can be turned into positive liberty – freedom to. (Some argue that Hayek's informational points can be taken up in Left-wing approaches; see Wainwright, 1994, 2018; Cumbers, 2012.)

## From Nozick and Hayek back to socialism

Collective obligations and economic equality can be a threat to freedom, as liberals point out. However, as outlined in relation to criticisms of Nozick and Hayek, they can also be a basis for positive freedom and the life chances of people, while a liberal regime that favours individualism and restricts redistribution can undermine freedom. So, a socialism of collectivism and egalitarianism needs to be extended to ensure that freedom and life chances in society are realized. Socialism can be better at achieving liberal goals of freedom than liberalism; a liberalism that really means it (see Hattersley, 1987) hence me arguing in this book for liberal goals within a socialist framework rather than for liberalism. However, many social democrats, democratic socialists, and even more anarchist socialists accept a role for markets and private ownership, on principled grounds that voluntary choice should be allowed and not prohibited. They should also be allowed for the pragmatic reasons that they give some dynamism in society – as there are at least some incentives in private property and markets, such incentives having a role alongside altruistic ones – as well as informational advantages, as long as regulated and limited.

A key point is that socialism alone, without liberal and plural inputs, comprises just collective ownership and economic equality. A society defined wholly by these inherently limits plurality, property rights and markets, and individual dissent from the collective majoritarian decision. To be open to a society that allows individual freedom and plurality in types of economic and social organization, socialism would have to be limited. In a socialist society, private property rights and markets would have to be strictly regulated and limited or they may take over and create a society homogenized in their image. But so also must socialism be limited if society is to be plural and individual difference allowed to exist. Of course, you may say that society should be totally socialist, but that would involve force and totalitarianism, which is where attempts at socialism have gone wrong in the past and made society an unfree and oppressive place to live. It can be answered that unlimited socialism may develop voluntarily, which is fine if that's the case. But given even strong capitalism contains big pools of altruistic behaviour and wide support for public services planned for need, despite the thrust of neoliberal capitalism against that, then it is plausible that, similarly, drives for diversity would also exist in a society based on collective ownership and economic equality. So, to avoid force and repression, socialism needs to limit itself.

Hayek's critique does not apply well to social democracy in practice. Attempts to assess and deliver to needs through institutions like the welfare state and nationalization could have been more efficient and sensitive, but they have not fundamentally failed at meeting needs on the whole, nor led to dictatorship or totalitarianism. But his critique may be more relevant to Marxist-inspired state socialism where there were informational and incentives problems with central state planning, and political dictatorships. While recognizing that these societies were not socialist, they had socialist ambitions and, in a form, some socialist institutions, and these, in part, may have been behind economic stagnation and political authoritarianism, for the sort of reasons Hayek suggested. Reforms to state socialism responded to this but ultimately threw the baby out with the bathwater. A limited role for markets providing incentives and information in restricted areas, and for private ownership alongside and subordinate to collective ownership, can promote economic efficiency, freedom, and pluralism – as can socialism, if not too monolithic. Protecting plurality in society, economically and politically, can be good for the economy and for political democracy and freedom. I am proposing maintaining socialism, but with a role within it for plurality, private ownership, and markets, for liberal and economic reasons (as argued for also by Nove, 1983, and Hodgson, 1984 on similar grounds). This is not social democracy, which is about capitalism with non-capitalist institutions within. It is pluralist socialism with dominant forms being socialist but with market and private institutions within.

It should not be controversial to advocate a subordinate role for small-scale private enterprise and restricted markets in a predominantly collectivist socialist economy. Allen (2011), a revolutionary Marxist and advocate of a collectively owned and planned economy, says, discussing Marx's concept of the alternative to capitalism, that while large corporations would be nationalized under communism, private ownership would be allowed to continue at the level of small enterprises (examples he gives are bike shops, cafés, and restaurants). This is unless them being transferred to co-operative ownership is consented to, rather than done on a forced basis. For Allen, while market forces would not determine the economy, market exchange would be expected to continue at least for a while – something also suggested by Lenin (Jossa, 2014). Hudis (2012: 192–3) says that for Marx, markets pre-existed capitalism so are not inherently capitalist. The key objective of socialism is to bring production under collective ownership and control, rather than be concerned with markets. The economy should not be characterized or dominated by market transactions, but this allows markets restricted in a subordinate and subsidiary role, rather than a governing autonomous one.

Examples discussed in this book, advocated enthusiastically by socialists, from the Zapatistas to Rojava and Marinaleda and many others, have a role for private enterprise and markets. Marxists like Ralph Miliband (1994) say that socialism should include economic pluralism and liberal rights in a predominantly collectivist system. Socialists like Sunkara (2019), who publishes the firmly Left magazines *Jacobin* and *Tribune*, argue for socialism incorporating liberal institutions. Advocates of democratic planning argue that markets have a place (see, for example, Macfarlane, 2019). A market forces economy which is driven by market criteria is not compatible with a democratically planned economy. But market exchange and socialized and regulated markets in a minority role, rather than a liberal or free-market economy, do not drive the economy. They are a different thing altogether to a market forces economy and market socialism, in which the market and commodification do have a determining role. (See the socialist economists Devine, 1988, an advocate of a democratically planned economy, and Elson, 1988, for this distinction. See Hodgson, 1998, for a critique of democratic planning and of Devine's position on markets. Adaman and Devine, 2001 and 2006, reply to his critique.)

At the same time, while restricted and regulated private ownership and markets should not be completely prohibited in a pluralist socialism, democratic planning can work in informational and motivational ways often associated primarily with private ownership and markets (see democratic planners Nieto and Mateo, 2020). Democratic planning can work informationally through participatory involvement and information and communication technology, the latter not available in past attempts at socialism and used now in fact by capitalist companies for planning. There can be incentives to innovate in planning systems, such as delivering for the collective good and rewards for innovation, including for that which has non-profit, social, and long-term ends (see Nieto and Mateo, 2020; Nieto, 2022). In fact, many innovations under capitalism have come through state and non-market processes, and in the private sector often from entrepreneurs who are not owners (that is, not capitalists) and are supported by collaborative platforms (Mazzucato, 2013; Nieto, 2022; Tarnoff, 2022).

So, on liberal and Right-wing criticisms, socialism needs to be extended to underpin the freedom liberals aim for but also undermine. But it also needs to be limited to allow liberal concerns and plurality to survive. Bobbio (1988, 2009) argues for liberal socialism. McManus (2020) argues socialism should maintain liberal institutions rather than abolishing them, expanding on them with democratic and egalitarian structures that allow liberal goals to be realized in a way they cannot be within liberalism. Brie (2021), discussing communism and embedded in Marxist philosophy, argues that socialism should be pluralist and retain liberal values and institutions. This is in recognition of the complexity and contradictions of modern society and so as not to oppress individuals or collectivities and some forms of creativity and developmentalism while within a collectivist framework. However, when it comes to ecological and feminist criticism, the situation is, I will argue, different. Here socialism needs to extend itself to support green and feminist objectives, just as it needs to expand to underpin liberal concerns. However, it can adapt without limiting itself for green and feminist objectives. These require adaptation rather than the self-limiting required in the case of responding to liberalism.

## Green and feminist criticisms

Some greens criticize socialism for being too committed to changing the relations of production – who owns production, but not the forces of production – technology and the components of industrialism – which are behind environmental problems (on ecology and socialism, see Ryle, 1988; Eckersley, 1992; Pepper, 1993). Socialism, both communist and social democratic, has been especially committed to growth and production to provide resources for a better-off society, addressing poverty and creating jobs for its historical constituency of the working class. When in work, they also pay taxes and create revenue for the social democratic welfare state and public services. Production and growth are seen as positive achievements, while for greens they create resource depletion and pollution, and need to be held back for a sustainable society based on less growth, low growth, no growth, or degrowth (see Latouche, 2009; D'Alisa et al, 2015; Jackson, 2017, 2021; Kallis et al, 2018). Socialism, like other ideologies, is also anthropocentric, putting the interests of humans first. So, where it is in the interests of humans for animals and nature to be protected, they will be; but where it is not, they will not be.

From a feminist perspective, socialism is too focused on class as the key division separating society in terms of benefits and power (on feminism and socialism, see Jaggar, 1983; Bryson, 2016; Tong and Botts, 2017). Its economic class perspective on inequality and power means it fails to take into account divisions that cross-cut with economic class but are different, such as those according to gender and ethnicity. Furthermore, socialism locates the source of exploitation, inequality, and power in society in capitalism. So, in terms of gender, women are seen as oppressed because capitalism needs a group who will reproduce the workforce in the family for free, and accept that role. It also needs a reserve army of labour who can be wheeled in and out of the workforce at times of boom and bust, and accept precarity and poor wages and conditions. This group keeps wages down by reducing the bargaining power of other workers, since they are available to replace them. Gender expectations construct women in such roles, as child rearers in the family and temporary low-paid precarious workers. Ideologies of gender are functional for the capitalist economic system.

This fails to understand, however, that gender oppression comes out of cultural and ideological structures that pre-existed capitalism and so are likely to continue in a socialist society. Inequalities of power and pay at work, for instance, are by gender as well as class, and the gender inequalities cross-cut class and cannot be explained in class terms alone. People of colour and women face dimensions of oppression in addition to those faced by White working-class men, and these are due to long-existing ideologies of racism and patriarchy, not, or not just, capitalist economic structures. So, a change to the economic system will not be enough, and socialism alone does not have an adequate explanation or solution to gender inequality. Changes to cultural and ideological structures of patriarchy will be needed as well as changes to structures of economic exploitation (on Marxism and feminism, see Barrett, 2014). Furthermore, socialism has focused on inequality and power in the public sphere of work, the economy, and politics. It has not paid much attention to the private sphere of the family and private relations, where women have suffered oppression as domestic labourers and the victims of male violence. So, socialism does not alone have an answer to oppression in the family and private sphere.

However, unlike liberal criticisms of socialism, the criticisms here point to absences in socialism rather than flaws in its inherent structures. Therefore, socialism does not need to limit itself to take on green and feminist concerns. It does need to adapt significantly, but conjuncturally rather than in its essence, in how it is at the moment rather than in its core identity, and does not need to restrict itself, but more add to itself.

## *Ecology and the implications for socialism*

Pro-capitalists argue that capitalist private property provides solutions to environmental problems and, in fact, that if it is spread even more, this will be good for the environment (see Saunders, 1995). If natural resources, like rare species or forests, are owned privately and people can make a profit out of them, there will be an incentive to protect them. So, not only can the environment be protected under capitalism, but capitalism can be positively beneficial for it if extended even further. Markets can be modified by the environment being priced in (Pearce et al, 1989). The environment is often external to the balance sheet (an 'externality'), free of cost, and so not counted in economic calculations of credit and debit, meaning money-oriented capitalists will not pay any attention to it. However, markets can be altered by the environment being given a price through depletion or pollution charges – for instance, in the form of taxes. Capitalists then effectively must pay for the environment, through a charge when they use it up or affect it by the pollution they create. This involves a change to the market, involving state intervention but inside capitalism rather than against it, and making markets work for the environment rather than getting rid of them. Consumers exert influence on capitalist production – as the latter responds to the former's behaviour in order to make money – so they can shift capitalism to being greener by practising green consumerism, using their purchasing power to make capitalism more environmentally friendly (Hailes, 2007). For example, one way of mitigating climate change is reducing the consumption of meat. So, adopting vegetarianism or veganism can shift companies to more environmentally friendly food production. Again, this is within the structures of capitalism, using the market and consumerism rather than abolishing market capitalism or going against it.

It may be that progressive change for the environment is possible within capitalism – for instance, by moving away from fossil fuels to renewable energy – if not in many cases *by* capitalism. Technological developments, regulation, and government incentives within capitalism have made progress in facilitating positive change of this sort for the environment. Some of this involves government modifications to capitalism. But many of these changes are mainly to and within capitalism and not, at least initially, by capitalism itself. Private ownership and profit-making alone will not protect parts of the environment in a global economy where they can be used up and capitalists move on. Rich corporations, rather than changing their behaviour, can pay the charges for environmental damage or pass these on to consumers. Green consumers can be duped by fraud, concealment, or misinformation.

So at the least, socialism needs to make changes to capitalism rather than accept capitalism as itself a solution to environmental problems. Under capitalism, those who cause and profit from environmental despoliation, private owners, have ownership of the process, while those most affected by it, society as a whole, are disenfranchised. Collective ownership, on the other hand, allows those who are affected by environmental problems, wider society, to have a collective input in control. It matches the effects of environmental damage with ownership of the process behind it. So, changes to the relations of production are needed to ensure the forces of production are geared to green ends. The market directs behaviour to where money can be made rather than where the environment can be protected. Modifications to deal with this involve the government sanctioning or incentivizing behaviour to make market capitalism greener. But planning by collective owners and controllers can more directly gear economic activity towards social and environmental concerns, whereas markets and capitalism do not intrinsically do so unless it is profitable or made profitable by intervention. Throughout this book, a key theme is that collective ownership is a necessary if not sufficient basis for a society that is responsive to social needs, and inclusive and democratized collective ownership within a pluralist socialism is a central proposal for an alternative society. I will focus on the democratic economy in the next chapter.

While socialism has conjuncturally been unecological, it is not necessarily so. It can broaden beyond a productivist class orientation and spread wealth by collectively owning and distributing it, rather than by expanding wealth in society through growth. There is no intrinsic reason why socialism cannot go beyond anthropocentrism. It is not inherently un-socialist to extend intrinsic ethical obligations to entities other than humans, such as animals. Capitalist progress on the environment has a lot to do with incentives and regulation introduced through government intervention adapting capitalism – for instance, towards renewable energy – so state interventionist rather than intrinsically capitalist measures. And collective ownership and planning bring those affected by environmental problems in line with control of the economy. Capitalism breaks that link and connects profit and private gain with ownership and control, divorcing the latter from those who are on the receiving end of its social and collective effects. Saving the planet requires socialism to extend rather than limit itself in its intrinsic dimensions.

## Feminism and the implications for socialism

As far as feminist criticisms go, socialism is focused on economic class inequality and exploitation. However, incorporating concerns to do with gender and patriarchy does not necessitate socialism dropping a focus on class inequality, but rather being more inclusive and adding gender and patriarchy, and linking capitalism and class dimensions with patriarchy and gender ones. For gender inequalities and power relations to be resolved, gender must be added to class and patriarchy added to capitalism as dimensions of power and inequality. Socialism can contribute to solving these problems but alone cannot resolve them. This involves adding to socialism and expanding its remit, rather than limiting socialism. This is because gender inequality does not expose intrinsic problems with class analysis, but its restrictedness. It does not show that class-focused socialism in itself is problematic, but that it is limited in the scope of what it can explain and solve. Similarly, socialism is not inherently tied only to the analysis of inequality and power in the public sphere at the expense of these in the private sphere. It can take on analysis and change in areas such as the family and personal violence by expanding its remit, by adapting and expanding rather than by limiting itself, by conjunctural revisions rather than revisions to its fundamental principles. In fact, socialists have been able to adapt to include feminist concerns, and many socialist feminists see socialism as compatible with feminism or even well suited to partnership with it.

This leads to the point that while socialism needs to take on gender and patriarchy to add to its class and capitalist analyses, the latter does help to contribute to an understanding of gender oppression, partially, with categories of social reproduction and the reserve army of labour, and the capitalist functions of these. Ideologies of gender justify for capitalism a group who reproduce the labour force for free and accept the role of low-paid, flexible, insecure workers who can be used in times of boom and disposed of in slumps. Meanwhile, they can be used as a reserve army that inhibits workers' struggles for pay and conditions, knowing that if workers go too far, they can be disposed of and replaced by women from outside the labour force. Furthermore, as an egalitarian doctrine, socialism may be well suited to taking an equality approach to areas outside economic and class divisions, and in other stratifications, such as of gender, race, and sexuality. So, the expansion of socialism in relation to gender involves enlarging to include gender and patriarchy in its concerns, but also broadening to bring socialist analysis to bear on understanding gender and patriarchy. Socialism does not need to be limited in the light of gender inequalities as it is not in itself a threat to gender equality in the way it can be to liberal principles. But it does need to be added to, to be adequate to solve gender and patriarchy inequalities and power, and expanded, as it partly, but not completely, provides a solution to them.

I have said earlier in this chapter that there are six ways socialism can respond to criticisms of it: 1) disagreement with the criticism and no change made to socialism; 2) expansion of socialism because it provides a solution to the point or perspective it is seen to fail on; 3) acceptance of the criticism, and of a need for the addition of extra dimensions to socialism to deal with it, because socialism is limited and in need of adding to; 4) adaptation, which is not just adding extra dimensions to socialism, but also changing elements of the ideology; 5) self-limitation, as socialism cannot answer the problem and, in fact, the problem strikes at inherent structural dimensions of socialism that need to be restricted to allow counter structures that can answer the problem, so plurality within a socialist society; and 6) rejection of socialism where the criticism is so fundamentally penetrating that socialism must be abandoned. The answers I have given on socialism's response to criticisms are summarized in Table 4.1.

This discussion has not been about socialism as a critique or analysis, and criticisms of that, but about a socialist society. So, my conclusions are about what the assessments I have discussed raise for socialism as a society, not as a form of explanation. I am not advocating pluralism or social democracy, a mixed economy of socialist and capitalist aspects. My focus is on a socialist society. So, the argument is not for a pluralism of equals, but socialism with plurality within. I am not advocating a social democratic mixed economy, as that is about a mix of forms within capitalism, whereas my discussion is about plurality in a post-capitalist socialist society. Similarly, my argument is not for market socialism, where there is a market economy with socialist forms like co-operatives. It is for a collectively owned and planned – that is, socialist – economy that allows a regulated role for markets within it.

## Conclusions

I have discussed liberal, neoliberal, Right-wing, green, and feminist criticisms of socialism. I have argued that liberal and neoliberal criticisms expose some fundamental problems in socialism. Socialism provides ways of meeting liberal objectives that liberalism cannot, so assessment of socialism on liberal grounds leads to the expansion of socialism to achieve liberal ends. However, it also shows some ways in which socialism is potentially inherently and structurally illiberal. This does not require the abandonment or rejection of socialism, because of its merits. But it does require its self-limitation and restriction, and its allowing of other ideologies and structures in a plural socialist society, where a liberal and pluralist socialism entails socialism as a dominant form but with a regulated and constrained role for non-socialist forms like liberal democracy, markets, and private ownership. So, liberal and neoliberal criticism requires the expansion but also self-limitation of socialism.

Green and feminist criticisms, however, do not require the self-limitation of socialism. While there can be progress on environmental concerns within capitalism, this is based on intervention to make corrections and modifications to it, so in capitalism and with it but, if anything, by socialist modifications. Furthermore, socialist institutions like collective ownership and planning can help solve environmental problems by matching those who are on the receiving end of the problems with those who control them, and so an expansion of socialism is required. So self-limitation is not necessary. Feminism shows the limits of socialism, but not an inherent structural

**Table 4.1:** Socialism and its responses to criticisms

| Critical perspective | The criticism | Socialism's answer to the criticism | How a socialism vulnerable to the criticism can adjust | Does the criticism show inherent and structural problems with socialism, so requiring rejection or self-limitation in a pluralist society? |
| --- | --- | --- | --- | --- |
| Liberal – for example, Mill | Socialism as collectivist and economically egalitarian may transgress individual rights | Collective ownership and equality contribute to freedom Political freedoms cannot provide freedom without economic democracy and equality too, which involves limiting some political freedoms and rights | Socialism can expand itself to underpin freedoms, but also limit itself to ensure political freedoms and rights are safeguarded | Socialism needs to include liberal rights This involves compromising socialism Socialism is potentially inherently anti-liberal (although not inherently anti-freedom), so being liberal involves restraints and limits on socialism to make space for liberal rights politically in a socialism with plurality |
| Neoliberal – for example, Nozick and Hayek | Socialism is contradictory to property rights; information and incentives are needed for the economy, and liberty | Socialism has an answer to property rights and market freedom arguments, but has to be mixed with constrained respect for restricted property rights in a socialism with plurality | Hayek is more of a problem for socialism than Nozick on incentives, information, and freedom | Incentives and freedom are issues. Socialism needs to accept liberalism and a role for the private sector and profit for those who need such incentives |

(continued)

**Table 4.1:** Socialism and its responses to criticisms (continued)

| Critical perspective | The criticism | Socialism's answer to the criticism | How a socialism vulnerable to the criticism can adjust | Does the criticism show inherent and structural problems with socialism, so requiring rejection or self-limitation in a pluralist society? |
|---|---|---|---|---|
| Neoliberal (continued) | | | Socialism needs to allow a regulated and restricted role for private ownership and markets, for information, incentives, pluralism, and freedom reasons | Socialism is not completely problematic on incentives or information grounds (there can be collectivist motivations and democratic planning) but is likely to be in part, so needs restraints on socialism and a constrained space for liberalism economically |
| Green | Socialism is oriented around growth, production, work, jobs, increasing standards of living – all incompatible to an extent with environmental care | Ecology needs collective ownership and planning to ensure collective environmental needs are met. Private ownership and profits will only work so far Socialism is the only answer | Socialism has been focused on growth, industry, and workers, but these are not inherent necessities, just strong contingent links There can be green forms of all these | Socialism is not inherently anti-green, because it is about collective ownership and equality, which are not inherently anti-ecological. But very often it has been about growth and production, so while not inherently |

**Table 4.1:** Socialism and its responses to criticisms (continued)

| Critical perspective | The criticism | Socialism's answer to the criticism | How a socialism vulnerable to the criticism can adjust | Does the criticism show inherent and structural problems with socialism, so requiring rejection or self-limitation in a pluralist society? |
|---|---|---|---|---|
| Green (continued) | Socialism is too concerned with relations of production and not enough with forces of production and industrialism | | | unecological, it is likely to be, so needs space for green principles This is adding to socialism though, limiting the often growth-oriented nature of socialism but not its inherent principles |
| Feminist | Socialism is too focused on class at the expense of gender, and on capitalism at the expense of patriarchy Gender oppression will not be solved by the abolition of class and capitalism | Capitalism and class are part of the explanation for gender inequality, so expanding socialism will help Socialism can adapt to incorporate gender and patriarchy more, adding to its approach and modifying socialism rather than rejecting it | Socialism does not have a full answer. Getting rid of capitalism will help, but otherwise socialism has no solution to patriarchy as a non-economic non-class issue, so it will have to ally with feminism But it does not necessarily restrict socialism to do so | Socialism is not inherently anti-feminist, so doesn't require limiting socialism, but does require adding to it |

antipathy to feminism. It shows the need for socialism to be expanded in the sense that capitalism benefits from gender inequality so its abolition can help with reversing gender inequality. However, while socialism is not structurally anti-feminist, it is also not structurally feminist, because of its economic class focus. So, while it does not need limiting, it does need greater incorporation and inclusion of gender and patriarchy as concerns, adding to and modifying socialism and linking with socialism.

While many socialists may quite roundly reject liberal and neoliberal criticism of socialism, I am saying such criticisms strike more at the heart of socialism as a society (rather than socialism as critique). They require socialism to limit itself, alongside its expansion, to meet liberal goals. Many socialists may be more friendly towards green and feminist criticism, but I am arguing that these show absences in socialism more than structural flaws. So, they do not require the more fundamental self-limiting of socialism but, alongside its expansion, a more moderate case of modifying, widening, and incorporating. On liberal concerns, socialism needs to be self-limiting for a socialism with pluralism. On green and feminist concerns, it needs to include and expand.

Collective ownership has been raised in this chapter, and through the chapters of this book so far, as a key form of socialism. I have defined socialism, in part, according to collective ownership. In the next chapter, I will return to this recurring theme and go into more depth on some more recent debates about it. I will be arguing for a socialism of collective ownership, but of a pluralist, inclusive, and democratized type.

**Further reading**

A good overview of types of socialism is Tony Wright's (1996) *Socialisms*. Bhaskar Sunkara's (2019) readable *The Socialist Manifesto* gives an overview of events in the history of socialism internationally and, like this book, says that socialism needs to include liberal structures and democracy, and be pluralist and based on conflict politics and non-reformist reforms. For a short discussion of socialism in the light of recent history, see Jeremy Gilbert's (2020) *Twenty-first Century Socialism*. For a great fictional introduction to socialism, see Robert Tressell's (1965) *The Ragged Trousered Philanthropists*. Richard Swift's (2016) *SOS: Alternatives to Capitalism* is an accessible, concise, and readable discussion of movements for alternatives to capitalism, with an international scope.

I have listed further reading on communism at the end of Chapter 1. On attempts at communism in practice, see David Lane's (1996) *The Rise and Fall of State Socialism* and Robin Blackburn's (1991) edited volume *After the Fall: The Failure of Communism and the Future of Socialism*.

On social democracy, see Adam Przeworski's (1986) *Capitalism and Social Democracy*, especially the essay on 'Social democracy as a historical phenomenon', a classic and influential Marxist–Leninist contribution to analyses of social democracy. In Gøsta Esping-Andersen's (1985) *Politics Against Markets*, the first chapter, 'Social democracy in theory and practice', discusses the meaning of social democracy, classical debates on it, and what its bases for success or failure are. Esping-Andersen is one of the leading theorists of social democracy. This chapter includes an assessment of Przeworski's work. In John Stephens' (1979) *The Transition from Capitalism to Socialism*, the third chapter, 'Revolution and reform', discusses classical and contemporary debates on whether socialism is better pursued through reform than revolution.

On Hayek, see Eamonn Butler's (1983) *Hayek*, especially Chapter 3 on Hayek's critique of socialism. Other chapters survey Hayek on markets, planning, egalitarianism, evolutionism, and constitutional reform, and are worth looking at. In Chandran Kukathis' (1989) *Hayek and Modern Liberalism*, Chapter 2 is on the critique of constructivism. Also worth looking at are Chapter 3 on individualism and spontaneous order and Chapter 4 on liberty and the rule of law. On Nozick, see Will Kymlicka's (2002) *Contemporary Political Philosophy*, the parts of Chapter 4 that focus on Nozick.

On ecology and socialism, see Chapters 4, 5, and 6 in Robyn Eckersley's (1992) *Environmentalism and Political Theory*, which is sceptical about Marx being green but sees socialism as amenable to an ecological perspective. Martin Ryle's (1988) *Ecology and Socialism*, especially Chapter 2, is a brief, readable discussion by an eco-socialist and includes a discussion of ecological critiques of socialism. See also David Pepper's (1993) *Eco-socialism: From Deep Ecology to Social Justice*.

On feminism and socialism, see Alison Jaggar's (1983) *Feminist Politics and Human Nature* – especially pp 229–44 on feminist criticisms of Marxist–Leninist politics and Chapters 8 and 10 on Marxism, socialism, and feminism. In Rosemarie Tong and Tina Botts' (2017) *Feminist Thought*, Chapter 3 is on Marxist and socialist feminism. In Valerie Bryson's (2016) *Feminist Political Theory*, Chapters 4, 5, 6, and 11 are on Marxist and socialist feminism.

5

# The Democratic Economy

I have discussed social and economic alternative societies or utopias, within and beyond capitalism and current societies. Many involve collective ownership or control on a democratic basis, often in the economy, and socialism has been distinguished by its commitment to collective ownership. In the last two chapters, I focused on utopia and socialism as core approaches that came out of the survey of alternatives in Chapters 1 and 2. In this chapter, I will go into more detail on collective ownership and control in the economy, especially on contemporary proposals for, and experiments in, a democratic economy. This is the third key approach I think came out of the alternatives surveyed in the opening chapters of the book.

On the social democratic as well as the revolutionary Left, public ownership has been a major commitment. In some parts of the world, as neoliberalism got a grip on the political agenda, public ownership moved from the mainstream to the margins. Centre-Left parties shifted away from state ownership and forms of planning – often indicative rather than direct planning anyway – towards a commitment to private ownership and markets.

In the austerity and post-austerity period, there was a rise of a 'radical' or 'populist' Left (see Mouffe, 2018); I prefer to call it the 'proper' or 'firm' Left. While social ownership never went away as a part of life in many countries, where it was pushed to the periphery it has returned more to the political agenda. Where the private sector and market became default policy choices, public ownership has come back into conventional politics. Social ownership can be combined with greater equality, but with equality coming as much through the structural change of social ownership as through redistribution of income. This a predistributional path to egalitarianism, with collective ownership of production and equality of distribution linked. The structure of the economy creates a more equal distribution (predistribution), rather than unequal distributions growing and then being corrected after the fact (redistribution). Social ownership can also ensure that public rather than private goals are achieved, including environmental objectives, greater accountability to society, long-term over short-term thinking, and more economically efficient operations in several ways.

Key public ownership policies in the revival of the firm Left have been for social ownership of energy, water, mail, and telecoms, the insourcing of local government services, municipal social ownership, assistance for the growth of the co-operative sector, transference of company shares to workers (on inclusive ownership funds, proposed by, among others, Bernie Sanders in the US, see Lawrence, 2019), and community wealth building, which I will return to later in the chapter. Proposals emphasize decentralized, local social ownership. Where national ownership is proposed, it is in a democratized form (McDonnell, 2016; Labour Party, 2017; *New Socialist*, 2017; Reynolds, 2017; Guinan and Hanna, 2018; Beckett, 2019). Proposals for social ownership and local wealth building are being pursued by think tanks like The Democracy Collaborative in the US and the Centre for Local Economic Strategies (CLES) in the UK. These agencies do not just suggest policy but are hands-on and guide implementation. Much-talked-about sites for the enactment of social ownership policies, with the assistance of such think-and-do tanks, are Cleveland, Ohio, in the US and Preston in the UK (O'Neill, 2016 and 2018, Howard, 2018a, and CLES and Preston City Council, 2019, highlight the action orientation of these think tanks). Key values and principles of the approaches in such places include: community and collaboration; place and locality; inclusion, good work, and the workforce; democratic ownership and systemic and institutional change; multiplier effects; and sustainability and ethical finance (see Kelly et al, 2015; Kelly and Howard, 2019). Policies pursued are often localist, but debates raise questions about the role of the centralized state and public ownership – whether the latter can be democratized – and about the democratic economy at national and public-wide levels. They also raise issues of internationalization and international development policy that I will come back to. (For brief and accessible introductions to what this chapter discusses, see *The Economist*, 2018; Beckett, 2019; Howard, 2019.)

## From an extractive to a circulatory economy

Some democratic economy initiatives involve community wealth building, where wealth is generated and retained in localities through political intervention to support socially owned companies. Local government builds links between anchor institutions and community businesses (summaries of this approach can be found in Brown et al, 2018, CLES and Preston City Council, 2019, and Guinan and O'Neill, 2019b; see also Kelly et al, 2015, on the US). Anchor institutions are ones quite tied to the locality – for example, hospitals, universities, and the local state. Local government encourages them to shift the outsourcing of services from large capitalist corporations to community, sometimes socially owned, providers, and to require contractors to have social or environmental objectives – for instance, the payment of a living wage. The result is that rather than money flowing outside the area to big corporations and their shareholders, an extractive economy (more 'trickle out' than 'trickle down'; Thompson, 2021), it stays in the hands of community members and their socially and privately owned businesses, a circulatory economy. Geographically, wealth is kept in the neighbourhood rather than being displaced beyond the local community; ethically, it is directed to the social needs of ordinary people rather than the wealth of the better off.

For Matthew Brown, leader of Preston City Council, community wealth building is about creating an alternative economic system locally. With the economy tied more to the locality than international investors, the area is more insulated from global economic shocks, like the financial crisis (O'Neill, 2016). There is an equality element in wealth being captured for local jobs, workers, other community owners, and reinvestment, rather than being allowed to disappear away to capital and uncommitted shareholders. In this sense, community wealth building is not just a technical approach to foster local economies, but also about power, rebalancing it from international capital to more democratic entities, be they local government or enterprises socially owned by community members (O'Neill, 2018).

Brown et al (2018) argue that key questions are who owns the wealth, who influences it, who benefits from it, and where does it go? The system that community wealth is departing from concentrates capital in the hands of capitalists; the place-based economy, on the other hand, invests it in the community. Brown et al argue, furthermore, that finance invests in property and land, rather than employment-rich sectors like manufacturing and services. Investment in automation leads to wealth being kept less in society through employment and going more to profits for capitalists (Labour Party, 2017, suggests social ownership of automation can make sure the benefits go to workers and society; see also Bastani, 2020). Proponents of the 'foundational economy' argue, relatedly, that investment should focus on basic infrastructure industries like energy distribution systems, education, and health, rather than areas like property and tech (see Foundational Economy Collective, 2018).

Preston Council assesses that between 2012/13 and 2016/17, procurement spending in the city rose from £38.3 million (5 per cent of spending that was locally retained) to £112.3 million (18.2 per cent), and within surrounding Lancashire from £288.7 million (18.2 per cent) to £488.7 million (79.2 per cent), despite spending overall declining by 15 per cent. Four thousand extra employees started to receive the living wage, and Preston won awards for its improvement on various social and economic indicators. It moved up on an index of social mobility and was lifted out of the 20 per cent most deprived areas in the UK, and unemployment dropped, falling below the national average (Manley, 2018; CLES and Preston City Council, 2019). (On the pursuit of related approaches internationally, in Canada, Italy, Spain, and the US, see Guinan and Hanna, 2018.)

These approaches fit with an international trend towards re-municipalization and municipal ownership, where services are returned to the local public sector. This often reverses outsourcing, privatization, and public–private partnerships favoured by the modernizing centre-Left and the Right. For the Transnational Institute (2017), municipal ownership offers cost advantages for the public, a likely greater commitment to worker welfare and social and environmental objectives, and, especially, more accountability (see Kishimoto, 2018). Examples of international municipalism include the building of public services in the Santiago commune of Recoleta in Chile, democratic water policies in Terrassa in Catalonia, the bringing back of waste management into public hands in Egypt, and public alternatives for managing waste in Algeria, Rwanda, Tanzania, and Tunisia (Kishimoto and Sunby, 2020; Pinto, 2020; Planas and Martinez, 2020; Weghmann, 2020).

## Institutional change and socialism

On the firm Left, radical change is envisaged as much in structural reform as in monetary and fiscal policy (*The Economist*, 2018). For Guinan and O'Neill (2018), proposals for a democratic economy involve an 'institutional turn'. As mentioned previously, rather than income inequality growing and being corrected by redistribution, more equal ownership of assets and distribution is encouraged from the start. Equality is pursued through wealth as much as income, a reason for social ownership (Brown et al, 2018: 126; also Howard, 2018b, talks about the approach in terms of assets; Piketty, 2017, has been important in drawing attention back to the link between wealth and inequality). The focus is on structural design and system (see Kelly et al, 2015). This involves a shift of power as well as income because ordinary people are empowered in ownership, which is less the case in social democratic redistribution. (On different types of ownership envisaged, see Kelly et al, 2015, on the US, and Labour Party, 2017.)

Part of the case for this approach is on democracy grounds. We do not have democracy unless it is widened to the economy as well as politics. Furthermore, political democracy is undermined if economic power can determine political decisions, so reducing the accountability of government to voters (see *New Socialist*, 2017; Beckett, 2019; Guinan and O'Neill, 2019a). The form of democracy envisaged is often participatory, with people playing a greater role in the governance of businesses and utilities. One issue is how to build support for the democratic economy, and the incorporation of people into its democratic structures and ownership is seen as a way of fostering this (Berry and Guinan, 2019).

Is there enough participatory consciousness in societies for this approach to work (see Beckett, 2019)? The pressure group We Own It (2019: 9) argue that people will participate if they have the chance to do so in an inspiring way (see also Guinan and O'Neill, 2019a). But participation may be biased towards those with time, money, and a sense of impactfulness (Heslop et al, 2019: 11). There have been problems motivating, for example, parents and other members of the community to participate in school governance. Research on co-ops suggests that offering opportunities for meaningful participation does not necessarily lead to these being taken up (Carter, 2006). Greater democratic participation needs more than structures. It also requires consciousness, a cultural and not just political shift. Furthermore, a question is whether individual participation in collective democracy can mobilize people behind the democratic economy, as Berry and Guinan (2019) propose, in the way that direct individual ownership stakes have behind capitalism. It involves people seeing their stake in a collective rather than in the individual sense. This will require a hegemonic narrative to mobilize people behind it, as Thatcher's popular capitalism of individual ownership did (see Hall, 1988).

The democratic economy is not an approach to overthrow capitalism, at least not yet, so is social democratic as much as socialist (see Brown et al, 2018: 134–5; Mason, 2019). But it replaces international corporate control in places with local socially owned democracy, so is also more than social democracy and has socialist aspects (Labour Party, 2017: 32; Guinan and Hanna, 2018: 109, 113; Guinan and O'Neill, 2018; *Financial Times*, 2019). It is structural and involves a shift in power and equality through social ownership, as under socialism, as much as after-the-fact redistribution and regulations of social democracy, which accepts a privately owned capitalist economy but tries to correct for its maldistributions. Berry and Guinan (2019) see the proposals as revolutionary or non-reformist reforms, changes within the system that gradually replace capitalism by the extension of democratized economic forms.

What, then, do democratic economy proposals mean for capitalism? Community wealth building does not amount to a dismantling of capitalism so much as a stepping away from contracting international capitalist companies in some places in favour of local community procurement. This does not systematically go after capital, but sidesteps or excludes it to create parallel social ownership. It competes with international capital and creates democratic capital, selectively nationalizing public services and spreading inclusive ownership, rather than widely nationalizing the economy. But the democratic economy excludes international capital, builds social ownership, and tries to enhance the direction of capital to social ends. It lives with capitalism but changes it by building non-capitalist forms and aims alongside continuing capitalism. Beckett (2019) asks whether community wealth policies regenerate capitalism and allow it to regroup. This is possible, but a key point of this book is that specific local experiments should not be seen in isolation. Democratic economy initiatives in places like Cleveland and Preston are compatible with approaches that nationalize private companies. So, the former can complement a politics that does not just dilute capitalism, but in part takes it over collectively. A main argument I am making in this book is that different approaches and levels should not be seen as mutually exclusive and opposed; there may be tensions between them, but they can be combined in a pluralist socialism.

## Plurality and reversibility

A democratic economy can involve a plurality of institutions, including socially owned enterprises created by the community or set up by local government, with government promoting social ownership and building relations between anchor institutions and co-operatives. The local and national state can provide or facilitate leadership, tax breaks, loans, investment, procurement support, and shelter organizations that will fund, promote, and back social ownership (Labour Party, 2017). There are the anchor institutions themselves and their procurement policy. Think tanks can be involved, as they have been in Preston and Cleveland. Institutions include municipal enterprises, public banks, and participatory budgeting. Initiatives may arise out of social movements (see Milburn and Russell, 2019a, for a discussion of their role) and support can come also from philanthropy and trade unions (Brown, 2018). The approach involves networks of agencies (CLES and Preston City Council, 2019, bring this out well), and Brown et al (2018: 135) describe it as social democracy plus plurality. There are diverse networks of actors in the co-operative regions of Mondragon in Spain and Emilia Romagna in Italy, mentioned in Chapter 1 (Guinan and Hanna, 2018). A lot is involved in the democratic economy, and being multiform makes it more systemic and institutional, so potentially more effective.

One wish is that institutional and system interrelatedness makes the democratic economy more difficult to dismantle than nationalized industries and utilities. Embedding change in society can outlast changes of government and avoid reversal by subsequent politicians. For Beckett (2019: 5), democratic economy proposals are for something more systemic and permanent than state ownership and tax. If they are less centrally linked to the state, as tax and nationalization are, then it is more difficult for a new government to remove them (Wainwright, 2017: 27, and We Own It, 2019: 9 and 38, argue for institutionalizing change to make it difficult for public services to be dismantled). Obstacles to reversal may come from plurality: of forms of ownership, actors, and approaches.

But if national publicly owned companies can be sold off, why not local social ownership too? Local and municipal social ownership and procurement policies are reversible, through competition regulation or changes in political control of local government. The democratic economy may be more complex to unravel than simple nationalizations or regulations, but this is still doable by a new government willing to change policy and dismantle. The question of reversibility is not countered by saying the democratic economy is systemic and institutionalized, because systems and institutions can be changed. Some argue that subsequent governments, even if of a different political complexion, may like the regenerative effects of community wealth building and keep it. But key actors who are disadvantaged by it include international capital. Even if the local economy stays mainly capitalist and for profit, international capital gets sidelined by the community wealth approach. Global capital may be as much a threat to community wealth building, and economic power as much a threat as political changes of government. And governments may find the appeal of local wealth retention less compelling when faced with the opposition of corporate power.

Berry and Guinan (2019) discuss how to deal with resistance to Left economic plans through finance and business strategies such as capital flight and investment strikes. They advocate restrictions on the movement of capital, international co-operation by governments to control capital, social value mandates on finance, taxation on financial transactions, regulation and reforms of banking, and building of democratic finance and public banks. They propose reforms to deal with civil service opposition: replacing civil service personnel from the corporate sector, creating units supportive of the government, and exploiting pockets of sympathy; introducing new norms of decision-making, a more pluralist economics, and more social criteria for directing the civil service's operations. Berry and Guinan argue that a Left government should democratize the system to create more participatory forms, which may require devolution in some areas; so the shift is not from one set of technocratic experts to another, but away from technocratic elite control. (See also Benn, 1981, and London Edinburgh Weekend Return Group, 2021.)

For some, the firm Left needs to build coalitions with wider liberal and Left actors to carry out its aims (see Gamble, 2019; Lawson, 2019). But this would require giving up already modest goals. On top of the reliance on systemic embeddedness I have mentioned, a strategy for maintaining community wealth and social ownership will need a basis in social movements and popular consciousness. The editors of *New Socialist* (2017) emphasize the role of values, culture, and movements supporting the democratic economy in the face of opposition from international capital, from within government institutions, and from the Right wing of centre-Left parties. Culture and socialization, they say, are as important as economic control and planning (see also Labour Party, 2017: 17). Culture and consciousness are important not just in defending the democratic economy, but are behind its development and realization in the first place – for instance, in building participation in democratic structures. *New Socialist* argue that democratic structures are important not just in themselves, but for bringing in and sustaining support for democracy, giving people a stake in the structures so they will want to hold on to them. But it will take more than structures to build a culture and values that make the democratic economy work and protect it from reversal.

Berry and Guinan emphasize the role of social movements in supporting the democratic economy against opposition. Alongside alternative mass media viewed beyond the converted, social movements and party members can be part of political education. This needs to be geared to the public, over and above meetings for members and activists, and exceeding the limits of social media, putting bodies on doorsteps and in workplaces directly explaining policies that are distorted in the media. It involves mass party membership, registered member schemes to expand the volunteer base, volunteer and non-member participation, 'big organizing', millions of doorstep 'persuasive conversations' that go deeper than data gathering, and community organizing mobilized beyond the electoral cycle. Some of this has been practised by the Labour Left movement Momentum in the UK and in Democrat organizing in the US (see Garland, 2019; Hilder, 2019; Klug and Rees, 2019). It requires policy knowledge on the part of party members and activists for when they talk to the public, so needs also political education and training within the party and movements.

Movements can also be forces for resistance against establishment opposition, through protest, education, or disruption – for instance, by trade union action (see German, 2019). Alongside the top-down use of social movements, alternative agendas and narratives that frame people's experiences and give them causal explanations and solutions (New Economics Foundation, 2013) and practical initiatives and experiments, such as alternative economies, often come from the bottom up (New Economics Foundation, 2015). So that is also a role for social movements, although coming up with ideas is less an issue for the Left than mobilizing understanding of and support for them (Guinan and McKinley, 2020).

## Scaling up

One limitation may be that experiments like Preston and Cleveland are too small-scale, piecemeal, incremental, and localist, and do not involve large-scale transformation. Can they be widened and scaled up (as discussed in

Howard, 2018b, and Guinan and O'Neill, 2019a)? Local approaches can be experimental, seeing whether the approach works, and if it does, then demonstrative, showing the way for others, as discussed in previous chapters (see Alperovitz, 2005). There is a prefigurative element (see Wainwright, 2017), building alternatives now as a basis for a wider economy along the same lines. Initiatives like those in Preston and Cleveland can spread across Left and liberal authorities, and have been doing so (see Leibowitz and McInroy, 2019).

The democratic economy can be scaled up not just by experiment and demonstration, but also through active political leadership at government level and in mainstream anchor institutions. It can show that things work, thus encouraging wider adoption, but also be positively led, facilitated, and built by the state, at local and national levels, and by public sector institutions (creating public–common partnerships; see Milburn and Russell, 2019a, 2019b). The Preston Model is more political than other social alternatives, less extra-political, more in public–public relationships, and so open to being developed by means other than just prefiguration – a political and not just social basis for change. It is more in the mainstream of society than on the margins of it or in separate spaces.

Cumbers and Hanna (2018) discuss the role of government in scaling up local initiatives. Government can pursue change through top-down nationalization, re-municipalization, economic incentives and public funding for social ownership, policy that gives first refusal for employees to buy companies at risk of closure or takeover, and public procurement policies that favour social and environmental goals and local co-ops. On-the-ground experimentation can be promoted at the national level by government (Howard, 2018a, discusses extending and scaling up the approach).

The approaches discussed involve funds being reinvested locally rather than disappearing out of the area, and this could appeal to Right-wing authorities, locally and nationally, interested in local economic regeneration (see O'Neill, 2018: 46–7, on the argument that community wealth building can appeal across the political spectrum). *New Socialist* (2017) argues that democratic economy approaches have a 'sober practicality' and that social ownership is popular with the public. They do not necessarily involve raising taxes, increasing public spending, or nationalization – off-putting from a Right-wing perspective – so can appeal across political divides. Matthew Brown sees them as common sense (although also ideological; O'Neill, 2016). This can make it easier to implement by the Left as they may encounter less Right-wing opposition, and easier to sustain across changes of government as the Right may be happy to allow local wealth building to continue.

However, the belief that the Right and capital can agree to democratic economy proposals puts a lot of faith in rational persuasion about policy and in overcoming historical polarizations between groups with conflicting interests. Furthermore, the appeal is to a Right that sees merits in place-based wealth building and local economic development. A Right seen more in class terms as representatives of international capital will be less convinced because, as mentioned previously, global capital is undermined by this approach. It loses business to local contractors, and some Right-wingers will be put off by this being to co-operative, that is a non-capitalist, enterprise. Despite *New Socialist* (2017) seeing democratic economy proposals as practical and crossing over Left–Right divides, they also warn that the democratic economy could be frustrated in its formulation and implementation.

## Localism and its limits

There are limits in the localism of democratic economy proposals. They are best suited to areas with a strong local identity, attachment among people to the area, and social infrastructure (Heslop et al, 2019: 9). The approach can work where there is a supportive culture and consciousness, but less well in places that lack this. Furthermore, it depends on the presence of anchor institutions and is not so useful where these are less prevalent (Brown says Preston is lucky with this: O'Neill, 2016. See the discussion of Tanzania later in the chapter).

Retention of wealth by the community, rather than its extraction by corporate capital, will be welcomed by most with Left-wing and community concerns. More contentious is the keeping of wealth locally at the expense of wider society. This could be seen to be parochial and insular. The approach can lead to competition and perhaps inequality between localities. In local wealth creation and retention, areas may be focused on their interests and become competitive with other areas, and in competition there are winners and losers, so inequalities grow. Competition can lead to wasteful duplication and reluctance to share resources or information. This could be the case with local authorities leading community wealth creation or local co-ops competing. For Hanna (2018b: 22), competition is as important an issue as ownership. Also, co-ops run the risk of being biased towards the sectional group that owns them – for instance, workers – as localism is towards the locality.

In poor communities, areas retaining wealth for local regeneration may be defensible. But more widely it could mean wealth is kept in better-off areas when redistribution to less well off communities would be desirable. A solution is pursuing such policies within a more regionally redistributive approach at national or supranational levels. Then, communities where wealth builds up could have some redistributed to poorer localities. This would require wealth generators not to lose the incentive to create and retain wealth locally if they know some will be redistributed. However, this is doable and is done under many redistributive structures.

The Democracy Collaborative's Ted Howard, who is involved in the Cleveland Model, rejects the 'beggar thy neighbour' criticism (O'Neill, 2018: 49), arguing that community wealth strategies are about resetting the balance between local communities and international capital as much as localities versus localities. O'Neill (2018) says that local government has to step up in the absence of other approaches and interest from national government. If national governments were more interested in equality, then local economic development could be different. Furthermore, what the local community wealth approach replaces is, for Howard, particularistic, where cities compete to attract investment at the expense of each other, but with the riches going to external corporate shareholders.

O'Neill (2016) suggests two paths: one is favouring local institutions; another is favouring those with more ethical standards. The two can go together, but the emphasis on ethical and social business involves supporting alternative economic structures as much as, or rather than, local regeneration. Favouring social business over local business where the two do not coincide would be hard for a local authority, but it gives an ethical rather than localist slant. CLES and Preston (2019: 23) say that choosing suppliers based on social value in Preston has not always meant choosing the local one (see also Eaton, 2018). Furthermore, the Preston policy has led to a shift in contracts away from London and the richer south-east of the UK but not from the rest of the country, so it has not necessarily meant abandoning a commitment to a wider community beyond the local one.

Wider forms of ownership can help counter the particularistic interest and competitive inequality of sectional ownership and localism. This brings us to national public ownership.

## National and public ownership

National public ownership can avoid wasteful competition, regional inequality, and replication of activities, and ensure more sharing of information than under decentralized forms (see Hanna, 2018a and 2018b, on the case for public ownership). This need not replace local ownership, as pluralism is beneficial for various reasons and in many cases greater local accountability and participation are positive. The experience of state ownership has suggested that democratization and decentralization of it are desirable. Another possible route is networks between co-ops and local authorities where agreements are made not to compete or conceal resources and information. This is a feature of the co-operative landscape in places like Mondragon and Emilia Romagna, mentioned in Chapters 1 and 5.

Hobbs (2018) argues that public ownership (her focus is on public services) represents society as a whole, not just particular groups (as in the representation of workers in worker co-ops) or communities (as in community wealth building). It can overcome insularity, sectionalism, and localism, and oversee equality between areas so that some do not get better off at the expense of others. *New Socialist* (2017) stresses national public ownership as an approach that guards against geographical economic inequalities and national inequality of services. We Own It (2019: 4) argue for local, regional, and national levels in social ownership. Relatedly, Common Wealth (2019) advocate pluralism in ownership against a monoculture of ownership types (see also We Own It, 2019: 5). For Hobbs and We Own It, we should not denigrate state ownership too much. It works or has worked, if not perfectly, for rail internationally and the National Health Service in the UK, for example. It allows economies of scale, consistency, equality, and cross-subsidy.

Cumbers and Hanna (2018: 15) also argue that local and national state public ownership is better for distributing benefits more equally. Forms such as community and worker ownership build wealth for specific groups, so can exacerbate inequality and create vested interests. Municipal ownership covers all local groups. Sectional groups face market pressures and so may externalize environmental costs (Cumbers and Hanna, 2018: 12, 15, 16). State ownership can be better on environmental grounds. Because of its scale, it can have a large impact if pursuing environmental policies like a green new deal (for *New Socialist*, 2017, national public ownership is the level at which to tackle issues like climate change).

Azmanova (2020) argues there is no guarantee that collective ownership will work for the common good, and often it has not. But it, at least, has a collective input that matches with deciding on collective goals. National ownership can be democratized via the inclusion of plural involved and affected stakeholder groups in governance – for example, local and national states, workers, consumers, managers, experts, and community groups (Labour Party, 2017: 27–31; Berry and Guinan, 2019; We Own It, 2019). This incorporates industrial democracy into public ownership to help ensure collective interests are the main aims (Berry and Guinan, 2019, 37–8). The past problems of public ownership may have been due to types of management as much as ownership itself and could be addressed by investigating new forms of governance and operation (Hobbs, 2018, makes a related point), which inclusive democratization is part of, rather than by a shift to private ownership.

Polling data shows support for public ownership (Hanna, 2018b; Kishimoto, 2018: 39; We Own It, 2019: 6). The Right-wing Legatum Institute found in 2017 that three quarters of the public in the relatively neoliberal UK, with majorities across generations and party allegiance, believed that water, electricity, gas, and rail should be publicly owned, and 50 percent thought that the banks should be nationalized (Elliott and Kanagasooriam, 2017: 14–17). Another 2017 poll shows a lower level of, but still majority, support for the nationalization of mail, water, rail, and energy across age, class, and region (Smith, 2017). Internationally, public ownership is not outlandish, even in the free-market US, where it is widespread (Guinan and Hanna, 2018: 118 ff; Hanna, 2018a, 2018b). It has been equated too easily with centralized, bureaucratic, inefficient, top-down organization despite evidence for efficiency (Hobbs, 2018: 42, makes this point; see also Cumbers and Hanna, 2018: 11).

Public ownership is a means governments use to centrally plan. The COVID-19 crisis highlighted the role of national planning, as huge levels of spending and direction by the state were used to respond to the spread of coronavirus. In some countries, this involved nationalization – for instance, of health services and transport. The market and private ownership are seen as insensitive to need, the market's focus being on demand and private owners' on profit. During the COVID-19 crisis, corporations often did not see their interests as being in line with provision for COVID-19 needs, and they had to be asked or directed to channel their operations in this direction. However, state direction is not necessarily best for the people, and many state COVID-19 responses have been about saving capitalists, big corporations, finance, and landlords as much as helping small businesses and the public. Blakeley (2020b) argues that state planning in itself is not socialist. It would need to be brought under democratic collective ownership and control to be so. She predicts that big corporations will eat up smaller ones hit by the crisis, reinforcing a shift to state monopoly capitalism, where states and big corporations dominate decision-making (see also Guinan and O'Neill, 2020, on post-COVID-19 'Amazon recovery'). The issues will be who controls state decisions, in whose interests, with what objectives, and how. She argues the Left should respond to this moment by making the case for democratic ownership and control of state planning by workers, consumers, and the public (see also Cooper and Aitchison, 2020; Keuchyan, 2020; Mair, 2020; Phillips and Rozworski, 2020a, 2020b; on socialism after Corbyn and COVID-19, see Blakeley, 2020a; more generally on post COVID-19, see Parker, 2020).

Murphy (2019) raises the issue of tensions between international, national, and decentralized levels. But an approach that combines decentralization with central state power may address those tensions. Central state power can provide an overarching context for decentralization, taking on those things that decentralization cannot do so well (for example, public services and environmental protection), overseeing equality and coherence between decentralized units, and linking upwards to the international level (see Adler,

2019, on the democratic economy internationally). Democratic economy proposals have implications for trade and globalization (Berry and Guinan, 2019; Pickard and Shrimsley, 2019). This leads us to community wealth building and the international level.

### Community wealth building internationally

Preston and Cleveland are prominent sites of community wealth building. But the approach can be seen in a wider global context in two ways: first, through its proliferation internationally, including in the Global South – a scaling outwards issue; second, through community wealth building being allied with international and foreign policy.

Community wealth building can release Global South countries from the hold of multinational corporations by generating and retaining wealth locally instead. In one example, advocates of the Preston Model have met with politicians, activists, and academics in Tanzania to discuss how community wealth building could be pursued in the north-western city of Kigoma (Collord, 2019). There is support from the town council and the member of parliament for Kigoma for greater ownership of the local economy, through co-operative unions and associations, and a history of pursuing co-operative enterprise in Tanzania. There are over 10,000 co-ops in Tanzania, whose membership comprises over 5 per cent of the Tanzanian population, so community wealth building can have resonance there. The approach adopted, though, must be adapted to local circumstances and supported by the community, so discussions between UK and Tanzanian representatives are about a theory and framework that will work for Kigoma. The discussions are based in equal peer-to-peer learning, in a two-way exchange, and can yield lessons for the further spread of community wealth building internationally. Kigoma is limited in anchor institutions, so one adaptation must be to that. Co-op membership in Kigoma is lower than nationally, and plans are afoot to build this up. Finance could come more through co-operative networks than donors or central government approval. The latter have proven less friendly to co-ops.

On a related side note, Clarke (2012) argues that North–South interurban partnerships predominantly involve policy transfer from North to South, imitative urbanism, despite the great gains that could be made from a more two-way cosmopolitan urbanism, which is not to say one-sidedness is what happened in the case discussed here. Abbey (2022), discussing social democracy, argues that African countries have more of a basis for consensus-based (*ubuntu*) democracy (relevant also in restorative justice practices discussed in Chapter 2) in contrast to more adversarial politics in western liberal democracy. This may be one way lessons can go from South to North.

Community wealth building can be built into overseas development policy towards Global South countries. Lessons can be learned from places like Kigoma about what the best method to support development is, reshaping it in a way that is less top-down and learns more from local, specific knowledge and circumstances. Overseas development policy could be oriented through peer-to-peer engagement across international co-operative networks and trade unions. This can replace development policies based on liberalized trade and favouring mutinational companies over co-operative enterprise. Such an international development policy would be more equal and more based in the local circumstances of places like Kigoma.

International and overseas development policy will only be progressive if allied with policies that include debt cancellation, reparations, and open borders, accompanied by measures that mean people do not feel compelled to leave their home countries if they do not want to. New international institutions can be built with equal votes for members, although as I argue later, this would still leave great inequality and power imbalances outside those institutions that would permeate the institutions themselves, however equal they are in formal democratic terms. As such, the global Left may make as much headway organizing with the global Left as through global government. There would have to be strong trade unions and labour rights for the Global South, organized internationally so workers of the rich North do not benefit at the expense of workers from the South. Democratic public ownership can make sure decisions are made in the interest of the community rather than for the profit of the few. Trade rules can get rid of investor protections and intellectual property rights that prevent governments from pursuing policies in the interest of their citizens, and rich-country protectionism can be dismantled. Social clauses and human rights should be built into trade agreements. The banking sector could be more regulated, and lower-income countries could be allowed to use capital controls to protect their economies, with democratic public banks to make sure loans favour the public interest. There can be extensions of growing international co-operation on the taxing of big corporations. (See Basu, 2019b, on a new internationalism.)

## Conclusions

The community wealth approach is about creating and retaining wealth in the community rather than making and extracting it from outside for uncommitted shareholders instead of citizens. Democratizing the economy involves marrying political and civil society, and the mainstream and margins. It includes the entrepreneurial state rather than rejecting active government – a local state but also national – and working in alliance with institutions rather than acting on them or wide-scale appropriation of private ownership. It involves social movements, trade unions, and charities.

The democratic economy institutionalizes the alternative and change via a system and assets rather than leaving these as they are and compensating by redistribution to correct inequalities. It is not socialism replacing social democracy, but socialist as well as social democratic. There is a rejuvenation of old social democracy, with greater emphasis on the local and decentralized. A question about social alternatives outside politics is how far they can be realized more widely, and politics can help with this. Political alternatives raise issues of entrenchment and institutionalization, and a basis in civil society is a response to this. Local decentralized social ownership needs to be allied with national public ownership if it is to be equally for all.

The democratic economy is pluralist. It is mainstream and political as well as alternative and social. There is a re-politicization of alternatives: going from extra-political alternatives to public–public political society links. Extra-political alternatives are built on and allied with political intervention and the mainstream public sector; a place for the political in social alternatives. Democratizing the economy involves formal as well as informal sectors. Scaling up can happen through experiment and demonstration and through political design and facilitation led by politics and party. It involves alternatives not just in isolated experiments on the fringes of society, but also via conventional politics, locally and nationally, set up downwards and scaled across as well as scaled up from below.

But this economy will face opposition from international capital who are disadvantaged by it. Complacency over parochialism, resistance, and the potential for reversal should be avoided. Embeddedness in society in the face of opposition from international capital and other interests will require going beyond just institutionalization. There should be reforms to capital, the civil service, and media, and a popular consciousness and social movement basis behind the democratic economy.

So, the democratic economy needs to be for all of society equally as well as localized, and geared to a fightback against powerful opposition and not complacent about its wider appeal. Key themes of this book raised in this chapter are pluralist socialism and multiple and multilevel combined measures for pursuing social goals – national and local alternatives, government and civil society alternatives, and political, social movement, and prefigurative alternatives, combined rather than some chosen over others. Common themes across these are utopianism, democratizing the economy, and, as such, socialist progress. Of the higher political levels discussed so far, the national one has been mentioned most often. Some argue that democratizing the economy needs to be pursued at higher levels, even global ones. Global alternative societies are the concern of the next chapter.

**Table 5.1:** The democratic economy

| Approaches to the democratic economy | Scale | Owners | Institutions | Actors | Relation to other forms of democratic economy |
|---|---|---|---|---|---|
| Communism | Society wide or international | Initially the state on behalf of the people, then society as a whole through worker and consumer councils | Worker and consumer councils National bureaucracy, but just as an administrative machinery for planning and execution of plans, not as a political agency | Working class and workers party in the transitional period Workers and consumers in communist society | Devolves economic democracy to workers and consumers Non-state organization May include co-ops and local councils but more society wide in focus Not as permissive of capitalist, market, and state institutions as social democracy or democratic socialism |
| Co-ops | Companies under co-operative ownership of workers, consumers, users or local community | Workers, consumers, users, community | Co-operatively owned company Government and shelter organizations may be involved in facilitating co-operative ownership | Government, shelter organizations, worker, consumer, or community owners | Not society wide Sectional ownership – for example, by the group who are owners rather than by all of society or representatives from across society or local community |
| Community wealth building | Usually local but could be national, and part of foreign and international policy | Co-ops owned by their members Municipal ownership | Government supports anchor institutions procuring services from local or national community (both privately and socially owned) rather than from global capitalist corporations | Government, anchor institutions, co-ops, think-and-do tanks, unions, charities | Not a form of ownership but can promote co-operative ownership as well as investment locally in the community rather than loss of money to global shareholders |

**Table 5.1:** The democratic economy (continued)

| Approaches to the democratic economy | Scale | Owners | Institutions | Actors | Relation to other forms of democratic economy |
|---|---|---|---|---|---|
| Social democracy | Society wide Usually national but can have supranational co-ordination | Public ownership in some areas, usually by the state on behalf of the people | State, publicly owned services, utilities, and sometimes corporations | Government, state, publicly owned services and utilities | Unlike communism and socialism, a mixed economy of public and private, state and market within capitalism Unlike co-ops, on a national scale |
| Socialism | Society wide Usually national but can have supranational co-ordination with other like-minded actors | State or other collective actors own the majority of the economy and public services | State ownership, but can also include co-ops Private ownership and markets can have a minority role within a socialist economy | Government, Left party, trade unions, social movements | Unlike social democracy, a predominantly socialist economy, publicly owned and planned Revolutionary reforms Unlike communism, it may allow a significant minority role for private ownership and markets Can include co-ops but is a society-wide system, not just at company level Not anarchist, because of the state dimension Not social democratic, because it is predominantly a socialist economy, not socialism within capitalism |

(continued)

**Table 5.1:** The democratic economy (continued)

| Approaches to the democratic economy | Scale | Owners | Institutions | Actors | Relation to other forms of democratic economy |
|---|---|---|---|---|---|
| Pluralist democratic socialism | Society wide Usually national | State and decentralized ownership, democratically inclusive of multiple actors with interests in and affected by the company or utility; also co-ops That is, not just social ownership by one group, like workers or government | Decentralized and state institutions, national and municipal state Plural institutions and groups are involved, not just state or workers; other groups are also included in democratized ownership, so more inclusive of all affected interests | Democratic socialist party, social movements, trade unions, variety of affected interests in society | Different emphasis from socialism more generically in that it emphasizes public ownership democratized and accountable to a variety of groups in society Protects a role for liberal and plural institutions in society to ensure socialism adheres to liberal, democratic, and pluralist principles |

**Further reading**

Joe Guinan and Martin O'Neill have written on the democratic economy and community wealth building in the much-mentioned 'The institutional turn' (2018) and their book *The Case for Community Wealth Building* (2019b). There are useful materials on the websites of The Democracy Collaborative, the Centre for Local Economic Strategies, and Common Wealth and in the journal *Renewal*. Andy Beckett's (2019) *Guardian* article on 'The New Left economics: how a network of thinkers is transforming capitalism' is useful, as is the Labour Party's (2017) report on *Alternative Models of Social Ownership*. Christine Berry and Joe Guinan (2019), in *People Get Ready*, are good on the challenges a Left government proposing economic democracy would face and how to overcome them. On the participatory, predistributive socialist approach, discussed in this chapter, compared to social investment state social democracy, see Celia Kerstenetzky's (2022) 'Horizons of social democracy', in *The Political Quarterly*.

Older and interesting books on the democratic economy include Pat Devine's (1988) *Democracy and Economic Planning*, which goes into some detail, Geoff Hodgson's (1984) more pro-market *The Democratic Economy*, the pluralist Robert Dahl's (1986) *A Preface to Economic Democracy*, and John Mathews' (1989) broader *Age of Democracy*. More recently, Simon Tremblay-Pepin's (2022) 'Five criteria to evaluate democratic economic planning models', in *Review of Radical Political Economics*, provides an overview of democratic planning models, and Christoph Sorg's (2022) 'Failing to plan is planning to fail', in *Critical Sociology*, looks at social, political, and ecological aspects of democratic planning using digital methods.

# 6

# Alternative Globalization

I have looked at alternative societies across the world, but mostly at local or national ones. How do these alternatives relate to international or global society (see Adler, 2019; Murphy, 2019)? In this chapter, I want to discuss alternatives at a more global level, to regimes such as global neoliberalism and the regulation of people movement.

In the 1970s and 1980s, globalization was defined, in part, by neoliberalism. For many, globalization meant the spread of economic liberalism as much as the globalization of capitalism. A movement grew in the 2000s, initially called anti-globalization, geared often, but not always, around global justice concerns (see Gill, 2000; Graeber, 2002; Pleyers, 2010). For instance, it was also in nationalist anti-globalization on the Left and the far Right. It was visible in large confrontational protests at meetings of world economic and political leaders. It was bottom-up and outside mainstream politics, not an elite or political movement. The movement was wide, comprising strands from socialist and union and labour positions to radical green and anarchist ones, among many others, both formally organized and informal. It was not against globalization per se but neoliberal globalization specifically and the form it took in imperialist corporate projects, free trade deals, international organizations, and capital mobility. The anti-globalization movement criticized the depoliticization of decisions, created by neoliberalism being inscribed in treaties and so beyond the control of governments and electors. It drew attention to the rising exploitation of labour as corporations moved their operations to areas where workers have the worst pay and conditions and countries with the weakest environmental and labour regulations. Anti-globalization highlighted issues previously more marginal in politics – such as health concerns about food, water, and pharmaceuticals, environmental problems, the rights of Indigenous people, and the extension of western media and consumerism in a homogenizing fashion – with a strong emphasis on global inequality.

Being against neoliberal globalization specifically rather than all globalization meant it was possible to be for an alternative globalization,

globalization still but of a non-neoliberal sort. So, 'alter-globalization' became a better term than 'anti-globalization'. This consisted of what was called 'one no but many yeses', the no to neoliberalism and the many yeses the alternatives. Anti-globalizers were against neoliberal globalization but for different reasons, leading to different proposals for the alternative. And it operated globally, though as we shall see, it has taken localist and less conflictual forms. (For other perspectives on alternatives to neoliberalism, see Jones and O'Donnell, 2018; Harris and Acaroğlu, 2022.)

## Political globalization

Anti- and alter-globalization were bottom-up movements. Parallel to them, another approach to alternative globalization developed, more through political power than civil society. This came from liberal and social democratically inclined advocates oriented to politics (for example, Held, 2004) more than the radical alter-globalizers, the latter being anarchist inclined and oriented to social movements.

Political alternative globalization is in part a response to the view that nation-states must compete to attract globally mobile capital, sometimes called competition state theory. Political liberalization and technological change from about the 1970s made it easier for capital to move across borders and invest where it can get the best deal. This has resulted in a race to the bottom by governments, stripping back regulations and protections for workers and the environment, and reducing tax and public spending, to attract capital that sees these as burdens. States competing for global capital undermine social democratic policies. Social democratic regulation at the national level is not possible, as it will put off capital that can just flee elsewhere (Huber and Stephens, 2002; Cerny and Evans, 2004).

Consequently, regulation must be pursued across nation-states so capital does not have anywhere to flee. This requires common international norms and standards agreed on at a global level. It can be implemented through existing institutions, such as the International Monetary Fund (IMF), the UN, and the World Trade Organization (WTO), beefed up in terms of power and enforcement, given more social as well as economic goals in their remit, and made more democratic and inclusive. There can be additional new global organizations pursuing social goals, on issues like labour rights, the environment, and global equality. There could be a world parliament with directly elected members, its composition in proportion to the populations of the countries represented. International bodies like the IMF, the UN, the World Bank, and the WTO could be agencies of the world parliament or institutions of its civil service (Monbiot, 2001). (Neilson, 2021, proposes a democratic socialist post-pandemic 'glocalist' version of global governance, from a Marxist perspective.)

However, this approach is ambitious. To be truly global, such structures need the states of the world involved in agreeing on common regulations. To be democratic, all states must have an equal say, at least in proportion to their populations. But for most governments to agree on significant regulatory, socially minded, and environmentally friendly policies requires a capacity for assent on such policies that does not exist and, because of diverse ideologies and interests, is unlikely to. Countries from Spain to Sudan and China to the US have such different ideologies and clashing interests that it is difficult to see how global governance can achieve agreements that are meaningful, sufficient, and effective. Outside global institutions, participants are unequal in power and economically, and these inequalities pass over into unequal sway in international fora and create different interests and conflicts there. Powerful states often use global institutions to impose their own aims as much as to pursue universal goals.

Opportunities for social democratic global governance have not been taken up. The financial crisis could have led to the global regulation of finance, and there was public support for this. But governments bailed out finance rather than reconstructing it. An ideological commitment to deregulation led to the opportunity for global regulation not being taken up. If the financial crisis did not lead to the global regulation of capitalism, it is difficult to see what would. Globalization to tackle development has often not benefitted poor countries, who get tied into investment and trade agreements that have many parts to their disadvantage, because of the power of actors from the North they are engaging with. Climate change calls out for global government, and there have been numerous attempts to come to international agreements to tackle the problem. But these have been around abstract targets, such as degrees of warming, rather than concrete means for achieving them. They have been weak in ambition, lacking the teeth and sanctions to ensure conformity, and have fallen because of the conflicting interests of actors involved in negotiations (but for a more optimistic appraisal after the UN Climate Change Conference in 2021 (COP26), see Jacobs, 2022). There are annual global meetings to tackle nuclear proliferation, but these have failed to make serious inroads into making the world a safer place and serious disarmament.

## Below global approaches

In such areas, national and bilateral approaches – international but below a fully global level – and pursuing concrete measures rather than abstract targets have been more successful. So below global and bottom-up seem to work better than global and top-down. When the COVID-19 crisis came, national governments took responsibility for responding, with international approaches not coming to the fore until the vaccination phase and then playing second fiddle to national government for much of the world. This is not necessarily misconceived, but perhaps a rational response to where real effectiveness and possibility lie. Zhou (2022) discusses how vaccine nationalism and global approaches to COVID-19 have shown processes of globalization and deglobalization, global inequalities, lagging consciousness of global interconnection, and barriers to global collaboration and multilateralism. (On similar themes and calls for global justice post pandemic, see Khondker, 2022, and Mittelman, 2022.)

This is not to say that global agreements cannot be made in areas like development, humanitarian aid, peacekeeping, international law, and human rights. There have been important achievements in such fields through international institutions like the UN. However, in terms of building an alternative that departs from and changes the neoliberal content of globalization, there are limits in ideology and interests to pursuing such a project through inclusive action at global political levels.

Global cosmopolitan aims are worthy but do not have the global cosmopolitan politics that will work for them. There is not sufficient global cosmopolitanism in values, aims, and politics internationally to provide a basis for it to be pursued at a global level. A more feasible approach is for cosmopolitan goals to be pursued at lower supranational or sub-global international levels, where state actors can seek out selected others with related material interests, like-minded ideological goals, or compatible geopolitical aims. This could be at regional levels, for instance via the EU, although what was supposed to be a social Europe ended up one of negative integration with the removal of regulations rather than enhancement of them. The G77, a non-aligned group of developing countries, formed a sub-global international alliance to pursue their shared interests. President Chávez of Venezuela tried to build an internationalism but one that was below global, with actors holding similar ideological aims or geopolitical interests. With conflict rather than consensus politics being what happens at the global level, the Left may be better off looking for a collaboration with the international Left than seeking global government. So, this is a sub-global selective internationalism.

For the Global South, Bello and Feffer (2009) advocate deglobalization and Amin (1990), delinking. Here, neoliberal globalization is replaced with more localized economies that work better for ecological and social justice. Production is done more for local markets than export, so countries have greater self-sufficiency and less dependence on the Global North. Trade policies involving quotas, subsidies, and tariffs protect local markets and manufacturing from corporate commodities from abroad. International institutions like the IMF and the World Bank are bypassed by regional ones based on co-operation and democracy rather than free markets, combining subsidiarity with confederal democracy. This compares with the sub-global internationalism I am arguing for, where those with like-minded ideas or related interests co-operate internationally more than pursuing change through global institutions that are ideologically, and in power, weighted against them (Amin, 1990; Bello and Feffer, 2009; Basu, 2019a; also Muhr, 2022, discusses the history of South–South delinking from a decolonial perspective; see also Gray and Gills, 2016, and Mawdsley, 2019, for overviews of South–South co-operation).

Furthermore, while global capital's power of exit should not be underestimated, the evidence does not support simple competition state theory. States can pursue a regulatory and social democratic approach without capital fleeing, and this has been possible in countries pursuing higher tax and spending programmes – for instance, in Scandinavia (Mosley, 2005; Calnitsky, 2022). States can retain global capital by means other than a race to the bottom. They may have skilled workers, an infrastructure of science, transport, education, and technology, a good health system and public spending policies that boost the economy, positive industrial relations that involve strong trade unions and fair employment practices, and targeted social and industrial investment. All of these, rather than the race to the bottom, can be attractive to capital. And for some businesses, the costs of relocating if a social democratic government comes to power are too great, so staying put ends up the best decision.

Alternative globalization can be pursued through national strategies, but as a response to global processes such as neoliberalism or climate change: so globally oriented if not global in means. This has followed the failure of global approaches to problems like climate change or their restricted role in responding to COVID-19. There have been on-the-ground, bottom-up concrete practices, such as carbon reduction and non-neoliberal economics, rather than top-down abstract targets. The former are national, intra-nationally regional, or local – for instance via local government. At the national level, there can be measures like bans on diesel or petrol car sales, support for renewable energy sources, financial transactions taxes diverting funds to environmental projects, ethical banking, and green new deal policies. National and local government strategies for democratizing the economy and community wealth building are sub-global approaches, but pursue solutions to global problems. These put community concerns over private profit for companies. Many such practices internationally have been at the municipal level (see Rushton, 2020).

So social objectives that cannot be pursued by regulation at a global or supranational level are furthered on national and local stages with cosmopolitan and global social concerns to the fore. These are alternatives to political globalization, with social, labour, and environmental aims, but pursued lower down rather than globally. Substitutes for neoliberal and anti-environmental globalization are at national and neighbourhood as much as international levels, but these are still responses to global economic and environmental processes, so address globalization and are globally minded.

## Alter-globalization in society

I have mentioned global, national, and local state approaches. There is also local civil society alter-globalization. This is in response to neoliberalism globally but constructs alternatives locally. The approach is more positive and literally constructive and less oppositional than anti-globalization. The positivity extends to reaching out to the local community and being open to them – for instance, migrants and the economically excluded – rather than building a, political force with just the like-minded and in conflict with the enemy, so it is less conflictual and more about outreach.

As discussed in Chapters 1 and 2, examples include sustainable economic activities, sharing economies, co-ops, alternative food production, eco-communities, intentional communities, community gardens, alternative social centres, alternative education, squats, occupations, and housing co-ops. Many are oriented around social rather than neoliberal or profit objectives and have green aims. They build sharing and decommodified economies, with exchange without markets or money but in kind and for free. They are co-operative or collectively run, often with horizontal rather than hierarchical decision-making. So, they are non-market and non-capitalist, with green and anti-waste values to the fore, and in an autonomous sphere separate from the state even if necessarily interacting with it. They can be supported by government procurement policy favouring initiatives that are sustainable and ethical, or funding, financial incentives, or infrastructure. These are anti- and alter- neoliberal globalization but at a local as much as a global level, while having a global consciousness and linked to global networks of similar initiatives.

The model of change is less about insurrectionary revolution, state oriented, politically reformist, or protest; and more about constructing local alternatives prefiguratively as a basis for transformation – so an alternative to the alternatives. It is less about changing the political agenda, more about constructing alternatives beyond it, though this does not exclude politics too. The alternatives are: experimental – worked out by trial and error, seeing whether an alternative society can work; demonstrative – if it works, showing how; and prefigurative – by example, laying a basis for a wider possible future society. This is not to say local alter-globalization cannot also be revolutionary, reformist in an incremental way, connected with state politics, or a form of protest via its constructive alternatives. It is materialist in its approach to change as much as about ideological persuasion, the change coming from the persuasiveness of material practice as much as argument or propaganda. The means of change can be an end as well, practised for its own benefits. Working out positive social relations in the alternatives is as much an objective as political goals. This is different to large-scale utopianism in the future, without being anti-utopian, because it is micro-utopianism in the here and now.

Pleyers (2010) describes one approach of these alter-globalizations as the 'way of subjectivity': bottom-up, local, participatory, networked, and an alternative to the political, playing out values in daily life and done by ordinary people on a participatory basis. This is different to what he calls the 'way of reason': by experts from above, with efficiency a priority, through institutions and political integration. As mentioned earlier, Holloway (2010) calls these 'way of subjectivity' alternatives 'cracks' where non-capitalist forms of life are built and can be expanded to undermine capitalism. He rejects using power to achieve change, but I believe the way of subjectivity and cracks needs to exist alongside and be intertwined with political institutional change. Pleyers says that the way of subjectivity and the way of reason can be related negatively, such as through dichotomy or absorption of one by the other. But they can be complementary, overlap, mutually support each other, cross-fertilize, and combine. This fits with my advocacy in this book of pluralist multilevel socialism.

Alter-globalization localisms may focus on their communities and so neglect opponents, power, change, and the possibilities of state and politics. They can become too separate from wider society and broader social change and be about alternative lifestyle and identity rather than political transformation. They can be multiplicities with a lack of overall coherence. But none of these possible drawbacks are necessary. Material extra-political change that creates contradictions with dominant forms can be linked in a multilevel way with political institutions. This allows wider uptake and engagement with political and social change, rather than just detachment from society, and politics can create bridges and coherence across multiple experiments and alternatives. The argument against false dichotomies between different approaches, and for a multilevel approach, is a key one of this book.

## A Fifth International

Such an approach has been taken up in the advocacy of a Fifth International ensuing from global movements of movements. This would follow four previous internationals – global organizations of workers and socialists, from the first, founded in 1864, to the fourth, set up in 1938. The advocacy of a Fifth International links with the emphasis of this book on a pluralist and dual approach, beyond polarizations, that emphasizes both the bottom-up in prefigurative alternatives and campaigning social movements, but necessarily in tandem with party and state politics.

In 2018 the Marxist world systems theorist Samir Amin called for a Fifth International, shifting the struggle for alternatives to capitalism from diverse movements to combination in political organization (Amin, 2018, 2019; Gills and Chase-Dunn, 2019; Moghadam, 2019). The global justice movement in the 1990s onwards led to the founding of the World Social Forum (WSF). Some participants in the WSF were involved in Leftist parties, but it was, in general, negative about political programmes or working with political parties. It was more of an open space for free exchanges among civil society actors. (See Chase-Dunn et al, 2009, on global Left movements and political regimes, North and South.) Before long, though, some felt the WSF should be moving towards a political strategy. Two books on the movements of movements (Sen, 2017, 2018) capture the belief in diverse movements with direct democracy and prefigurative approaches, and the views of those who want more engagement with political organization. (Soborski, 2018, criticizes progressive social movements for lack of political vision.)

Amin (2018) argues that emancipatory struggles have crumbled, are fragmented, or have been too focused on national issues where they have not had significant success. Transformational change has been abandoned. WSF movements are no longer the place, he says, to develop an alternative, and those looking for a world alternative society must build a political alliance for change. He calls for a platform for co-ordinating plural struggles and constructing a coherent programme. For Amin, lessons can be taken from entities like the communist Third International. He proposes a structured organization with the representation of workers and peoples from all continents, in unity and diversity. Amin calls for a meeting to establish a new international to develop a long-term unified strategy with political objectives, a political organization rather than a set of disparate movements.

Karatasli (2019) also suggests building on the historical legacy of global Left movements of the 20th century. But he says a new international, effectively a world political party (see also Pätomaki, 2019), should not replace horizontal diverse movements or local and community action, but rather supplement and connect them. The two do not have to be mutually exclusive. This gels with what I have argued for in this book on the process of transition from here to there, and on the end objective of an alternative society: going beyond dichotomy and polarizations, and seeing party and state politics, movements, and alternatives in combination. It also links with my argument in this chapter that global institutions may not, as it stands, yield a lot for the Left, but the international linkage of the global Left can. The Left should seek change in an international Left, I have argued, as much as in global government, although the former should of course be using international institutions where it can and seeking to transform or replace them.

# Open borders

Anti-globalization has adopted the form of alter-globalization, and this has been taken up in proposals for global regulation, a sort of international social democracy. However, this approach has obstacles to success. There is not a cosmopolitan political underpinning for its cosmopolitan ends. Sub-global internationalism, national, and local political and extra-political alternatives to globalization are more viable. These are a sub-global way of pursuing alter-globalization. They exist after, alongside, or as part of the more global anti-globalization movement. They have a global consciousness and global networks but are based in national or local places. However, I want to argue that there is an alternative globalization that should and can be pursued at a global level. This is an alternative globalization of open borders. A basis in cosmopolitan attitudes may also be lacking for this, but the prospects for openness to global borders may not be as dim in the long term as at first it seems.

There are philosophical and practical arguments for open borders, the former based on principle and the latter more on economic and social grounds. The case for migration from both perspectives is strong. However, there are differing opinions over which is the best to use. There are two reasons why the philosophical and principled ones could be preferred. First, if you throw statistics at people about the economic and social benefits of immigration, this frequently does not work. People have personal anecdotal experience they feel casts doubt on contrary systematic evidence. If an immigrant gets a job that your friend also applied for, that, for some, trumps data showing that immigration creates employment. Some people believe that migrants take jobs and use public services funded by taxpayers' money, and no amount of numbers will dissuade them from this evocative story. So, it can be argued, the way to persuade people about the case for immigration is with a narrative based more on humanitarianism and morality – for instance, about fellow humans fleeing difficult circumstances, compassion, obligations that can be shown to them, and our appreciation for what they give. A second reason for scepticism about pursuing empirical economic and social arguments in support of migration concerns how you argue for immigration if it ends up not having economic and social gains. Those in favour of open borders may want to argue for them irrespective of whether they benefit receiving societies or bring problems. A focus on economic and social arguments leads you to having to question immigration where it does not bring improvements. So, the better thing is to focus on the argument for migration in its own right, regardless of economic and social consequences for receiving communities, because the moral case stands even if the empirical one does not.

To be plausible, an argument has to be well informed. But some misleading impressions underlie negativity about immigration. Rather than there being great waves of them, international migrants make up just 3.3 per cent of the world's population. In the 19th century, the percentage was 10 per cent (OECD/UN-DESA, 2013: 2; Dicken, 2015: 345). The quantity has grown because the world population has enlarged, so the numbers of people doing lots of things, such as not migrating, have increased. But, proportionately, international migration has gone down since the 19th century. Rich countries have more international immigration than the global average: about 10 per cent of immigration is in OECD countries. But people in those places often think the numbers are far greater than they are. In many rich countries, people think there are three times as many migrants as there are (Duffy and Frere-Smith, 2014; Gorodzeisky and Semyonov, 2020). Most international migration is not from poor to rich countries: 33 per cent is between developing countries, and 22 per cent is between developed countries (IOM, 2013: 25). 72% of refugees are hosted in countries neighbouring their country of origin (UNHCR, 2022). Also 83 per cent of refugees are hosted in low and middle income countries, 27 per cent in the Least Developed Countries, and 16 per cent in high income countries (UNHCR, 2022). In 2021 the countries that hosted the most refugees were Turkey, Colombia, Uganda, and Pakistan while those accommodating the highest number relative to their national population were Lebanon, Curaçao, Jordan, and Turkey (UNHCR, 2022). So, any image that rich Europe and North America are being flooded with refugees is off the mark. The key issue here is that much opposition to international migration is based on the idea that there are huge waves of it from poor to rich countries. The facts do not back this up, so the negativity must be put into question. Furthermore, much attention in anti-immigration discourses is on receiving rather than on sending countries or the migrants themselves. If you look at the providing states and the migrants, you can see many gains for both.

*Philosophical and principled arguments*

What is the case for open borders in their own right – the philosophical and principled arguments? (For a philosophical defence, see Carens, 2013; see also, Bertram, 2018.) Some are based on freedom and rights. Liberals are for freedom of speech, belief, and assembly. From this perspective, it is proposed, it is inconsistent to not also be in favour of other freedoms which allow people to be autonomous and express self-determination, in this case freedom of movement. It is not defensible to support liberty and self-determination in some areas and not others. This is equally the case if you believe you should be free to emigrate to pursue liberty or a better life elsewhere, but do not favour the freedom of others to immigrate to your country in pursuit of the same things. Furthermore, restrictions on free movement are related to other transgressions of liberty and rights, such as the right to family life, freedom of association, the right to a trial before detention, and freedom from undue surveillance. These are eroded by immigration restrictions and state coercion in the management of people's movements. In addition, denial of entry may lead to immigrants' loss of freedoms in their home countries up to the extent of torture and death.

Other principled arguments for immigration are based on obligation – we should help others, especially those less well off than ourselves. This is allied with cosmopolitanism – our commitments should be to others regardless of their origins, and not only or first to people from our own nation. The latter involves a more communitarian approach, that duties are primarily to people from our community, defined in this case in terms of country. A cosmopolitan perspective puts the emphasis not on common membership of community, unless the community is the whole globe, and it extends our obligations to all. From this viewpoint, there is no justifiable reason why we should favour people from our own populace. All humans are equally deserving of our commitment, and this includes welcoming those from beyond our national borders to enjoy the benefits and freedoms we have in our own country where those are lacking in theirs. Some may say that to access the resources of our nation, immigrants should have made a contribution that entitles them to these. But exclusion from our borders stops them from doing that. So, the answer to this argument is to allow migrants entry so they can contribute.

This links to arguments for open borders based on equality. One equality argument concerning immigration is about the equal worth of all humans. At the moment, people have very different opportunities and life chances because of the arbitrary fact of the country they were born in. They are restricted from changing that situation through freedom to move to where they can advance their chances, whether in terms of economic well-being, freedom, or other factors. Others, because of the luck of where they were born, have much greater freedoms and life chances where they live. So, people are not treated equally and do not have equal life chances because of a fact out of their control. Allowing free movement would enable them to have the same chances as other people globally. Not allowing free movement prevents this. This is an issue of injustice based on the moral equality of all humans.

Another argument based on equality concerns economic equality. Many who migrate do so to advance their material life chances, and from a position of material inequality to somewhere where they can better their economic situation. Migration, in this case, does not itself essentially lessen structures of economic inequality but helps some escape a more unequal situation. It helps some move from a poorer position to a better-off one and, in that position, to send money to their home country, which helps that country become better off too. So, while it may not overturn basic structures of economic inequality, it may be one factor that can mitigate them.

A narrative on open borders and immigration can focus on these issues of justice, freedom, obligation, and equality. Some, however, argue that even if there is a justification in these arguments, borders should not be opened too much and complete free movement cannot be allowed, because of the negative economic and social consequences for receiving countries. But there are several myths about these consequences, and often the effects for receiving countries are economically and socially very positive.

## Economic and social arguments

Immigration, it is argued by some, leads to lower wages in rich receiving countries, the loss of jobs from domestic citizens to migrant workers, a greater burden on welfare and social services, and social problems to do with a decline of community, trust, and national identity. However, for most of these claims, there is very little reliable evidence. The evidence is that immigration into rich countries has mostly beneficial effects in these areas.

As far as wages go, immigration may be connected sometimes to lower wages at the bottom of the ladder. However, insofar as this is the case, these lower wages are not caused by migration. They are imposed by employers who use times of higher immigration to employ migrants on lower wages and so decrease wage rates at the bottom. The cause, therefore, is employers operating on the labour market rather than migration. The solution, it follows, is not to cut immigration but to bring about a more ethical approach by employers or, lacking that, stronger trade unions and labour market regulations to ensure decent minimum living wages. Average wages, meanwhile, do not seem to come down in times of high immigration (Blanchflower et al, 2007; TUC, 2007).

The argument that migrant workers take domestic workers' jobs is based on the assumption that there are a fixed number of positions. If the number of job seekers increases through factors such as a higher birth rate or more migrant labourers, then there is less work to go around, and the new young breadwinners or migrants take some of the domestic employees' jobs. However, a supply of new workers can lead to more employment being created. Areas of the economy where it is difficult to find domestic employees willing to do the work – perhaps low-paid occupations such as farm labouring, construction, or health services – find a supply of labour, are boosted, and can grow. More work is done in such areas, creating employment and increased consumption of the goods and services produced. Migrants do paid work, so tax revenue increases, which can be used to fund public services. The wage-earners spend money in shops so boost demand, leading to more production and more employment in manufacturing, services, and retail. So, overall, the economy expands, and while migrant employees may sometimes take jobs that domestic workers have applied for, the overall supply of work in the economy increases. Chiefly, the effect is an increase in employment and chances of work for domestic workers, not a decrease (TUC, 2007).

Overall, studies of immigration suggest that it leads to economic growth because migrants move from being unproductive to being productive and businesses are better able to match the supply of labour to demand. The evidence from economics is almost universal on the positive effects of international migration economically (Dustmann and Preston, 2019).

One problem that affects sending countries is 'brain drain'. Less rich states suffer a loss of skilled labour to better-off countries, in some cases in big numbers (Campbell, 2022, discusses the increasing 'poaching' in the UK of doctors from poorer countries where they are much needed). This is a serious issue but may be offset by the remittances the workers send back. The migrants get experience and training in the countries they go to that they can take back. They benefit economically and in other ways. There can be political ways of dealing with brain drain other than immigration restrictions, such as labour swaps where rich-country workers go abroad, compensation, and requirements placed by sending societies, such as that skilled workers work in their country of origin for a short period in return for training before being free to travel abroad. Root causes for people leaving their countries can be tackled. Brain drain is a serious problem for some states, but it is not irremediable. (On brain drain and remittances, see de Haas, 2007.)

The argument that immigrants put an undue burden on welfare and public services is also off the mark. The opposite seems frequently the case. Most migrants work. Furthermore, they are often net contributors to welfare and public services, paying more in than the value of what they get out, while domestic citizens are sometimes net beneficiaries. By entering employment and so stimulating economic growth, migrant workers facilitate greater tax revenue to fund public services (Dustmann and Frattini, 2013, 2014; OECD, 2013; Office for Budget Responsibility, 2013; Vargas-Silva, 2015). They also often do work in public services that domestic workers are less keen to. One of the costs of immigration is immigration control, so more open borders would reduce that burden on public spending.

Igarashi and Laurence (2021), among others, suggest that immigration leads to anti-immigrant sentiment. Some studies (a prominent example is Putnam, 2007) suggest that community and trust decline in areas of diversity or high immigration. But loss of community and trust is one thing; blaming it on immigration is another. It can be as much to do with the hostility of the receiving population as an effect of the arriving one, and developing cohesion takes time as new forms grow and are forged. Snapshots should be resisted, and a longer-term perspective taken. Furthermore, the subject is complex, and studies that tease out layers of the phenomenon show there is more to it.

Dinesen et al (2020) review the literature on ethnic diversity and trust, and say in general it shows a negative relationship, but this is modest rather than to an extent that supports apocalyptic claims about heterogeneity being a severe threat to cohesion. Furthermore, studies are mostly of residential contexts where people live alongside each other and have exposure to other groups more than connection with them, unlike situations such as work or education, where there is more contact. Greater contact may increase trust, and its effect is often not covered in studies that are negative about diversity and cohesion. There is mixed evidence, but that includes information that shows trust improves with interaction. Green et al (2020) say data from European countries shows association reduces negative attitudes towards immigrants, and they suggest this can be further facilitated by policies that pursue tolerant and inclusive integration policies, increasing contact and consequently reducing anti-immigration attitudes.

Sturgis et al (2014) carried out a study of London, a city with high levels of immigration and diversity. The authors found that where there is more contact in diverse areas, people have stronger feelings of trust, but where diversity takes more segregated forms and people live side by side with less association, heterogeneity goes along with people feeling less cohesion. They also found that diversity is connected with greater trust among the young than the old, the former being more likely to have grown up in a pluralist context. The implication is that if contact increases between varied groups over time and the young, more used to diversity, grow older and make up a greater proportion of the population, then trust in mixed areas will grow.

Demireva and Heath's (2014) study of data on Britain delves further into the complexity of the phenomenon. They conclude that fear of crime, economic deprivation at the neighbourhood level, and social renting as opposed to private ownership, have a stronger link to lack of civic spirit than diversity. Bridging contacts between groups has a positive relationship with cohesion and decreases strong identification among the White British with their own ethnicity. Residential diversity in itself, they argue, does not tell us much about intergroup interactions, but when you look at where these interactions involve more contact, they conclude that cohesion increases. Overall, then, contact between groups in diverse areas seems to be associated with trust holding up.

To suggest national identity is eroded by immigration takes it at one point in time and sees it as the then true character to be measured against. But national identity at any stage is itself a result of development and progress over time, the change being affected by, among other things, immigration and diversity historically. So, modifications in national identity should not be seen in terms of one fixed moment, but as processual. One of the positive things about immigration is the way it does change national identity, introducing diversity, novelty, and new and rich cultures, and all that is positive about that.

## Are open borders possible?

If open borders are defensible morally and in terms of their economic and social effects, are they feasible and will anyone support such an idea? Is it utopian and unrealistic to pursue open borders and the free moment of people? A first issue is whether open borders would lead to huge and unsustainable population movements. Evidence from where borders are open does not support that this would be the case. Before the 1970s, immigration controls were less prevalent, and before the First World War, people moved internationally in much higher proportions, although the world population was smaller so numbers were less. But in this case, as in others involving long-term cross-border movements, such as within the EU, there were not huge and impossible people movements. In large states like Canada, Russia, and the US, similarly, there is not unmanageable mobility of people across long-distance open borders even though there are few obstacles to crossing them. Extrapolating from cases of relaxed border restrictions, Moses (2006) estimates open borders would double international migration. At this time, that means an increase from about 3.3 per cent of the world's population to about 6.6 per cent.

Economists may look at wage levels and hypothesize that if borders are opened, people will travel across them to where they can achieve higher wage levels. But this relies on the assumption that people are individual economic maximizers. Sociologists will tell you that humans are social animals, and their decisions are motivated by a wider range of social, emotional, and psychological factors and not simply economic ones. So, given open borders and the means for making more money, many people will stay where they are because of attachments to community and family, and practical issues like expense and language. In short, open borders would not lead to huge and unmanageable population movements.

But even so, will anyone support open borders? In rich countries of immigration, there is strong negativity towards immigrants and immigration. The data on hostility to immigration makes it seem almost inconceivable that there could be any prospect of advancing the case for open borders. However, there is variability and there are chinks in the picture. In the UK, it has been found that 75 per cent of people want immigration to be reduced and only 3 per cent want an increase (Ford et al, 2012: 30; Ford and Heath, 2014: 79). The UK is a country with higher-than-average immigration and strong anti-immigration attitudes, so if there is hope for positive attitudes to immigration there, then there may be elsewhere. UK and European attitudes show that some types of immigration are less unpopular than others. Temporary, student, skilled, and legal migration, and reunification with close family are looked on more positively than other forms (Migration Observatory, 2011; Ford et al, 2012; Blinder, 2014; Heath and Richards, 2019; Blinder and Richards, 2020; Ford and Mellon, 2020), and this may also be the case for refugees (De Coninck, 2020). The more unpopular sorts are illegal and permanent immigration. In the US, which has the highest number of international migrants of any country, if not the largest proportion, a minority of 39 per cent of people want it decreased and 57 per cent think immigrants strengthen the country (Kohut, 2015). Furthermore, some sections of the population are more pro-immigration than others. Young, educated, and metropolitan groups in Europe see immigration as having brought benefits and are less likely to be anti-immigrant. These are groups that will make up more of the population as the young get older and as the proportion of the population educated to degree level is growing. Those in high-immigration areas are more pro-immigration and, as we have seen, contact is associated with higher levels of trust between diverse groups, suggesting that immigration itself can lead to more positive attitudes to it (Clarke and Gibson, 2012; Goodwin, 2012; Duffy and Frere-Smith, 2014; Ford and Heath, 2014: 82; ESS, 2016; Heath and Richards, 2019; McLaren and Paterson, 2020). There is evidence that attitudes to immigration may be softening in some places (ESS, 2016; Blinder and Richards, 2020).

Furthermore, attitudes are not a fixed, objective truth. They are the product, in part, of narratives and explanations. Important sections of the mainstream media encourage anti-immigration sentiment and racism. Politicians are mostly so fearful of the electoral consequences of a pro-immigration stance that they will not challenge anti-immigration attitudes. But if they were to do so, they could help change those attitudes. They could explain, for instance, that low wage levels are caused by employers setting pay, not immigrants, and that housing shortages are due to a lack of homes, especially state housing, rather than immigration. They could tell a story of compassion and the benefits of migration to frame it in a new way. So, amid high levels of anti-immigration sentiment, there are bases for thinking support for open borders can be gradually built in certain groups, some of whom will become more preponderant in the future.

Open borders are worth fighting for. An alternative global society with open borders would have the benefits of past societies with more open borders and current societies where migration is more open. It would be a world society with more equal rights, freedom extended, and greater opportunities and life chances for all. There would be greater freedom from war, poverty, and persecution. Societies welcoming migrants would enjoy multiculturalism and hybridity, and globally there would be greater productivity and growth. Economies and public services would benefit. Toleration and trust would grow with time and intermingling.

## Conclusions

Thinking about alternative societies in a globalized world requires us to look at international forms this could take. Anti- and alter-globalization movements have opposed current globalization and steered towards alternative types. Anti-globalization has grown into alter-globalization, where people advocate a different globalization on a world level. Alter-globalization does not just protest for an alternative to neoliberal globalization, but tries to constructively put it into place, often on a local basis rather than globally, and positively as much as through negative conflict.

At a political level, global regulation has been advocated as a way of shifting neoliberal globalization to a more social democratic kind via global institutions. The practical implementation of this has been limited, at least in part because of ideological and material differences, divisions of an enduring sort, and the dominance of neoliberalism. This does not rule out political internationalism, and of course global governance should be used as far as possible to make the world a better place. But political international change can take place at the level of a more sub-global selective internationalism where interests and ideology are more likely to coincide. The Left is better off seeking out a global Left than global government. Local alter-globalization and selective sub-global internationalist politics can be supplemented by alternatives to neoliberal globalization at a national level through democratizing the economy to more collectively oriented forms.

While cosmopolitan goals and alternatives to neoliberal globalization may be best pursued beyond cosmopolitan politics and at sub-global international, local, and national levels, a cosmopolitan alternative globalization may be possible through open borders and the free movement of people. Achieving this may seem like an enormous hill to climb, but a narrative of compassion and common humanity can be built. This can be supplemented by the evidence (that is difficult to argue with) on the benefits of global population movements for rich countries, and by building on chinks in attitudes to immigration where some forms of global people movements have a basis of support among key growing groups and increasing contact among diverse groups appears to foster community. ·

**Table 6.1:** Alternative globalization

| Responses to globalization that try to build an alternative | Alternative to | Scale/level | Institutions | Approach/method | Actors | Political ideology | Relations to other alternatives to globalization |
|---|---|---|---|---|---|---|---|
| Anti-globalization | Against global capitalism but does not in itself provide a clear identifiable alternative | Global | Global social movements | Conflictual Protest | Social movements | Variety, as it is oppositional as much as positive Socialist, social democratic, labour, anarchist, green; some would even include the nationalist Right | Mainly anti with less emphasis on what the alternative is More conflictual and about protest An alternative agenda but very diverse and critical as much as singularly positive Global rather than national or local |
| Alter-globalization and localist alternatives | Anti-globalization, against global corporate capitalism, but with a clearer emphasis on alternative structures | Often local alternatives, but with global consciousness and globally connected | Local positive alternative societies | Often constructive of alternatives and outreach to the community as much as oppositional and protest Ends in themselves but also prefigurative of wider change | Local builders of alternatives Community grassroots Sometimes facilitated by local or national state | Often effectively socialist or communist, but not generally dogmatic and ideological Green and anarchist elements | More positive than anti-globalization Less about protest and more about constructing alternatives More bottom-up and localist than political globalization or national approaches |

(continued)

**Table 6.1:** Alternative globalization (continued)

| Responses to globalization that try to build an alternative | Alternative to | Scale/level | Institutions | Approach/method | Actors | Political ideology | Relations to other alternatives to globalization |
|---|---|---|---|---|---|---|---|
| Political globalization | Neoliberal global capitalism, if not against capitalism itself | Global | Global institutions of regulation and social democracy seeking global agreements on social rather than neoliberal criteria | Change via global political institutions | Global institutions State actors who build and fund those institutions and are members of them | Social democracy | More open to mixed economy in capitalism than anti- and alter-globalization More centralist and less grassroots Less localist |
| Sub-global internationalism | Global capitalism, in the alternative's leftist forms | Sub-global international agreements and co-ordination between ideologically like-minded states and groups or those with related geopolitical interests | Sub-global international agreements or supranational organizations | Agreements and co-ordination between states or groups with shared ideological or geopolitical interests | Primarily states in international co-ordination, but can include social movements and NGOs | In the formulation I am envisaging, socialist, but could be on different ideological bases | Does not attempt full political globalization More state focused than anti- or alter-globalization or localism More internationalist than national approaches |

**Table 6.1:** Alternative globalization (continued)

| Responses to globalization that try to build an alternative | Alternative to | Scale/level | Institutions | Approach/method | Actors | Political ideology | Relations to other alternatives to globalization |
|---|---|---|---|---|---|---|---|
| National Left alternatives | Global capitalism | National | Nation-state and Left national governments | Use of nation-state, public ownership, national planning, national regulation | National governments and Leftist political parties | Socialist | More state oriented than anti- and alter-globalization. More nation-state oriented than political globalization. More socialist than mixed economy, regulatory, global social democracy |
| Open borders | Restrictions on global people movements. Post-colonialism | National and global | Opening of national borders | State and supranational action under pressure from social movements and human rights organizations | Governments, supranational organizations, social movements, migration rights organizations | Liberal, libertarian, internationalist, including international socialist | Less oriented to socialist or capitalist content of programmes, and more to free movement of individuals. Not against political or nation-state structures, but against them restricting immigration |

Note: These alternatives overlap and are not mutually exclusive or opposed. Many people will be involved in two or more of these and see many as possibilities.

## Further reading

Geoffrey Pleyers' *Alter-globalization* (2010) is good on alter-globalization movements and separates them into two strands: 'the way of subjectivity' and 'the way of reason'. Cristina Flesher Fominaya's (2020) *Social Movements in a Globalized World* and Donatella della Porta's (2015) *Social Movements in Times of Austerity: Bringing Capitalism Back into Protest Analysis* are more up to date with the later post-financial crisis period. A bottom-up decolonial grouping of initiatives for global alternatives, from the Global Tapestry of Alternatives to Progressive International, can be found at the Adelante website (adelante.global).

David Held's (2004) *Global Covenant: The Social Democratic Alternative to the Washington Consensus* states the case for the social democratic global governance I am sceptical about in this chapter.

Samir Amin's (2018) 'Letter of intent for an inaugural meeting of the International of Workers and Peoples' sets out the case for a new international moving on from the fragmentation and, in his view, ineffectiveness of the movements of movements. Discussions of this proposal were published in overlapping special issues of *Globalizations* (Gills and Chase-Dunn, 2019) and the *Journal for World Systems Research* (Amin, 2019). These are also in book form in Gills and Chase-Dunn (2021). See the Focus on the Global South website (focusweb.org) for a Global South deglobalization perspective.

Christopher Bertram's (2018) *Do States Have the Right to Exclude Immigrants?* is a short accessible statement of the philosophical case that they do not, except in rare cases. Joseph Carens is a leading philosophical advocate of open borders: see his *The Ethics of Immigration* (2013). The website openborders.info, founded by Vipul Naik, is good on this area. *Why Immigration is Good for All of Us*, by the think tank Class (2014), is an introduction to evidence on why immigration is positive economically and socially for rich countries.

The spotlight of this book is on alternatives rather than how we got to where we are, and in this chapter, open borders rather than the history behind borders. But important sources on the context for borders can be found in Nadine El-Enany's (2020) *Bordering Britain*, Maya Goodfellow's (2020) *Hostile Environment*, and Harsha Walia's *Border and Rule* (2021) and 'Why climate justice must go beyond borders' (2022). They put borders and immigration controls in the context of imperialism, violent colonialism, anti-colonial resistance, nationalism, xenophobia, global capitalism, racism, and class. The wealth of rich former colonialist countries is based on a history of exploitation and domination globally, the wealth benefitting the rich countries but coming historically from colonies. For open borders advocates, migrants from former colonies have a claim to that wealth (Basu, 2020b).

Reading on localized alternatives is covered in recommended reading for Chapter 1. National Left alternatives are covered in further reading for Chapter 4.

# Conclusion

The first and second chapters of this book outlined economic and social alternatives, theoretical and actual: from communism to co-ops, participatory communities, low work, slow society, eco-localism, and digital alternatives; and from communes to alternative social centres, food alternatives, free education, alternatives to prison, and welfare. They discussed how changing to alternatives can happen through many means. Of course, I have not been able to include everything. Alternatives like Christiania in Copenhagen (Smith, 2020), alternative currencies (see North, 2019 and 2020), and alternative sexualities are among areas a second edition could deal with! The rest of the book probed in more depth the issues raised by the social alternatives discussed in Chapters 1 and 2.

Many of the alternatives discussed in Chapters 1 and 2 are seen as utopias, now or in the future. The third chapter discussed Marxist and liberal criticisms of utopianism. It gave a Marxist answer to the Marxist criticisms and argued that utopianism can include liberal dimensions. The fourth chapter discussed ideas and practices of socialism, including historical attempts to implement socialism. It discussed green, feminist, and liberal criticisms of socialism. The chapter argued that the expansion of socialism can deal with many issues raised by these perspectives. In some areas, though, socialism needs to limit itself to deal with problems it has faced in the past and potential tendencies within it. This chapter argues for a liberal socialism with plurality, and multilevel means for getting to socialism and organizing it. This is a pluralist socialism, a core theme of the book.

The fifth chapter continued with alternative economies, focusing on the revival of calls for democratizing the economy, especially through decentralized and more inclusively democratic collective ownership. It addressed challenges such approaches face, in themselves and in opposition they may encounter. I argued that local social ownership should be pursued within the context of state public ownership. The sixth chapter looked at global forms alternative societies can take, arguing that regulatory and progressive global government is unlikely given different interests and ideologies in the world. Anti- and alter-globalization has, in fact, taken national and localized forms. But I argued for sub-global internationalist political globalization. And I proposed that what can happen at a fully global level is an alternative of the free movement of people across open borders.

I have tried to focus in this book on empirical examples as well as theory, on complexity and plurality within a socialist framework, and on alternatives in the present and future. I have also tried to bring together many routes for changing to alternatives, making the case for interlinkages between them rather than exclusive routes one way or another. What I have been arguing for is a socialism of democratized collective ownership and control that takes on board the need for plural, liberal, and utopian dimensions. The argument for a pluralist and complex socialist alternative society has been made in several ways.

On utopianism and liberalism, I am arguing that utopianism need not be problematic from Marxist and liberal perspectives, but can be compatible with both Marxist and liberal concerns. In the case of Marxism, this is by utopianism being materialist rather than idealist, as some Marxists say, and so utopianism is compatible with Marxism. In the case of liberalism, utopianism need not be totalitarian, as liberals argue, because a utopia can and should be – especially given past failed attempts to pursue socialism – open to liberal and plural structures within the overall framework. So, utopianism is compatible with Marxist and liberal concerns rather than opposed to them, as in the more simplified contrast made by some. An argument throughout this book is against false dichotomies between approaches and levels, not downplaying tensions in such combinations but making the case for a socialistically plural and multilevel approach.

The means for alternative societies have come up throughout the book, both for getting there and for administering the alternative in a future society. In terms of means, the book explores utopian and prefigurative experiments in alternative societies and economies, saying that they can be the basis for change. This is beyond just political and state methods, because on-the-ground alternatives offer examples and experiments in alternatives and tests them, exemplary and demonstrative. In the Global South, they provide decolonial alternatives to models from the Global North. This is unlike the traditional insurrectionary route which has (but needn't have) tended towards changing to something which has been formulated in theory but not tried much in practice. So, an alternative society should be committed to not just state, political, and government means of change, but also practical experimentation in society, which can be built on and allied with state-oriented change. At the same time, the alternatives-alongside-capitalism dimension has to be allied with political means of change, and the latter parts of the book discuss socialism, the democratic economy, and alternative globalization as pursued through politics. Politics needs prefigurative experimental change in society, and anti-politics needs politics. The argument is for socialism with complex and plural means as well as complexity and pluralism in ends. This is not just eclecticism; I have set this out within the framework of political socialism.

Fuchs (2020b) talks about 'class struggle social democracy'. This aims to move to democratic socialism and involves: a pluralist convergence of radical reforms and the gradual transformation of institutions; trade union industrial action with working-class struggle (trade unions are another topic that could get more attention when discussing alternative societies and routes to them); new social combinations across classes and other divisions and identities; electoral parliamentary politics, social movements and movement parties; organization spontaneity and new prefigurative forms of social co-operation; the building of democratically controlled commons within as well as beyond capitalism; leadership and mass action; both conflict antagonistic politics and taking power. This includes different but complementary political strategies and rejects seeing these as contradictory or mutually exclusive. There are parallels here with what I am advocating in this book. I may not use the term 'social democracy' for this approach as that implies staying within capitalism, although in this context it refers to building from political reformism within capitalism to something beyond. Fuchs discusses thinkers as diverse as Rosa Luxemburg (2008), Michael Hardt and Antonio Negri (2017), and Bhaskar Sunkara (2019) as advocating change along these lines. Likewise, Eagleton (2022: 191), discussing a post-Corbyn Left in the UK, argues that the 'the priority must be to grow this movement through every available channel', numerous existing and thriving examples of which he gives.

At the centre of this is an argument for collective ownership and the democratic economy, of a pluralist and complex kind. Public ownership has returned to mainstream politics, as have approaches like community wealth building linked to social ownership. Public ownership should be more democratically inclusive so that it has the interests of all at heart and not just particular groups. Forms of collective ownership other than state or public ownership need to be included – co-ops, for example. So, the argument is for plurality and complexity within a socialist and political framework.

This is argued for at a global level too. More socialist global governance is seen as a limited possibility because of inbuilt conflict and contending interests in international politics. But I have said that politics at the level of nation-states, while important and effective in many ways, needs to be supplemented by a more possible sub-global internationalism based on shared material interests, ideology, or geopolitical interest. Real globalism, though, can come at the level of open national borders and the free movement of people internationally. Again, the argument is for an alternative society of a plural and complex kind, including many levels.

An overall perspective of the book is that clean and clear arguments rarely work, and arguments for the new breaking from the old are also often problematic. A socialism of complexity and plurality, in both means and ends, is needed. But what is proposed is not just an open pluralism of all that is available and including socialism, but a perspective based on socialism, collective ownership, and the state with pluralism and complexity within this. Not a utopia of many utopias, but a utopia with plurality within it; not pluralism with socialism, but socialism with pluralism.

This book tries to contribute to the debate about alternative societies and alternatives to capitalism by including a broad range of possibilities, economically and socially, focusing on plural, multilevel aspects to change. I have included theory with practice and argued that locally based, prefigurative experiments, to be effective and scaled up, have to be complemented by state-led and sub-global international political initiatives. At the same time, the dangers of the latter can be averted by supporting and building from current-day utopian, decentralized, prefigurative experimentation. The result is a plural, liberal, utopian, multilevel, political, democratic socialism.

# Acknowledgements

Many people, too numerous to mention, have given me advice over the years on alternative societies and socialism, and discussed the issues covered in this book with me. I am very grateful to them all and to the great students who have taken my courses on these topics. Thanks to the following who gave me advice on this book or feedback on parts or all of it: Onur Acaroğlu, Sebastian Berg, David Berry, Esra Demirkol Colosio, Aaron Gain, Danë Goodsman, Richard Mangas, Charlie Masquelier, Paul McGuinness, Laura Morosanu, Rafal Soborski, and anonymous referees. Thanks to Shannon Kneis and all at Bristol University Press. Much love to Sally, Katie, Jake, Felix, Brian, and Christina. This book is dedicated to Mim.

# Bibliography

Abbey, M. (2022) 'The state of African social democracy', *IPS Journal*, [online] 11 July, Available from: www.ips-journal.eu/topics/future-of-soc ial-democracy/the-state-of-african-social-democracy-6030/

Abensour, P. (2008) 'Persistent utopia', *Constellations*, 15(3): 406–21.

Acaroğlu, O. (2019) 'Paris 1871 and Fatsa 1979: revisiting the transition problem', *Globalizations*, 16(4): 404–23.

Adaman, F. and Devine, P. (2001) 'Participatory planning as a deliberative democratic process: a response to Hodgson's critique', *Economy and Society*, 30(2): 229–39.

Adaman, F. and Devine, P. (2006) 'The promise of participatory planning: a rejoinder to Hodgson', *Economy and Society*, 35(1): 141–7.

ADILKNO (The Foundation for the Advancement of Illegal Knowledge) (1994) *Cracking the Movement: Squatting Beyond the Media*, New York: Autonomedia.

Adler, D. (2019) 'The international institutional turn: the missing ingredient in Labour's new political economy', *Renewal*, 27(4): 11–22.

Akuno, K. (2017) 'Build and fight: the program and strategy of Cooperation Jackson', in K. Akuno and A. Nangwaya (eds) (2017) *Jackson Rising: The Struggle for Economic Democracy and Black Self-determination in Jackson, Mississippi*, Québec: Daraja Press, pp 3–41.

Akuno, K. and Nangwaya, A. (eds) (2017) *Jackson Rising: The Struggle for Economic Democracy and Black Self-determination in Jackson, Mississippi*, Québec: Daraja Press.

Albert, M. (2003) *Parecon: Life after Capitalism*, London: Verso.

Albert, M. (2006) *Realizing Hope: Life beyond Capitalism*, London: Zed Books.

Albert, M. (2012) 'Summarizing participatory economics', *ZCommunications*, [online] 1 December, Available from: https://zcomm.org/znetarticle/ summarizing-participatory-economics-by-michael-albert/

Albert, M. and Spannos, C. (2006) 'Parecon today', *ZCommunications*, [online] 27 April, Available from: https://zcomm.org/znetarticle/pare con-today-by-michael-albert/

Alderman, L. (2016) 'In Sweden, an experiment turns shorter workdays into bigger gains', *New York Times*, [online] 20 May, Available from: www. nytimes.com/2016/05/21/business/international/in-sweden-an-experim ent-turns-shorter-workdays-into-bigger-gains.html?_r=0

Allen, K. (2011) *Marx and the Alternative to Capitalism*, London: Pluto Press.

Alperovitz, G. (2005) *America beyond Capitalism: Reclaiming Our Wealth, Our Liberty, and Our Democracy*, Hoboken, NJ: John Wiley.

Amin, S. (1990) *Delinking: Towards a Polycentric World*, London: Zed Books.

Amin, S. (2018) 'Letter of intent for an inaugural meeting of the International of Workers and Peoples', *Pambazuka News*, [online] 23 August, Available from: www.pambazuka.org/global-south/letter-intent-inaugural-meet ing-international-workers-and-peoples

Amin, S. (2019) 'Forum on Samir Amin's proposal for a New International of Workers and Peoples', *Journal of World-Systems Research*, 25(2): 247–53.

Andrews, G. (2008) *The Slow Food Story: Politics and Pleasure*, Montreal: McGill-Queen's University Press.

Arando, S., Gago, M., Jones, D.C. and Kato, T. (2015) 'Efficiency in employee-owned enterprises: an econometric case study of Mondragon', *ILR Review*, 68(2): 398–425.

Arcilla, C.A. (2022) 'Disrupting gentrification: from barricades and housing occupations to an insurgent urban subaltern history in a southern city', *Antipode*, [online] 22 March, Available from: https://onlinelibrary.wiley. com/doi/abs/10.1111/anti.12827

Aslan, A. and Akbulut, B. (2019) 'Democratic economy in Kurdistan', in A. Kothari, A. Salleh, A. Escobar, F. Demaria and A. Acosta (eds) *Pluriverse: A Post-development Dictionary*, New Delhi: Tulika Books, pp 151–3.

Avineri, S. (1968) *The Social and Political Thought of Karl Marx*, Cambridge: Cambridge University Press.

Avineri, S. (1973) 'Marx's vision of future society and the problem of utopianism', *Dissent*, 20(3): 323–31.

Azmanova, A. (2020) *Capitalism on Edge: How Fighting Precarity Can Achieve Radical Change Without Crisis or Utopia*, New York: Columbia University Press.

Bajpai, S., Crespo, J.M. and Kothari, A. (2022) 'Nation-states are destroying the world. Could "bioregions" be the answer?', *Open Democracy*, [online] 7 March, Available from: www.opendemocracy.net/en/oureconomy/nat ion-states-are-destroying-the-world-could-bioregions-be-the-answer/

Barnard, A. (2011) '"Waving the banana" at capitalism: political theater and social movement strategy among New York's "freegan" dumpster divers', *Ethnography*, 12(4): 419–44.

Barrett, M. (2014) *Women's Oppression Today: The Marxist/Feminist Encounter*, London: Verso.

Bartkowski, F. (1989) *Feminist Utopias*, Lincoln: University of Nebraska Press.

Bartlett, L. (2005) 'Dialogue, knowledge, and teacher-student relations: Freirean pedagogy in theory and practice', *Comparative Education Review*, 49(3): 344–64.

Bartlett, T. and Schugurensky, D. (2020) 'Deschooling society 50 years later: revisiting Ivan Illich in the era of COVID-19', *Sisyphus: Journal of Education*, 8(3): 65–84.

Bastani, A. (2020) *Fully Automated Luxury Communism: A Manifesto*, London: Verso.

Basu, L. (2019a) 'The "Washington Consensus" is dead. But what should replace it?', *Open Democracy*, [online] 13 April, Available from: www.opendemocracy.net/en/oureconomy/washington-consensus-dead-what-should-replace-it/

Basu, L. (2019b) 'An agenda for a new internationalism', *Open Democracy*, [online] 18 July, Available from: www.opendemocracy.net/en/oureconomy/agenda-new-internationalism/

Basu, L. (2020a) 'How to fix the world', *Open Democracy*, [online] 29 April, Available from: www.opendemocracy.net/en/oureconomy/how-fix-world/

Basu, L. (2020b) 'The post-pandemic city beyond state and market: a thought experiment', *Metapolis*, [online] June, Available from: https://metapolis.net/project/the-post-pandemic-city-beyond-state-and-market-a-thought-experiment/

Basu, L. (2020c) 'Step aside progressive patriotism – intergalactic humanism has arrived', *Open Democracy*, [online] 18 December, Available from: www.opendemocracy.net/en/oureconomy/step-aside-progressive-patriotism-intergalactic-humanism-has-arrived/

Bate, P. and Carter, N. (1986) 'The future for producers' co-operatives', *Industrial Relations Journal*, 17(1): 57–70.

Bauman, Z. (1976) *Socialism: The Active Utopia*, Abingdon: George Allen and Unwin.

Bauman, Z. (1998) *Globalization: The Human Consequences*, Cambridge: Polity Press.

Bauman, Z. (2003) 'Utopia with no topos', *History of the Human Sciences*, 16(1): 11–25.

BBC (2021) 'Four-day week "an overwhelming success" in Iceland', *BBC*, [online] 6 July, Available from: www.bbc.com/news/business-57724779

Beckett, A. (2019) 'The New Left economics: how a network of thinkers is transforming capitalism', *The Guardian*, [online] 25 June, Available from: www.theguardian.com/news/2019/jun/25/the-new-left-economics-how-a-network-of-thinkers-is-transforming-capitalism

Bello, W. and Feffer, J. (2009) 'The virtues of deglobalization', *Foreign Policy in Focus*, [online] 9 September, Available from: https://fpif.org/the_virtues _of_deglobalization/

Benjamin, R. (2019) *Race after Technology: Abolitionist Tools for the New Jim Code*, Cambridge: Polity Press.

Benn, T. (1981) *Arguments for Democracy* (edited by C. Mullin), London: Penguin.

Ben-Rafael, E., Oved, Y. and Topel, M. (eds) (2013) *The Communal Idea in the 21st Century*, Boston: Brill.

Berg, M. and Seeber, B.K. (2017) *The Slow Professor: Changing the Culture of Speed in the Academy*, Toronto: University of Toronto Press.

Berger, B.M. (1981) *The Survival of a Counterculture: Ideological Work and Everyday Life among Rural Communards*, New Brunswick: Transaction Publishers.

Bernstein, E. (1968) 'Summerhill: a follow-up study of its students', *Journal of Humanistic Psychology*, 8(2): 123–36.

Berry, C. and Guinan, J. (2019) *People Get Ready: Preparing for a Corbyn Government*, London: OR Books.

Berry, D. (2008) *Copy, Rip, Burn: The Politics of Copyleft and Open Source*, London: Pluto Press.

Bertram, C. (2018) *Do States Have the Right to Exclude Immigrants?* Cambridge: Polity Press.

Bhatia, B. (2015) 'Auroville: a utopian paradox', *Columbia Academic Commons*, [online] 5 March, Available from: https://academiccommons.columbia. edu/doi/10.7916/D8RR1X4S

Bhattacharya, T. (2015) 'How not to skip class: social reproduction of labor and the global working class', *Viewpoint Magazine*, [online] 31 October, Available from: https://viewpointmag.com/2015/10/31/how-not-to-skip-class-social-reproduction-of-labor-and-the-global-working-class/

Bigo, D., Issin, E. and Ruppert, E. (eds) (2019) *Data Politics: Worlds, Subjects, Rights*, London: Routledge.

Blackburn, R. (ed) (1991) *After the Fall: The Failure of Communism and the Future of Socialism*, London: Verso.

Blagg, H. (2017) 'Doing restorative justice "otherwise": decolonizing practices in the Global South', in I. Aertsen and B. Pali (eds) *Critical Restorative Justice*, Oxford: Hart Publishing, pp 61–78.

Blakeley, G. (ed) (2020a) *Futures of Socialism: The Pandemic and the Post-Corbyn Era*, London: Verso.

Blakeley, G. (2020b) 'The era of state monopoly capitalism', *Tribune*, Spring: 26–31.

Blanchflower, D.G., Saleheen, J. and Shadforth, C. (2007) *The Impact of the Recent Migration from Eastern Europe on the UK Economy*, London: Bank of England.

Blinder, S. (2014) *UK Public Opinion toward Immigration: Overall Attitudes and Level of Concern*, Oxford: Oxford Migration Observatory.

Blinder, S. and Richards, L. (2020) *UK Public Opinion toward Immigration: Overall Attitudes and Level of Concern*, Oxford: Oxford Migration Observatory.

Bloch, E. (1995) *The Principle of Hope*, Cambridge: MIT Press.

Bobbio, N. (1988) *Which Socialism? Marxism, Socialism and Democracy*, Cambridge: Polity Press.

Bobbio, N. (1996) *Left and Right: The Significance of a Political Distinction*, Cambridge: Polity Press.

Bobbio, N. (2009) *The Future of Democracy*, Cambridge: Polity Press.

Bonnett, A. (2013) 'Something new in freedom', *Times Higher Education*, [online] 23 May, Available from: www.timeshighereducation.com/featu res/something-new-in-freedom/2003930.article#

Bradley, K. and Hedrén, J. (2015) *Green Utopianism: Perspectives, Politics and Micro-practices*, London: Routledge.

Brand, S. (2010) 'How slums can save the planet', *Prospect*, [online] 27 January, Available from: www.prospectmagazine.co.uk/magazine/how-slums-can-save-the-planet

Bregman, R. (2017) *Utopia for Realists: And How We Can Get There*, London: Bloomsbury Publishing.

Breslin, T. (2021) *Lessons from Lockdown: The Educational Legacy of COVID-19*, Abingdon: Routledge.

Bria, F. (2018) 'Our data is valuable. Here's how we can take that value back', *The Guardian*, [online] 5 April, Available from: www.theguardian. com/commentisfree/2018/apr/05/data-valuable-citizens-silicon-valley-barcelona

Brie, M. (2021) 'Uniting communism and liberalism: an unsolvable task or a most urgent necessity?', in M. Musto (ed) *Rethinking Alternatives with Marx: Economy, Ecology and Migration*, Cham: Palgrave Macmillan, pp 309–37.

Briy, A. (2020) 'Zapatistas: lessons in community self-organisation in Mexico', *Open Democracy*, [online] 25 June, Available from: www.opende mocracy.net/en/democraciaabierta/zapatistas-lecciones-de-auto-organiz aci%C3%B3n-comunitaria-en/

Brock, A., Jr (2020) *Distributed Blackness: African American Cybercultures*, New York: New York University Press.

Brown, M. (2018) 'Applying "the Preston Model" to the cooperative economy', *Open 2018 Conference* [video] 24 September, Available from: www.youtube.com/watch?v=rLPxFkghfYs

Brown, M., Howard, T., Jackson, M. and McInroy, N. (2018) 'A new urban economic system: the UK and the US', in J. McDonnell (ed) *Economics for the Many*, London: Verso, pp 126–41.

Browne, S. (2015) *Dark Matters: On the Surveillance of Blackness*, Durham, NC: Duke University Press.

Bruno-Jofré, R. and Zaldívar, J.I. (2012) 'Ivan Illich's late critique of *Deschooling Society*: "I was largely barking up the wrong tree"', *Educational Theory*, 62(5): 573–92.

Brunton, F. and Nissenbaum, H. (2016) *Obfuscation: A User's Guide for Privacy and Protest*, Cambridge, MA: MIT Press.

Bryson, A. and MacKerron, G. (2013) *Are You Happy While You Work?* CEP Discussion Paper No 1187, London: Centre for Economic Performance, LSE.

Bryson, V. (2016) *Feminist Political Theory*, Basingstoke: Palgrave.

Büchi, M., Festic, N. and Latzer, M. (2022) 'The chilling effects of digital dataveillance: a theoretical model and an empirical research agenda', *Big Data & Society*, 9(1), [online] 6 January, Available from: https://journals.sagepub.com/doi/10.1177/20539517211065368

Buckingham, D. (2021) 'Deschooling society? Revisiting Ivan Illich after lockdown', *David Buckingham*, [online] 14 April, Available from: https://davidbuckingham.net/2021/04/14/deschooling-society-revisiting-ivan-illich-after-lockdown/

Bugan, C. (2012) *Burying the Typewriter: Childhood under the Eye of the Secret Police*, London: Picador.

Butler, E. (1983) *Hayek: His Contribution to the Political and Economic Thought of Our Time*, London: Temple Smith.

Calnitsky, D. (2022) 'The policy road to socialism', *Critical Sociology*, 48(3): 397–422.

Campbell, D. (2022) 'NHS hiring more doctors from outside UK and EEA than inside for first time', *The Guardian*, [online] 8 June, Available from: www.theguardian.com/society/2022/jun/08/nhs-hiring-more-doctors-from-outside-uk-and-eea-than-inside-for-first-time

Carens, J. (2013) *The Ethics of Immigration*, Oxford: Oxford University Press.

Carmichael, S. (2018) 'Black power in the USA', in D. Austin (ed) *Moving against the System: The 1968 Congress of Black Writers and the Making of Global Consciousness*, London: Pluto Press.

Carrier, N. and Piché, J. (2015) 'The state of abolitionism', in *Champ Pénal/ Penal Field*, XII, [online] 21 August, Available from: https://journals.openedition.org/champpenal/9164

Carter, N. (2006) 'Political participation and the workplace: the spillover thesis revisited', *The British Journal of Politics and International Relations*, 8(3): 410–26.

Castillo, R.A.H. (2021) 'Building alliances in pandemic times: the Zapatista journey through Europe', *International Work Group for Indigenous Affairs*, [online] 30 August, Available from: www.iwgia.org/en/news/4511-building-alliances-in-pandemic-times-the-zapatista-journey-through-europe.html

Cato, M.S. (2018) 'The bioregional economy: reclaiming our local land', in M. Parker, G. Cheney, V. Founier and C. Land (eds) *The Routledge Companion to Alternative Organization*, London: Routledge, pp 220–35.

Cerny, P.G. and Evans, M. (2004) 'Globalization and public policy under New Labour', *Policy Studies*, 25(1): 51–65.

Chase-Dunn, C., Niemeyer, R., Saxena P., Kaneshiro, M., Love, J. and Spears, A. (2009) *The New Global Left: Movements and Regimes*, Riverside, CA: IROWS.

Chatterton, P. (2010) 'So what does it mean to be anti-capitalist? Conversations with activists from urban social centres', *Urban Studies*, 47(6): 1205–24.

Chatterton, P. (2013) 'Towards an agenda for post-carbon cities: lessons from Lilac, the UK's first ecological, affordable cohousing community', *International Journal for Urban and Regional Research*, 37(5): 1654–74.

Chatterton, P. (2018) *Unlocking Sustainable Cities: A Manifesto for Real Change*, London: Pluto Press.

Chennault, C. (2021) 'Relational life: lessons from Black feminism on Whiteness and engaging new food activism', *Antipode*, 54(2): 357–77.

Clarence-Smith, S. and Monticelli, L. (2022) 'Flexible institutionalization in Auroville: a prefigurative alternative to development', *Sustainability Science*, [online] 1 March, Available from: https://link.springer.com/article/10.1007/s11625-022-01096-0

Clark, D. (2004) 'The raw and the rotten: punk cuisine', *Ethnology*, 43(1): 19–31.

Clark, S. and Teachout, W. (2012) *Slow Democracy*, White River Junction, VT: Chelsea Green Publishing.

Clark, S. and Teachout, W. (2013) 'Slow democracy', *Open Democracy*, [online] 20 September, Available from: www.opendemocracy.net/transformation/susan-clark-woden-teachout/slow-democracy

Clarke, N. (2012) 'Actually existing comparative urbanism: imitation and cosmopolitanism in North-south interurban partnerships', *Urban Geography*, 33(6): 796–815.

Clarke, T. and Gibson, O. (2012) 'London 2012's Team GB success sparks feelgood factor', *The Guardian*, [online] 10 August, Available from: www.theguardian.com/sport/2012/aug/10/london-2012-team-gb-success-feelgood-factor

Class (Centre for Labour and Social Studies) (2014) *Why Immigration is Good for All of Us*, London: Class.

Class War University (2013) 'Occupying the city with The Social Science Centre – an interview with Mike Neary', *Class War University*, [online] 2 September, Available from: https://classwaru.org/2013/09/02/occupying-the-city-with-the-social-science-centre/

CLES and Preston City Council (2019) *How We Built Community Wealth in Preston: Achievements and Lessons*, Preston: Preston City Council.

Collord, M. (2019) 'Building community wealth globally: the Kigoma-Preston collaboration', *Democracy Collaborative*, [online] 22 November, Available from: https://democracycollaborative.org/learn/publication/building-community-wealth-globally-kigoma-preston-collaboration

Common Wealth (2019) *Owning the Future: Toward the Democratic Economy*, London: Common Wealth.

Cooper, D. (2014) *Everyday Utopias: The Conceptual Life of Promising Spaces*, Durham, NC: Duke University Press.

Cooper, L. and Aitchison, G. (2020) *The Dangers Ahead: Covid-19, Authoritarianism and Democracy*, London: LSE Conflict and Civil Society Research Unit.

Coote, A. (2019) 'Universal basic income doesn't work. Let's boost the public realm instead', *The Guardian*, [online] 6 May, Available from: www.theguardian.com/commentisfree/2019/may/06/universal-basic-income-public-realm-poverty-inequality

Coote, A. and Yazici, E. (2019) *Universal Basic Income: A Union Perspective*, Ferney-Voltaire: Public Services International.

Corbyn, J. (2018) 'Full text of Jeremy Corbyn's 2018 Alternative MacTaggart Lecture', *Labour Party*, [online] 23 August, Available from: https://labour.org.uk/press/full-text-jeremy-corbyns-2018-alternative-mactaggart-lecture/

Cornforth, C. (1983) 'Some factors affecting the success or failure of worker co-operatives', *Economic and Industrial Democracy*, 4(2): 163–90.

Cornforth, C. (1995) 'Patterns of co-operative management: beyond the degeneration thesis', *Economic and Industrial Democracy*, 16(4): 487–523.

Cornforth, C., Thomas, A., Lewis, J. and Spear, R. (1988) *Developing Successful Worker Co-operatives*, London: Sage.

Coughlan, S. (2012) 'Human rights activists taught online tactics', *BBC*, [online] 5 November, Available from: www.bbc.co.uk/news/business-20085559

Cowburn, A. (2020) 'Coronavirus: Rishi Sunak urged to consider four-day working week in response to pandemic', *Independent*, [online] 21 June, Available from: www.independent.co.uk/news/uk/politics/coronavirus-four-day-week-rishi-sunak-furlough-economy-a9573446.html

Coyle, M.J. and Scott, D. (eds) (2021) *The Routledge International Handbook of Penal Abolition*, London: Routledge.

Crosland, A. (2006) *The Future of Socialism*, London: Constable and Robinson.

Crossan, J., Cumbers, A., McMaster, R. and Shaw, D. (2016) 'Contesting neoliberal urbanism in Glasgow's community gardens: the practice of DIY citizenship', *Antipode*, 48(4): 937–55.

Cumbers, A. (2012) *Reclaiming Public Ownership: Making Space for Economic Democracy*, London: Zed Books.

Cumbers, A. and Hanna, T. (2018) 'Democratic ownership', in L. Macfarlane (ed) *New Thinking for the British Economy*, London: Open Democracy, pp 10–22.

Cutcher, L. and Mason, P. (2018) 'Credit unions' in M. Parker, G. Cheney, V. Founier and C. Land (eds) *The Routledge Companion to Alternative Organization*, London: Routledge, pp 253–66.

Dahl, R.A. (1986) *A Preface to Economic Democracy*, Oakland: University of California Press.

Dahrendorf, R. (1958) 'Out of utopia: toward a reorientation of sociological analysis', *American Journal of Sociology*, 64(2): 115–27.

D'Alisa, G., Demaria, F. and Kallis, G. (eds) (2015) *Degrowth: A Vocabulary for a New Era*, London: Routledge.

Davidson, J.P.L. (2022) 'The sociology of utopia, modern temporality and Black visions of liberation', *Sociology*, [online] 7 October, Available from: https://journals.sagepub.com/doi/10.1177/00380385221117360

Davis, A. (2003) *Are Prisons Obsolete?* New York: Seven Stories Press.

Davis, M. (2020) 'How to save the postal service', *The Nation*, [online] 6 April, Available from: www.thenation.com/article/politics/usps-profiteering-nationalize-amazon/

Dawson, M. (2016) *Social Theory for Alternative Societies*, London: Palgrave.

De Coninck, D. (2020) 'Migrant categorizations and European public opinion: diverging attitudes towards immigrants and refugees', *Journal of Ethnic and Migration Studies*, 46(9): 1667–86.

de Haas, H. (2007) *Remittances, Migration and Social Development: A Conceptual Review of the Literature*, Geneva: United Nations Research Institute for Social Development.

della Porta, D. (2015) *Social Movements in Times of Austerity: Bringing Capitalism Back into Protest Analysis*, Cambridge: Polity Press.

Demireva, N. and Heath, A. (2014) 'Diversity and the civic spirit in British neighbourhoods: an investigation with MCDS and EMBES 2010 data', *Sociology*, 48(4): 643–62.

Devine, P. (1988) *Democracy and Economic Planning*, Cambridge: Polity Press.

Dicken, P. (2015) *Global Shift: Mapping the Changing Contours of the World Economy*, London: Sage.

Diefenbach, T. (2019) 'Why Michels' "iron law of oligarchy" is not an iron law – and how democratic organisations can stay "oligarchy-free"', *Organization Studies*, 40(4): 545–62.

Dinerstein, A.C. (2017) 'Concrete utopia: (re)producing life in, against and beyond the open veins of capital', *Public Seminar*, [online] 7 December, Available from: https://publicseminar.org/2017/12/concrete-utopia/

Dinerstein, A.C. and Pitts, F.H. (2018) 'From post-work to post-capitalism? Discussing the basic income and struggles for alternative forms of social reproduction', *Journal of Labor and Society*, 21(4): 471–91.

Dinerstein, A.C. and Pitts, F.H. (2021) *A World beyond Work? Labour, Money and the Capitalist State between Crisis and Utopia*, Bingley: Emerald Publishing.

Dinesen, P.T., Schaeffer, M. and Sonderskøv, K.M. (2020) 'Ethnic diversity and social trust: a narrative and meta-analytical review', *Annual Review of Political Science*, 23: 441–65.

Drousioti, K. (2019) 'What is and is not utopia', in K. Kujawińska Courtney, T. Fisiak, A. Miksza and G. Zinkiewicz (eds) *What's New in the New Europe? Redefining Culture, Politics, Identity*, Łódz: Łódź University Press.

Drousioti, K. and Papastephanou, M. (2022) 'Incriminatory utopias: utopian visions creating scapegoats', *Thesis Eleven*, [online] 19 June, Available from: https://journals.sagepub.com/doi/10.1177/07255136221098474

Duff, K. (ed) (2021) *Abolishing the Police*, London: Dog Section Press.

Duffy, B. and Frere-Smith, T. (2014) *Perceptions and Reality: Public Attitudes to Immigration*, London: Ipsos MORI.

Dustmann, C. and Frattini, T. (2013) *The Fiscal Effect of Immigration to the UK*, London: UCL Press.

Dustmann, C. and Frattini, T. (2014) 'The fiscal effects of immigration to the UK', *Economic Journal*, 124(580): 593–643.

Dustmann, C. and Preston, I.P. (2019) 'Free movement, open borders and the global gains from labor mobility', *Annual Review of Economics*, 11: 783–808.

Eagleton, O. (2022) *The Starmer Project: A Journey to the Right*, London: Verso.

Eaton, G. (2018) 'Corbynism 2.0: the radical ideas shaping Labour's future', *New Statesman*, [online] 19 September, Available from: www.newstatesman.com/politics/uk/2018/09/corbynism-20-radical-ideas-shaping-labour-s-future

Eckersley, R. (1992) *Environmentalism and Political Theory*, London: UCL Press.

*The Economist* (2018) 'Corbynomics would change Britain – but not in the way most people think', [online] 17 May, Available from: www.economist.com/britain/2018/05/17/corbynomics-would-change-britain-but-not-in-the-way-most-people-think

*The Economist* (2022) 'In praise of slow sport', [online] 23 June, Available from: www.economist.com/culture/2022/06/23/in-praise-of-slow-sport

Edwards, F. and Mercer, D. (2007) 'Gleaning from gluttony: an Australian youth subculture confronts the ethics of waste', *Australian Geographer*, 38(3): 279–96.

Egan, D. (1990) 'Towards a Marxist theory of labor-managed firms: breaking the degeneration thesis', *Review of Radical Political Economics*, 22(4): 67–86.

El-Enany, N. (2020) *Bordering Britain: Law, Race and Empire*, Manchester: Manchester University Press.

Eliçin, Y. (2011) 'Social capital, leadership and democracy: rethinking Fatsa', *International Journal of Social Sciences and Humanity Studies*, 3(2): 509–18.

Elliott, J.E. (1987) 'Karl Marx: founding father of workers' self-governance?', *Economic and Industrial Democracy*, 8(3): 293–321.

Elliott, M. and Kanagasooriam, J. (2017) *Public Opinion in the Post-Brexit era: Economic Attitudes in Modern Britain*, London: Legatum Institute.

Elson, D. (1988) 'Market socialism or socialization of the market?', *New Left Review*, I/172: 3–44.

Ergas, C. (2010) 'A model of sustainable living: collective identity in an urban ecovillage', *Organization and Environment*, 23(1): 32–54.

Esping-Andersen, G. (1985) *Politics against Markets: The Social Democratic Road to Power*, Princeton, NJ: Princeton University Press.

ESS (European Social Survey) (2016) *Attitudes towards Immigration and their Antecedents: Topline Results from Round 7 of the European Social Survey*, London: European Research Infrastructure Consortium.

Esteva, G., Parakash, M. and Stuchul, D. (2008) 'From a pedagogy of liberation to liberation from pedagogy', in M. Hern (ed) *Everywhere All the Time: A New Deschooling Reader*, Oakland, CA: AK Press, pp 13–30.

Eubanks, V. (2018) *Automating Inequality: How High-tech Tools Profile, Police, and Punish the Poor,* New York: St Martin's Press.

Evans, M. (1975) *Karl Marx*, London: Allen and Unwin.

Evans, M. and Kay, J. (2009) 'Parecon or libertarian communism', *Libcom*, [online] 7 August, Available from: https://libcom.org/library/participat ory-society-or-libertarian-communism

Fanon, F. (2008) *Black Skin, White Masks*, London: Pluto Press.

Featherstone, M. (2017) *Planet Utopia: Utopia, Dystopia and Globalization*, Abingdon: Routledge.

Federici, S. (2019) *Re-enchanting the World: Feminism and the Politics of the Commons*, Oakland, CA: PM Press.

Fenton, N., Freedman, D., Schlosberg, J. and Deack, L. (2020) *The Media Manifesto*, Cambridge: Polity Press.

*Financial Times* (2019) 'Labour's agenda is not the answer for Britain', *Financial Times*, [online] 5 September, Available from: www.ft.com/content/439d7 270-cfb8-11e9-99a4-b5ded7a7fe3f

Finchett-Maddock, L. (2017) *Protest, Property and the Commons: Performances of Law and Resistance*, London: Routledge.

Firestone, S. (2015) *The Dialectic of Sex*, London: Verso.

Firth, R. (2012) *Utopian Politics: Citizenship and Practice*, London: Routledge.

Firth, R. (2022) *Disaster Anarchy: Mutual Aid and Radical Action*, London: Pluto Press.

Fischer, F. (2017) *Climate Crisis and the Democratic Prospect: Participatory Governance in Sustainable Communities*, Oxford: Oxford University Press.

Fitzpatrick, T. (1999) *Freedom and Security: An Introduction to the Basic Income Debate*, Basingstoke: Palgrave MacMillan.

Flesher Fominaya, C. (2020) *Social Movements in a Globalized World*, London: Red Globe Press.

Forbis, M. and Brenner, J. (2014) 'The Zapatistas at 20: building autonomous community', *Solidarity*, [online] 23 March, Available from: https://solidarity-us.org/p4135/

Ford, R. and Heath, A. (2014) 'Immigration: a nation divided?', in A. Park, J. Curtice and C. Bryson (eds) *British Social Attitudes 31*, London: NatCen Social Research, pp 78–94.

Ford, R. and Mellon, J. (2020) 'The skills premium and the ethnic premium: a cross-national experiment on European attitudes to immigrants', *The Journal of Ethnic and Migration Studies*, 46(3): 512–32.

Ford, R., Morrell, G. and Heath, A. (2012) 'Immigration: "fewer but better"? Public views about immigration', in A. Park, E. Clery, J. Curtice, M. Phillips and D. Utting (eds) *British Social Attitudes 29*, London: NatCen Social Research, pp 26–44.

Foundational Economy Collective (2018) *Foundational Economy: The Infrastructure of Everyday Life*, Manchester: Manchester University Press.

Frankel, B. (2018) *Fictions of Sustainability: The Politics of Growth and Post-capitalist Futures*, Melbourne: Greenmeadows.

Frankel, B. (2020) *Capitalism versus Democracy? Rethinking Politics in the Age of Environmental Crisis*, Melbourne: Greenmeadows.

Fraser, N. (1994) 'After the family wage: gender equity and the welfare state', *Political Theory*, 22(4): 591–698.

Freire, P. (1970) *Pedagogy of the Oppressed*, London: Continuum.

Freud, S. (1985) 'Civilisation and its Discontents', in A. Dickson (ed) *S. Freud: Civilisation, Society and Religion*, London: Penguin.

Fuchs, C. (ed) (2020a) 'Communicative Socialism/Digital Socialism', *tripleC*, 18(1), [online] 13 January, Available from: www.triple-c.at/index.php/tripleC/issue/view/41

Fuchs, C. (2020b) 'Communicative socialism/digital socialism', *tripleC*, 18(1): 1–31, [online] 13 January, Available from: www.triple-c.at/index.php/tripleC/article/view/1144/1308

Fuchs, C. and Unterberger, K. (eds) (2021) *The Public Service Media and Public Service Internet Manifesto*, London: University of Westminster Press.

Fukuyama, F. (1989) 'The end of history?', *The National Interest*, 16: 3–18.

Fürst, J. and McLellan, J. (eds) (2018) *Dropping out of Socialism: The Creation of Alternative Spheres in the Soviet Bloc*, Lanham, MD: Lexington Books.

Gabagambi, J.J. (2018) 'A comparative analysis of restorative justice practices in Africa', *Hauser Global Law School Program*, [online] October, Available from: www.nyulawglobal.org/globalex/Restorative_Justice_Africa.html

Gahman, L., Mohamed, N., Penados, F., Reyes, J-R., Mohamed, A. and Smith, S-J. (2022) *A Beginner's Guide to Building Better Worlds: Ideas and Inspiration from the Zapatistas*, Bristol: Bristol University Press.

Gamble, A. (2019) 'The Left v. authoritarian populism' in M. Perryman (ed) *Corbynism from Below*, London: Lawrence and Wishart.

Gander, K. (2016) 'The university where you can get a BA-level degree for free', *The Independent*, [online] 24 June, Available from: www.independ ent.co.uk/news/education/tuition-fees-degrees-free-university-brigh ton-fub-universities-bachelor-degree-ba-if-project-ragged-a7100421.html

Ganesh, S. and Zoller, H. (2018) 'Organizing transition: principles and tensions in eco-localism', in M. Parker, G. Cheney, V. Founier and C. Land (eds) (2018) *The Routledge Companion to Alternative Organization*, London: Routledge, pp 236–50.

Garforth, L. (2018) *Green Utopias: Environmental Hope before and after Nature*, Cambridge: Polity Press.

Garland, J. (2019) 'Members not only', in M. Perryman (ed) *Corbynism from Below*, London: Lawrence and Wishart.

Geoghegan, V. (2008) *Utopianism and Marxism*, Bern: Peter Lang.

German, L. (2019) 'An extra-parliamentary affair', in M. Perryman (ed) *Corbynism from Below*, London: Lawrence and Wishart, pp 189–207.

Gibson-Graham, J.K. and Dombroski, K. (eds) (2020) *The Handbook of Diverse Economies*, Cheltenham: Edward Elgar.

Gilbert, J. (2020) *Twenty-first Century Socialism*, Cambridge: Polity Press.

Gill, S. (2000) 'Towards a postmodern prince? The battle in Seattle as a moment in the new politics of globalization', *Millennium: Journal of International Studies*, 29(1): 131–40.

Gills, B. and Chase-Dunn, C. (2019) 'An instrument for the global Left? Samir Amin's Proposal for a Fifth International', *Globalizations*, 16(7): 967–72.

Gills, B.K. and Chase-Dunn, C. (eds) (2021) *Unity on the Global Left: Critical Reflections on Samir Amin's Call for a New International*, London: Routledge.

Gilmore, R.W. (2007) *Golden Gulag: Prisons, Surplus, Crisis, and Opposition in Globalizing California*, Berkeley: University of California Press.

Gilmore, R.W. (2022) *Change Everything: Racial Capitalism and the Case for Abolition*, Chicago: Haymarket Books.

Goodfellow, M. (2020) *Hostile Environment: How Immigrants Became Scapegoats*, London: Verso.

Goodsman, D. (1991) *Summerhill: Theory and Practice*, PhD thesis, University of East Anglia.

Goodwin, B. and Taylor, K. (2009) *The Politics of Utopia: A Study in Theory and Practice*, Bern: Peter Lang.

Goodwin, M. (2012) 'Far Right ideas: Britain's generation gap', *The Guardian*, [online] 16 September, Available from: www.theguardian.com/commentisfree/2012/sep/16/far-right-britains-generation-gap

Gorodzeisky, A. and Semyonov, M. (2020) 'Perceptions and misperceptions: actual size, perceived size and opposition to immigration in European societies', *Journal of Ethnic and Migration Studies*, 46(3): 612–30.

Gorz, A. (1982) *Farewell to the Working Class: An Essay on Post-industrial Socialism*, London: Pluto Press.

Gottesdiener, L. (2014) 'Visiting a revolution that won't go away', *TomDispatch*, [online] 23 January, Available from: https://tomdispatch.com/laura-gottesdiener-visiting-a-revolution-that-won-t-go-away/

Gradin, S. (2015) 'Radical routes and alternative avenues: how cooperatives can be non-capitalist', *Review of Radical Political Economics*, 47(2): 141–58.

Graeber, D. (2002) 'The new anarchists', *New Left Review*, 13: 61–73.

Graeber, D. (2018) *Bullshit Jobs: A Theory*, New York: Simon and Schuster.

Gray, J. (2008) *Black Mass: Apocalyptic Religion and the Death of Utopia*, London: Penguin.

Gray, K. and Gills, B.K. (2016) 'South–South cooperation and the rise of the Global South', *Third World Quarterly*, 37(4): 557–74.

Green, E.G.T, Visintin, E.P, Sarrasin, O. and Hewstone, M. (2020) 'When integration policies shape the impact of intergroup contact on threat perceptions: a multilevel study across 20 European countries', *Journal of Ethnic and Migration Studies*, 46(3): 631–48.

Greenberg, E.S. (1981) 'Industrial self-management and political attitudes', *American Political Science Review*, 75(1): 29–42.

Greenberg, E.S. (1983) 'Context and co-operation: systematic variations in the political effects of workplace democracy', *Economic and Industrial Democracy*, 4(2): 191–223.

Gribble, D. (1998) *Real Education: Varieties of Freedom*, Bristol: Libertarian Education.

Griffith, M. (2010) *The Unschooling Handbook: How to Use the Whole World as Your Child's Classroom*, New York: Three Rivers Press.

Guinan, J. and Hanna, T. (2018) 'Democratic ownership in the new economy', in J. McDonnell (ed) *Economics for the Many*, London: Verso, pp 108–25.

Guinan, J. and O'Neill, M. (2018) 'The institutional turn: Labour's new political economy', *Renewal*, 26(2): 5–16.

Guinan, J. and O'Neill, M. (2019a) *From Community Wealth Building to System Change: Local Roots for Economic Transformation*, London: IPPR.

Guinan, J. and O'Neill, M. (2019b) *The Case for Community Wealth Building*, Cambridge: Polity Press.

Guinan, J. and McKinley, S. (2020) 'Hanging in the balance: the democratic economy after Corbyn', *Renewal*, 28(1): 16–25.

Guinan, J. and O'Neill, M. (2020) 'Only bold state intervention will save us from a future owned by corporate giants', *The Guardian*, [online] 6 July, Available from: www.theguardian.com/commentisfree/2020/jul/06/state-intervention-amazon-recovery-covid-19

Hailes, J. (2007) *The New Green Consumer Guide*, London: Simon and Schuster.

Hall, S. (1988) *The Hard Road to Renewal: Thatcherism and the Crisis of the Left*, London: Verso.

Hancox, D. (2013) *The Village against the World*, London: Verso.

Hanna, T. (2018a) *Our Common Wealth: The Return of Public Ownership in the United States*, Manchester: Manchester University Press.

Hanna, T. (2018b) 'The next economic settlement: the return of public ownership', *Renewal*, 26(2): 17–32.

Hardt, M. and Negri, A. (2017) *Assembly*, Oxford: Oxford University Press.

Harris, N. and Acaroğlu, O. (eds) (2022) *Thinking beyond Neoliberalism: Alternative Societies, Transition, and Resistance*, London: Palgrave Macmillan.

Hart, H. (ed) (1970) *Summerhill: For and Against*, New York: Hart Publishing Company.

Hart, I. (2001) 'Deschooling and the web: Ivan Illich 30 years on', *Educational Media International*, 38(2–3): 69–76.

Harvey, D. (2000) *Spaces of Hope*, Berkeley: University of California Press.

Harvey, D. (2012) *Rebel Cities: From the Right to the City to the Urban Revolution*, London: Verso.

Hattersley, R. (1987) *Choose Freedom: The Future for Democratic Socialism*, London: Penguin.

Hayek, F. (1962) *The Road to Serfdom*, London: Routledge.

Hayek, F. (1980) 'The principles of a liberal social order', in *Studies in Philosophy, Politics and Economics*, Chicago: University of Chicago Press, pp 160–77.

Heath, A. and Richards, L. (2019) *How do Europeans Differ in their Attitudes to Immigration: Findings from the European Social Survey 2002/3–2016/17*, Paris: OECD.

Held, D. (2004) *Global Covenant: The Social Democratic Alternative to the Washington Consensus*, Cambridge: Polity Press.

Held, D. (2006) *Models of Democracy*, Cambridge: Polity Press.

Hemmings, R. (1972) *Fifty Years of Freedom: A Study of the Development of the Ideas of A.S. Neill*, London: Allen and Unwin.

Hern, M. (ed) (2008) *Everywhere All the Time: A New Deschooling Reader*, Oakland, CA: AK Press.

Heslop, J., Morgan, K. and Tomaney, J. (2019) 'Debating the foundational economy', *Renewal*, 27(2): 5–12.

Hicks, J. (2022) 'The future of data ownership: an uncommon research agenda', *Sociological Review*, [online] 16 May, Available from: https://journals.sagepub.com/doi/10.1177/00380261221088120

Hicks, M. (2017) *Programmed Inequality: How Britain Discarded Women Technologists and Lost Its Edge in Computing*, Cambridge, MA: MIT Press.

Hilder, P. (2019) 'The revolution will be networked', in M. Perryman (ed) *Corbynism from Below*, London: Lawrence and Wishart, pp 160–70.

Hind, D. and Mills, T. (2018) 'Media democracy: a reform agenda for democratic communications', in L. Macfarlane (ed) *New Thinking for the British Economy*, London: Open Democracy, pp 160–71, Available from: www.opendemocracy.net/en/opendemocracyuk/new-thinking-for-the-british-economy/

Hobbs, C. (2018) 'Doing public ownership: centralisation, decentralisation, bureaucracy and control', *Renewal*, 26(3): 40–3.

Hodgson, G. (1984) *The Democratic Economy: A New Look at Planning, Markets and Power*, London: Penguin.

Hodgson, G. (1998) 'Socialism against markets? A critique of two recent proposals', *Economy and Society*, 27(4): 407–33.

Hodkinson, S. and Chatterton, P. (2006) 'Autonomy in the city? Reflections on the social centres movement in the UK', *City*, 10(3): 305–15.

Hogg, D.J. (2022) '"The Left will find that it has bought a Trojan horse": the dialectics of universal basic income', *Critical Sociology*, [online] 25 April, Available from: https://journals.sagepub.com/doi/10.1177/0261018322 1092151

Holloway, J. (2010) *Crack Capitalism*, London: Pluto Press.

Holloway, J. (2012) 'Crack capitalism: "we want to break"', *Roarmag*, [online] 4 December, Available from: https://roarmag.org/essays/john-holloway-crack-capitalism-we-want-to-break/

Honneth, A. (2017) *The Idea of Socialism: Towards a Renewal*, Cambridge: Polity.

Honoré, C. (2004) *In Praise of Slowness: Challenging the Cult of Speed*, Glasgow: HarperCollins.

Honoré, C. (2008) *Under Pressure: Putting the Child Back into Children*, London: Orion.

Hopewell, T. (2018) 'I spent 3 days with the Zapatistas. Here's what happened', *Global Justice Now*, [online] 9 April, Available from: www.globaljustice.org.uk/blog/2018/04/i-spent-three-days-zapatistas-heres-what-happened/

Hopkins, R. (2019) 'Transition movement', in A. Kothari, A. Salleh, A. Escobar, F. Demaria and A. Acosta (eds) *Pluriverse: A Post-development Dictionary*, New Delhi: Tulika Books, pp 317–20.

Horowitz, I.L. (1989) 'Socialist utopias and scientific utopias: primary fanaticisms and secondary contradictions', *Sociological Forum*, 4(1): 107–13.

Howard, T. (2018a) 'The Democracy Collaborative joins Jeremy Corbyn's new Community Wealth Building Unit as advisors', *The Democracy Collaborative*, [online] 8 February, Available from: https://democracyco llaborative.org/content/democracy-collaborative-joins-jeremy-corbyns-new-community-wealth-building-unit-advisors

Howard, T. (2018b) 'The making of a democratic economy', *Royal Society of Arts*, [video] 19 November, Available from: www.thersa.org/events/2018/11/the-making-of-a-democratic-economy

Howard, T. (2019) 'Trickle up economics', *Prospect Magazine*, [online] 13 July, Available from: www.prospectmagazine.co.uk/sponsored/trickle-up-economics

Huber, E. and Stephens, J.D. (2002) 'Globalization, competitiveness and the social democratic model', *Social Policy and Society*, 1(1): 47–57.

Hudis, P. (2012) *Marx's Concept of the Alternative to Capitalism*, Leiden: Brill.

Hwang, T. (2020) *Subprime Attention Crisis: Advertising and the Time Bomb at the Heart of the Internet*, Danvers, MA: Farrar, Strauss, and Giroux.

ICCA Consortium (2021) *Territories of Life*, ICCA Consortium.

Igarashi, A. and Laurence, J. (2021) 'How does immigration affect anti-immigrant sentiment, and who is affected most? A longitudinal analysis of the UK and Japan cases', *Comparative Migration Studies*, 9: Article 24, [online] 21 June, Available from: https://comparativemigrationstudies.springeropen.com/articles/10.1186/s40878-021-00231-7

Illich, I. (1971a) *Deschooling Society*, London: Calder and Boyars.

Illich, I. (1971b) 'The alternative to schooling', *Saturday Review*, 19 June.

Illich, I. (2008) 'Foreword', in M. Hern (ed) *Everywhere All the Time: A New Deschooling Reader*, Oakland, CA: AK Press, pp iii–v.

Internationalist Commune of Rojava (2018) *Make Rojava Green Again*, London: Dog Section Press.

IOM (International Organization for Migration) (2013) *IOM World Migration Report 2013: Migrant Well-being and Development*, Geneva: IOM.

Issin, E. and Ruppert, E. (2020) *Being Digital Citizens*, London: Rowman & Littlefield.

Jackson, T. (2017) *Prosperity without Growth: Foundations for the Economy of Tomorrow*, London: Routledge.

Jackson, T. (2021) *Post Growth: Life after Capitalism*, Cambridge: Polity Press.

Jacobs, M. (2022) 'Reflections on COP26: international diplomacy, global justice and the greening of capitalism', *The Political Quarterly*, 93(2): 270–7.

Jaggar, A.M. (1983) *Feminist Politics and Human Nature*, Brighton: Harvester Press.

Jameson, F. (2007) *Archaeologies of the Future: The Desire Called Utopia and Other Science Fictions*, London: Verso.

Jeffrey, C. and Dyson, J. (2021) 'Geographies of the future: prefigurative politics', *Progress in Human Geography*, 45(4): 641–58.

Jervis, R. (2022) 'Co-operatives and socialism: the promises and contradictions of a system of worker ownership', in N. Harris and O. Acaroğlu (eds) *Thinking Beyond Neoliberalism: Alternative Societies, Transition, and Resistance*, Cham: Palgrave MacMillan, pp 49–74.

Ji, M. (2020) 'With or without class: resolving Marx's Janus-faced interpretation of worker-owned cooperatives', *Capital & Class*, 44(3): 345–69.

Johnston, J. (2008) 'Counter-hegemony or bourgeois piggery? Food politics and the case of FoodShare', in W. Wright and G. Middenhorf (eds) *The Fight over Food: Producers, Consumers, and Activists Challenge the Global Food System*, University Park, PA: Penn State University Press, pp 93–120.

Jones, B. and O'Donnell, M. (eds) (2018) *Alternatives to Neoliberalism: Towards Equality and Democracy*, Bristol, Policy Press.

Jossa, B. (2005) 'Marx, Marxism and the cooperative movement', *Cambridge Journal of Economics*, 29(1): 3–18.

Jossa, B. (2014) 'Marx, Lenin and the cooperative movement', *Review of Political Economy*, 26(2): 282–302.

Jossa, B. (2017) *Labour Managed Firms and Post-capitalism*, Abingdon: Routledge.

Judt, T. (2011) *Ill Fares the Land: A Treatise on Our Present Discontents*, London: Penguin.

Kahn, R. and Keller, D. (2007) 'Paulo Freire and Ivan Illich: technology, politics and the reconstruction of education', *Policy Futures in Education*, 5(4): 431–48.

Kallis, G., Kostakis, V., Lange, S., Muraca, B., Paulson, S. and Schmelzer, M. (2018) 'Research on degrowth', *Annual Review of Environment and Resources*, 43: 291–396.

Kanter, R.M. (1972) *Commitment and Community: Communes and Utopias in Sociological Perspective*, Cambridge, MA: Harvard University Press.

Karatasli, S.S. (2019) 'The world is in a revolutionary moment – how can the global Left be a serious player?', *Open Democracy*, [online] 1 November, Available from: www.opendemocracy.net/en/oureconomy/the-world-is-in-a-revolutionary-moment-how-can-the-global-left-be-a-serious-player/

Karlin, J.R. (2022) 'Battles for socio-spatial hegemony in the exilic space of Exarcheia', *Antipode*, 54(2): 1112–40.

Kasparian, D. (2022) *Co-operative Struggles: Work Conflicts in Argentina's New Worker Co-operatives*, Boston: Brill.

Kelley, R.D.G. (2002) *Freedom Dreams: The Black Radical Imagination*, Boston: Beacon Press.

Kelly, M. and Howard, T. (2019) *The Making of a Democratic Economy: Building Prosperity for the Many, Not Just the Few*, Oakland, CA: Berrett-Koehler.

Kelly, M., McKinley, S. and Duncan, V. (2015) 'Community wealth building: America's emerging asset-based approach to city economic development', *Renewal*, 24(2): 51–68.

Kerstenetzky, C.L. (2022) 'Horizons of social democracy: social investment or transcending capitalism?', *The Political Quarterly*, 93(1): 130–41.

Keuchyan, R. (2020) 'Economic planning can succeed where the market fails', *Tribune*, [online] 26 April, Available from: https://tribunemag.co.uk/2020/04/democratic-planning-can-succeed-where-the-market-fails

Khondker, H.H. (2022) 'The post-pandemic world and the prospect for global justice: a commentary', *Globalizations*, 19(3): 513–17.

Kingsley, P. (2010) 'The art of slow reading', *The Guardian*, [online] 15 July, Available from: www.theguardian.com/books/2010/jul/15/slow-reading

Kirwan, S., Dawney, L. and Brigstocke, J. (eds) (2016) *Space, Power and the Commons: The Struggle for Alternative Futures*, Abingdon: Routledge.

Kishimoto, S. (2018) 'The unstoppable rise of remunicipalisation', *Transnational Institute*, [online] 23 April, Available from: www.tni.org/en/article/the-unstoppable-rise-of-remunicipalisation

Kishimoto, S. and Sunby, E. (2020) 'Public ownership in times of coronavirus', *Open Democracy*, [online] 20 April, Available from: www.opendemocracy.net/en/oureconomy/public-ownership-times-coronavirus/

Kitchin, R. and Fraser, A. (2020) *Slow Computing: Why We Need Balanced Digital Lives*, Bristol: Bristol University Press.

Klein, H. (2019) 'A spark of hope: the ongoing lessons of the Zapatista revolution 25 years on', *North American Congress on Latin America*, [online] 18 January, Available from: https://nacla.org/news/2019/01/18/spark-hope-ongoing-lessons-zapatista-revolution-25-years

Klug, A. and Rees, E. (2019) 'How big organising works', in M. Perryman (ed) *Corbynism from Below*, London: Lawrence and Wishart, pp 120–35.

Koduvayur Venkitaraman, A. and Joshi, N. (2022) 'A critical examination of a community-led ecovillage initiative: a case of Auroville, India', *Climate Action*, 1: Article 15, [online] 8 July, Available from: https://link.springer.com/article/10.1007/s44168-022-00016-3

Kohut, A. (2015) '50 years later, Americans give thumbs-up to immigration law that changed the nation', *Pew Research Center*, [online] 4 February, Available from: www.pewresearch.org/fact-tank/2015/02/04/50-years-later-americans-give-thumbs-up-to-immigration-law-that-changed-the-nation

Kollewe, J. (2022) 'Thousands of UK workers begin world's biggest trial of four-day week', *The Guardian*, [online] 6 June, Available from: www.theguardian.com/business/2022/jun/06/thousands-workers-worlds-biggest-trial-four-day-week

Kothari, A. (2014) '10 principles of radical ecological democracy: a way to achieve global human happiness without destroying the planet', *Films for Action*, [online] 22 April, Available from: www.filmsforaction.org/articles/towards-alternatives-radical-ecological-democracy/

Kothari, A. (2021) 'These alternative economies are inspirations for a sustainable world', *Scientific American*, [online] 1 June, Available from: www.scientificamerican.com/article/these-alternative-economies-are-inspirations-for-a-sustainable-world/

Kothari, A., Salleh, A., Escobar, A., Demaria, F. and Acosta, A. (eds) (2019) *Pluriverse: A Post-development Dictionary*, New Delhi: Tulika Books.

Kropotkin, P. (2007) *Mutual Aid: A Factor in Evolution*, Gloucester: Dodo Press.

Kukathis, C. (1989) *Hayek and Modern Liberalism*, Oxford: Clarendon Press.

Kumar, K. (1987) *Utopia and Anti-utopia in Modern Times*, Oxford: Blackwell.

Kumar, K. (1991) *Utopianism*, Milton Keynes: Open University Press.

Kumar, K. (2010) 'The ends of utopia', *New Literary History*, 41(3): 549–69.

Kymlicka, W. (2002) *Contemporary Political Philosophy: An Introduction*, Oxford: Clarendon Press.

Labour Party (2017) *Alternative Models of Ownership*, London: Labour Party.

Lamble, S. (2021) 'Practising everyday abolition', in K. Duff (ed) *Abolishing the Police*, London: Repeater Books, pp 147–60.

Lane, D. (1996) *The Rise and Fall of State Socialism*, Cambridge: Polity Press.

Langmead, K. (2016) 'Challenging the degeneration thesis: the role of democracy in worker cooperatives?', *Journal of Entrepreneurial and Organizational Diversity*, 5(1): 79–98.

Lansley, S. and Reed, H. (2019) *Basic Income for All: From Desirability to Feasibility*, London: Compass.

Latouche, S. (2009) *Farewell to Growth*, Cambridge: Polity Press.

Lawrence, M. (2019) 'Inclusive ownership funds: a transatlantic agenda for transformative change', *Renewal*, 27(4): 60–6.

Lawson, N. (2019) 'Labouring under illusions', in M. Perryman (ed) (2019) *Corbynism from Below*, London: Lawrence and Wishart, pp 170–88.

Leahy, T. (2019) 'Permaculture', in A. Kothari, A. Salleh, A. Escobar, F. Demaria and A. Acosta (eds) (2019) *Pluriverse: A Post-development Dictionary*, New Delhi: Tulika Books, pp 274–77.

Leibowitz, J. and McInroy, N. (2019) 'Beyond Preston: how local wealth building is taking the UK by storm', *CityMonitor*, [online] 25 March, Available from: https://citymonitor.ai/government/beyond-preston-how-local-wealth-building-taking-uk-storm-4533

Leopold, D. (2005) 'The structure of Marx and Engels' considered account of utopian socialism', *History of Political Thought*, 26(3): 443–66.

Leopold, D. (2007) 'Socialism and (the rejection of) utopia', *Political Ideologies*, 12(3): 219–37.

Leopold, D. (2016) 'On Marxian utopophobia', *Journal of the History of Philosophy*, 54(1): 111–34.

Level (2020) 'Abolition for the people', [online] 6 October, Available from: https://level.medium.com/abolition-for-the-people-397ef29e3ca5

Levin, M. (1989) *Marx, Engels and Liberal Democracy*, Basingstoke: Macmillan.

Levitas, R. (1979) 'Sociology and utopia', *Sociology*, 13(1): 19–33.

Levitas, R. (2003) 'Introduction: the elusive idea of utopia', *History of the Human Sciences*, 16(1): 1–10.

Levitas, R. (2011) *The Concept of Utopia*, Witney: Peter Lang.

Levitas, R. (2013) *Utopia as Method: The Imaginary Reconstitution of Society*, Basingstoke: Palgrave.

Lewis, S. (2020) 'The coronavirus crisis shows it's time to abolish the family', *Open Democracy*, [online] 24 March, Available from: www.opendemocracy.net/en/oureconomy/coronavirus-crisis-shows-its-time-abolish-family/

Lister, I. (ed) (1974) *Deschooling: A Reader*, London: Cambridge University Press.

Liu, W. (2020) *Abolish Silicon Valley: How to Liberate Technology from Capitalism*, London: Repeater Books.

London Edinburgh Weekend Return Group (2021) *In and Against the State: Discussion Notes for Socialists*, London: Pluto Press.

Longxi, Z. (2002) 'The utopian vision: east and west', *Utopian Studies*, 13(1): 1–20.

Lopez, A. and Bush, M.E.L. (2020) 'Technology for transformation is the path forward', *Global Tapestry of Alternatives Newsletter*, [online] July, Available from: https://globaltapestryofalternatives.org/newsletters:01:index

Lovell, D. (2004) 'Marx's utopian legacy', *The European Legacy: Toward New Paradigms*, 9(5): 629–40.

Lucas, H. (2011) *After Summerhill: What Happened to the Pupils of Britain's Most Radical School?* Bristol: Herbert Adler Publishing.

Luxemburg, R. (1973) *Reform or Revolution*, New York: Pathfinder Press.

Luxemburg, R. (2008) *The Essential Rosa Luxemburg*, Chicago: Haymarket Books.

Macfarlane, L. (2019) 'We already live in a planned economy – we just need to take the steering wheel', *Open Democracy*, [online] 11 March, Available from: www.opendemocracy.net/en/oureconomy/we-already-live-in-a-planned-economy-we-just-need-to-seize-the-steering-wheel/

Maheshvarananda, D. (2012) *After Capitalism: Economic Democracy in Action*, San Germán: InnerWorld Publications.

Mair, S. (2020) 'How will coronavirus change the world?', *BBC*, [online] 31 March, Available from: www.bbc.com/future/article/20200331-covid-19-how-will-the-coronavirus-change-the-world

Malm, A. (2020) *Corona, Climate, Chronic Emergency: War Communism in the Twenty-First Century*, London: Verso.

Malmgren, E. (2018) 'Socialized media', *The Baffler*, [online] 19 September, Available from: https://thebaffler.com/latest/socialized-media-malmgren

Mandel, E. (1975) 'Self-management: dangers and possibilities', *International*, 2(4): 3–9.

Manley, J. (2018) 'Preston changed its fortunes with "Corbynomics" – now other cities are doing the same', *The Conversation*, [online] 7 November, Available from: https://theconversation.com/preston-changed-its-fortunes-with-corbynomics-now-other-cities-are-doing-the-same-106293

Mannheim, K. (1979) *Ideology and Utopia*, London: Routledge & Kegan Paul.

Manuel, F.E. and Manuel, F.P. (1979) *Utopian Thought in the Western World*, Cambridge, MA: Belknap.

Marthews, A. and Tucker, C. (2017) 'The impact of online surveillance on behavior', in D. Gray and S.E. Henderson (eds) *The Cambridge Handbook of Surveillance Law*, Cambridge: Cambridge University Press, pp 437–54.

Marx, K. (1864) 'Inaugural address of the International Working Men's Association', *Marxists.org*, [online], Available from: www.marxists.org/arch ive/marx/works/1864/10/27.htm

Marx, K. (1975) 'Economic and philosophical manuscripts', in L. Colletti (ed) *Marx: Early Writings*, London: Penguin, pp 279–400.

Marx, K. (1998) *The Civil War in France*, Chicago: Charles H. Kerr Publishing Company.

Marx, K. (2009) *Critique of the Gotha Programme*, Gloucester: Dodo Press.

Marx, K. and Engels, F. (1968) 'Manifesto of the Communist Party', in *Selected Works in One Volume*, London: Lawrence and Wishart, pp 31–63.

Marx, P. (2020) 'Nationalize Amazon', *Jacobin*, [online] 29 March, Available from: www.jacobinmag.com/2020/03/nationalize-amazon-coronavirus-delivery-usps

Mason, P. (2012) 'Viewpoint: Manuel Castells on the rise of alternative economic cultures', *BBC*, [online] 31 October, Available from: www.bbc.co.uk/news/business-20027044

Mason, P. (2019) 'Could a progressive phoenix arise from the ashes of the UK's political meltdown?', *Social Europe*, [online] 10 September, Available from: www.socialeurope.eu/could-a-progressive-phoenix-arise-from-the-ashes-of-the-uks-political-meltdown

Masquelier, C. (2017a) 'Beyond co-optation: revisiting the transformative function of "workers' self-directed enterprises"', *Socialism and Democracy*, 31(2): 53–72.

Masquelier, C. (2017b) *Critique and Resistance in a Neoliberal Age: Towards a Narrative of Emancipation*, London: Palgrave.

Mathews, J. (1989) *Age of Democracy: The Politics of Post-Fordism*, Oxford: Oxford University Press.

Mawdsley, E. (2019) 'South–South cooperation 3.0? Managing the consequences of success in the decade ahead', *Oxford Development Studies*, 47(3): 259–74.

Mazzucato, M. (2013) *The Entrepreneurial State: Debunking Public vs. Private Sector Myths*, London: Anthem Press.

McDonnell, J. (2016) 'The Tories are just as vicious as they have ever been – John McDonnell speech in Preston', *Labourlist*, [online] 20 April, Available from: https://labourlist.org/2016/04/the-tories-are-just-as-vici ous-as-they-have-always-been-john-mcdonnell-speech/

McIlwain, C. (2020) *Black Software: The Internet & Racial Justice, from the AfroNet to Black Lives Matter*, Oxford: Oxford University Press.

McLaren, L. and Paterson, I. (2020) 'Generational change and attitudes to immigration', *Journal of Ethnic and Migration Studies*, 46(3): 665–82.

McLeod, A.M. (2015) 'Prison abolition and grounded justice', *UCLA Law Review*, 62(5): 1156–239.

McManus, M. (2020) 'Socialists don't want to destroy liberalism. We want to go beyond it', *Jacobin*, [online] 2 October, Available from: https://jacobinmag.com/2020/10/socialism-liberalism-marx

Mehta, V. (2019) 'The great Indian basic income debate', *Open Democracy*, [online] 14 November, Available from: www.opendemocracy.net/en/beyond-trafficking-and-slavery/great-indian-basic-income-debate/

Mendick, H. (2014), 'Social class, gender and the pace of academic life: what kind of solution is slow?' *Forum: Qualitative Social Research*, 15(3): Article 7, [online] 26 September, Available from: www.qualitative-research.net/index.php/fqs/article/view/2224

Migration Observatory (2011) *Thinking Behind the Numbers: Understanding Public Opinion on Immigration in Britain*, Oxford: Migration Observatory.

Milburn, K. and Russell, B. (2019a), 'How "public-common partnerships" can help us take back what's ours', *Novara Media*, [online] 10 July, Available from: https://novaramedia.com/2019/07/10/how-public-common-partnerships-can-help-us-take-back-whats-ours/

Milburn, K. and Russell, B. (2019b) *Public-Common Partnerships: Building New Circuits of Collective Ownership*, London: Common Wealth.

Miles, M. (2008) *Urban Utopias: The Built and Social Architectures of Alternative Settlements*, Abingdon: Routledge.

Miliband, R. (1994) *Socialism for a Sceptical Age*, Cambridge: Polity Press.

Mill, J.S. (1989) 'Chapters on socialism', in S. Collini (ed) *On Liberty and Other Writings*, Cambridge: Cambridge University Press, pp 219–80.

Mittelman, J.H. (2022) 'Global transitioning: beyond the Covid-19 pandemic', *Globalizations*, 19(3): 439–49.

Moghadam, V.M. (2019) 'On Samir Amin's call for a Fifth International', *Globalizations*, 16(7): 998–1005.

Monbiot, G. (2001) 'How to rule the world', *The Guardian*, [online] 17 July, Available from: www.theguardian.com/politics/2001/jul/17/greenpolitics.globalization

Monticelli, L. (2018) 'Embodying alternatives to capitalism in the 21st century', *tripleC*, 16(2): 501–71, [online] 4 May, Available from: www.triple-c.at/index.php/tripleC/article/view/1032

Monticelli, L. (2021) 'On the necessity of prefigurative politics', *Thesis Eleven*, 167(1): 99–118.

Monticelli, L. (ed) (2022) *The Future Is Now: An Introduction to Prefigurative Politics*, Bristol: Bristol University Press.

More, T. (1892) *Utopia*, London: Cassell and Company.

Morozov, E. (2019) 'Digital socialism? The calculation debate in the age of big data', *New Left Review*, 116/17: 33–67.

Moses, J. (2006) *International Migration: Globalization's Last Frontier*, London: Zed Books.

Mosley, L. (2005) 'Globalization and the state: still room to move?', *New Political Economy*, 10(3): 355–62.

Mouffe, C. (2018) *For a Left Populism*, London: Verso.

Mountz, A., Bonds, A., Mansfield, B., Loyd, J., Hyndman, J., Walton-Roberts, M., Basu, R., Whitson, R., Hawkins, R., Hamilton, T. and Curran, W. (2015) 'For slow scholarship: a feminist politics of resistance through collective action in the neoliberal university', *ACME*, 14(4): 1235–59, [online] 18 August, Available from: www.acme-journal.org/index.php/acme/article/view/1058

Moylan, T. (1986) *Demand the Impossible: Science Fiction and the Utopian Imagination*, London: Methuen.

Muhr, T. (2022) 'Reclaiming the politics of South-South cooperation', *Globalizations*, [online] 1 June, Available from: www.tandfonline.com/doi/full/10.1080/14747731.2022.2082132

Muldoon, J. (2020) 'Don't break up Facebook – make it a public utility', *Jacobin*, [online] 16 December, Available from: https://jacobinmag.com/2020/12/facebook-big-tech-antitrust-social-network-data/

Muldoon, J. (2022) *Platform Socialism: How to Reclaim our Digital Future from Big Tech*, London: Pluto Press.

Murphy, C. (2019) 'Editorial: the unspoken dilemmas of Corbynomics', *Renewal* 27(3): 5–13, [online] 6 August, Available from: https://renewal.org.uk/wp-content/uploads/2020/09/ren27.3_01editorial-1.pdf

Mutisi, M. and Sansculotte-Greenidge, K. (eds) (2012) *Integrating Traditional and Modern Conflict Resolution: Experiences from Selected Cases in Eastern and the Horn of Africa*, Durban: Accord.

Nalla, M.K. and Newman, G.R. (eds) (2013) *Community Policing in Indigenous Communities*, Boca Raton, FL: CRC Press.

Neill, A.S. (1962) *Summerhill: A Radical Approach to Education*, London: Victor Gollancz.

Neill, A.S. (1986) *A Dominie's Log*, London: Hogarth Press.

Neilson, D. (2021) 'Reversing the catastrophe of neoliberal-led global capitalism in the time of coronavirus: towards a democratic socialist alternative', *Capital and Class*, 45(2): 191–213.

Ness, I. and Azzellini, D. (eds) (2011) *Ours to Master and to Own: Workers' Control from the Commune to the Present*, Chicago: Haymarket Books.

Neustatter, A. (2011) 'Summerhill school and the do-as-yer-like kids', *The Guardian*, [online] 19 August, Available from: www.theguardian.com/education/2011/aug/19/summerhill-school-at-90

New Economics Foundation (2010) *21 Hours: Why a Shorter Working Week Can Help Us All to Flourish in the 21st Century*, London: New Economics Foundation.

New Economics Foundation (2013) *Framing the Economy: The Austerity Story*, London: New Economics Foundation.

New Economics Foundation (2015) *Responses to Austerity: How Groups across the UK are Adapting, Challenging and Imagining Alternatives*, London: New Economics Foundation.

*New Socialist* (2017) 'Labour's alternative models of ownership report', *New Socialist*, [online] 11 June, Available from: https://newsocialist.org.uk/labo urs-alternative-models-of-ownership-report/

Nieto, M. (2022) 'Entrepreneurship and decentralised investment in a planned economy: a critique of the Austrian reading', *Historical Materialism*, 30(1): 133–63.

Nieto, M. and Mateo, J.P. (2020) 'Dynamic efficiency in a planned economy: innovation and entrepreneurship without markets', *Science and Society*, 84(1): 42–66.

Noble, S.U. (2018) *Algorithms of Oppression: How Search Engines Reinforce Oppression*, New York: NYU Press.

Noorani, T., Blencowe, C. and Brigstocke, J. (eds) (2013) *Problems of Participation: Reflections on Authority, Democracy, and the Struggle for Common Life*, Lewes: ARN Press.

North, P. (2019) 'Alternative currencies', in A. Kothari, A. Salleh, A. Escobar, F. Demaria and A. Acosta (eds) *Pluriverse: A Post-development Dictionary*, Delhi: Tulika Books, pp 92–5.

North, P. (2020) 'Alternative currencies: diverse experiments', in J.K. Gibson-Graham and K. Dombroski (eds) *The Handbook of Diverse Economies*, Cheltenham: Edward Elgar, pp 230–37.

Nove, A. (1983) *The Economics of Feasible Socialism*, Hemel Hempstead: Allen and Unwin.

Nozick, R. (1974) *Anarchy, State and Utopia*, Oxford: Blackwell.

O'Brien, M.E. (2019a) 'Communizing care', *Pinko*, [online] 15 October, Available from: https://pinko.online/pinko-1/communizing-care

O'Brien, M.E. (2019b) 'Six steps to abolish the family', *Commune*, 5, Winter, [online] 30 December, Available from: https://communemag.com/six-steps-to-abolish-the-family/

OECD (Organisation for Economic Co-operation and Development) (2013) *International Migration Outlook 2013*, Paris: OECD.

OECD/UN-DESA (Organisation for Economic Co-operation and Development/United Nations Department for Economic and Social Affairs) (2013) *World Migration in Figures*, Paris: OECD.

Office for Budget Responsibility (2013) *2013 Fiscal Sustainability Report*, London: Office for Budget Responsibility.

O'Flaherty, K. (2021) 'How private is your Gmail, and should you switch?', *The Guardian*, [online] 9 May, Available from: www.theguardian.com/technology/2021/may/09/how-private-is-your-gmail-and-should-you-switch?

Omale, J. (2006) 'Justice in history: an examination of African restorative traditions and the emerging restorative justice paradigm', *African Journal of Criminology and Justice Studies*, 2(2): 33–63.

O'Neill, J. (2002) 'Socialist calculation and environmental valuation: money, markets and ecology', *Science and Society*, 66(1): 137–51.

O'Neill, J. (2003) 'Socialism, associations and the market', *Economy and Society*, 32(2): 184–206.

O'Neill, M. (2014) 'The slow university: work, time and well-being', *Forum: Qualitative Social Research*, 15(3): Article 14, [online] 26 September, Available from: www.qualitative-research.net/index.php/fqs/article/view/2226

O'Neill, M. (2016) 'The road to socialism is the A59: the Preston Model', *Renewal*, 24(2): 69–78, [online] 31 May, Available from: https://journals.lwbooks.co.uk/renewal/vol-24-issue-2/article-8868/

O'Neill, M. (2018) 'Beyond extraction: the political power of community wealth building: Ted Howard interviewed by Martin O'Neill', *Renewal*, 26(2): 46–53.

Orwell, G. (1987a) *1984*, London: Penguin.

Orwell, G. (1987b) *Animal Farm*, London: Penguin.

Pachamama Alliance (2021) 'A bioregional plan to permanently protect the Amazon Sacred Headwaters', [online] 1 July, Available from: https://news.pachamama.org/a-plan-to-permanently-protect-the-amazon-sacred-headwaters

Paden, R. (2002) 'Marx's critique of the utopian socialists', *Utopian Studies*, 13(2): 67–91.

Parker, M. (ed) (2020) *Life after COVID-19: The Other Side of Crisis*, Bristol: Bristol University Press.

Parker, M., Fourier, V. and Reedy, P. (2007) *The Dictionary of Alternatives*, London: Zed Books.

Parker, M., Cheney, G., Founier, V. and Land, C. (eds) (2018) *The Routledge Companion to Alternative Organization*, London: Routledge.

Parkin, F. (2002) *Max Weber*, Milton Park: Routledge.

Parsons, A. (2014) 'The sharing economy: a short introduction to its political evolution', *Open Democracy*, [online] 5 March, Available from: www.opendemocracy.net/transformation/adam-parsons/sharing-economy-short-introduction-to-its-political-evolution

Pätomaki, H. (2019) 'The rational kernel within Samir Amin's mythological shell: the idea of a democratic and pluralist world political party', *Globalizations*, 16(7): 1006–11.

Pearce, D., Markandya, A. and Barbier, E.B. (1989) *Blueprint for a Green Economy*, London: Earthscan.

Pearce, J. (2018) 'Free and open-source appropriate technology', in M. Parker, G. Cheney, V. Fournier and C. Land (eds) *The Routledge Companion to Alternative Organization*, London: Routledge, pp 308–28.

Peat, J. (2020) 'Burgon calls for Labour to print free tabloid newspaper for commuters', *The London Economic*, [online] 11 February, Available from: www.thelondoneconomic.com/news/burgon-calls-for-labour-to-print-free-tabloid-newspaper-for-commuters-177196/

Pels, D. (2003) *Unhastening Science: Autonomy and Reflexivity in the Social Theory of Knowledge*, Liverpool: Liverpool University Press.

Penney, J. (2016) 'Chilling effects: online surveillance and Wikipedia use', *Berkeley Technology Law Journal*, 31(1): 117–82.

Penney, J. (2022) 'Understanding chilling effects', *Minnesota Law Review*, 106(3), [online] 25 April, Available from: https://minnesotalawreview.org/article/understanding-chilling-effects/

Pepper, D. (1993) *Eco-socialism: From Deep Ecology to Social Justice*, London: Routledge.

Pepper, D. (1991) *Communes and the Green Vision: Counterculture, Lifestyle and the New Age*, London: Green Print.

Phillips, L. and Rozworski, M. (2020a) 'Why we need economic planning', *Tribune*, [online] 31 March, Available from: https://tribunemag.co.uk/2020/03/why-we-need-economic-planning

Phillips, L. and Roworski, M. (2020b) 'Planning the future', *Tribune*, [online] 19 July, Available from: https://tribunemag.co.uk/2020/07/planning-the-future

Pickard, J. and Shrimsley, R. (2019) 'Jeremy Corbyn's plan to rewrite the rules of the UK economy', *Financial Times*, [online] 1 September, Available from: www.ft.com/content/e1028dda-ca49-11e9-a1f4-3669401ba76f

Piketty, T. (2017) *Capital in the Twenty-first Century*, Cambridge, MA: Belknap Press.

Piketty, T. (2021) *Time for Socialism: Dispatches from a World on Fire, 2016–2021*, New Haven, CT: Yale University Press.

Pinto, A.P. (2020) 'How a communist mayor is defeating privatization in Chile', *Open Democracy*, [online] 21 April, Available from: www.opendemocracy.net/en/oureconomy/how-communist-mayor-defeating-privatization-chile/

Planas, M. and Martinez, J. (2020) 'Water should be a public good, not a commodity. Catalonia is showing how', *Open Democracy*, [online] 30 April, Available from: www.opendemocracy.net/en/oureconomy/water-should-be-public-good-not-commodity-catalonia-showing-how/

Pleyers, G. (2010) *Alter-globalization: Becoming Actors in the Global Age*, Cambridge: Polity Press.

Popper, K. (2011) *The Open Society and its Enemies*, Abingdon: Routledge.

Prakash, M. and Esteva, G. (2008) *Escaping Education: Living as Learning within Grassroots Cultures*, New York: Peter Lang.

Preston, J. and Firth, R. (2020) *Coronavirus, Class and Mutual Aid in the United Kingdom*, Cham: Palgrave Macmillan.

Przeworski, A. (1986) *Capitalism and Social Democracy*, Cambridge: Cambridge University Press.

Putnam, R.D. (2007) '*E pluribus unum*: diversity and community in the twenty-first century. The 2006 Johan Skytte Prize Lecture', *Scandinavian Political Studies*, 30(2): 137–74.

Raddi, G. (2018) 'Nationalize Facebook', *Politico*, [online] 9 October, Available from: www.politico.eu/article/nationalize-facebook-data-priv acy-hackers-advertisement-social-media/

Raekstad, P. (2018) 'Revolutionary practice and prefigurative politics: a clarification and defense', *Constellations*, 25(3): 359–72.

Raekstad, P. and Gradin, S.S. (2020) *Prefigurative Politics: Building Tomorrow Today*, Cambridge: Polity Press.

Ranger, J. (2020) 'Slow down! Digital deceleration towards a socialist social media', *tripleC*, 18(1): 254–67.

Rasillo, X.B. and Wirth, M. (2022) 'Alternative economies and commoning practices in Catalonia: unpacking *ecoxarxes* from a social studies of economisation perspective', *Antipode*, [online] 19 July, Available from: https://onlinelibrary.wiley.com/doi/10.1111/anti.12867

Reynolds, J. (2017) 'Could Preston provide a new economic model for Britain's cities?' *Citymetric*, [online] 10 August, Available from: www.cit ymetric.com/politics/could-preston-provide-new-economic-model-brit ain-s-cities-3243

Rikap, C. (2020) 'What would a state-owned Amazon look like? Ask Argentina', *Open Democracy*, [online] 24 November, Available from: www. opendemocracy.net/en/oureconomy/what-would-state-owned-amazon-look-ask-argentina/

Rossiter, N. and Zehle, S. (2018) 'Toward a politics of anonymity: algorithmic actors in the constitution of collective agency and the implications for global economic justice movements', in M. Parker, G. Cheney, V. Founier and C. Land (eds) *The Routledge Companion to Alternative Organization*, London: Routledge, pp 151–62.

Rushton, S. (2020) 'People-powered local politics can save democracy from populism', *Equal Times*, [online] 16 April, Available from: www.equalti mes.org/can-people-powered-local-politics

Ryle, M. (1988) *Ecology and Socialism*, London: Century Hutchinson.

Sadowski, J. (2019) 'Privacy is just the beginning of the debate over tech', *OneZero* [online] 6 June, Available from: https://onezero.medium.com/ privacy-is-just-the-beginning-of-the-debate-over-tech-8807c2f8458f

Sadowski, J. (2020) *Too Smart: How Digital Capitalism is Extracting Data, Controlling our Lives, and Taking Over the World*, Cambridge, MA: MIT Press.

Sadowski, J. (2021) 'Facebook is a harmful presence in our lives. It's not too late to pull the plug on it', *The Guardian*, [online] 6 October, Available from: www.theguardian.com/commentisfree/2021/oct/06/facebook-scandals-social-media

Sale, K. (2000) *Dwellers in the Land: The Bioregional Vision*, Athens, GA: University of Georgia Press.

Samuel, S. (2020) 'Everywhere basic income has been tried, in one map', *Vox*, [online] 20 October, Available from: www.vox.com/future-perfect/2020/2/19/21112570/universal-basic-income-ubi-map

Sargent, L.T. (1994) 'Three faces of utopianism revisited', *Utopian Studies*, 5(1): 1–37.

Sargent, L.T. (2010) *Utopianism: A Very Short Introduction*, Oxford: Oxford University Press.

Sargisson, L. (1996) *Contemporary Feminist Utopianism*, London: Routledge.

Sargisson, L. (2012) *Fool's Gold: Utopianism in the Twenty-first Century*, London: Palgrave.

Saros, D.E. (2014) *Information Technology and Socialist Construction: The End of Capital and the Transition to Socialism*, London: Routledge.

Saunders, P. (1995) *Capitalism: A Social Audit*, Milton Keynes: Open University Press.

Savage, M. (2017) 'What really happened when Swedes tried six-hour days?' *BBC*, [online] 8 February, Available from: www.bbc.co.uk/news/business-38843341

Schugurensky, D. (1998) 'The legacy of Paulo Freire: a critical review of his contributions', *Convergence*, 31(1/2): 17–29.

Schumacher, E.F. (1973) *Small Is Beautiful: Economics as if People Mattered*, London: Sphere.

Schwab, A-K. and Roysen, R. (2022) 'Ecovillages and other community-led initiatives as experiences of climate action', *Climate Action*, 1(12), [online] 12 June, Available from: https://link.springer.com/article/10.1007/s44168-022-00012-7

Sen, J. (ed) (2017) *The Movements of Movements. Part 1: What Makes Us Move?* New Delhi: OpenWord.

Sen, J. (ed) (2018) *The Movements of Movements. Part 2: Rethinking Our Dance*, New Delhi: OpenWord.

Sharzer, G. (2017) 'Cooperatives as transitional economics', *Review of Radical Political Economics*, 49(3): 456–76.

Shepherd, J. (2007) 'So, kids, anyone for double physics? (But no worries if you don't fancy it)', *The Guardian*, [online] 1 December, Available from: www.theguardian.com/uk/2007/dec/01/ofsted.schools

Silverstein, S. (2020) 'Family abolition isn't about ending love and care. It's about extending it to everyone', *Open Democracy*, [online] 24 April, Available from: www.opendemocracy.net/en/oureconomy/family-abolit ion-isnt-about-ending-love-and-care-its-about-extending-it-to-everyone/

Simmel, G. (1976) 'The metropolis and mental life', in K.H. Wolff (ed) *The Sociology of Georg Simmel*, Free Press: New York, pp 409–26.

Simonetti, L. (2012) 'The ideology of slow food', *Journal of European Studies*, 42(2): 168–9.

Sitrin, M. and Colectiva Sembrar (eds) (2020) *Pandemic Solidarity: Mutual Aid during the Covid-19 Crisis*, London: Pluto Press.

Sjøgren, K. (2013) 'The boss, not the workload, causes workplace depression', *ScienceNordic*, [online] 27 October, Available from: https:// sciencenordic.com/denmark-depression-diseases/the-boss-not-the-workl oad-causes-workplace-depression/1392177

Smith, M. (2017) 'Nationalization vs privatization: the public view', *YouGov*, [online] 19 May, Available from: https://yougov.co.uk/topics/politics/ articles-reports/2017/05/19/nationalization-vs-privatization-public-view

Smith, P.B. (2009) 'Reflections on aspects of Marxist anti-utopianism', *Critique,* 37(1): 99–120.

Smith, T. (2020) 'Freetown Christiania: an economic "nowtopia" at the heart of a European capital city', *Open Democracy*, [online] 7 January, Available from: www.opendemocracy.net/en/oureconomy/freetown-christiania-economic-nowtopia-heart-european-capital-city/

Snider, A.C. (nd) *After Deschooling What? A Review by A.C. Snider*, University of Vermont, Source unknown.

Soborski, R. (2018) *Ideology and the Future of Progressive Social Movements*, London: Rowman & Littlefield.

Solnit, R. (2013) 'Diary', *London Review of Books*, 35(16), [online] 29 August, Available from: www.lrb.co.uk/v35/n16/rebecca-solnit/diary

Solnit, R. (2022) 'A planet in peril and our embrace of Big Brother: George Orwell would have been shocked', *The Guardian*, [online] 24 June, Available from: www.theguardian.com/commentisfree/2022/jun/24/big-brother-george-orwell-climate-change-surveillance

Sorg, C. (2022) 'Failing to plan is planning to fail: toward an expanded notion of democratically planned postcapitalism', *Critical Sociology*, [online] 17 March, Available from: https://journals.sagepub.com/doi/full/10.1177/ 08969205221081058

Spannos, C. (ed) (2008) *Real Utopia: Participatory Society for the 21st Century*, Oakland, CA: AK Press.

Spencer, D. (2014) 'The case for working less', *British Policy and Politics at LSE*, [online] 24 January, Available from: https://blogs.lse.ac.uk/politicsan dpolicy/the-case-for-working-less/

Srnicek, N. (2019) 'The only way to rein in big tech is to treat them as a public service', *The Guardian*, [online] 23 April, Available from: www.theg uardian.com/commentisfree/2019/apr/23/big-tech-google-facebook-uni ons-public-ownership

Srnicek, N. and Williams, A. (2015) *Inventing the Future: Postcapitalism and a World without Work*, London: Verso.

Stall, J. (2020) 'Collectivize Facebook', *Jonastaal*, [online], Available from: www.jonasstaal.nl/projects/collectivize-facebook/

Stanley, E.A. and Smith, M. (eds) (2011) *Captive Genders: Trans Embodiment and the Prison Industrial Complex*, Edinburgh: Oakland Press.

Stephens, J.D. (1979) *The Transition from Capitalism to Socialism*, Chicago: University of Illinois Press.

Stirling, A. and Arnold, S. (2019) *Nothing Personal: Replacing the Personal Tax Allowance with a Weekly National Allowance*, London: New Economics Foundation.

Stirner, M. (2010) *The Ego and Its Own*, London: Dodo Press.

Stuart, F. and White, A. (2019) 'ourVoices episode 1: whose data? Our data!', *Open Democracy*, [online] 12 November, Available from: www. opendemocracy.net/en/podcasts/ourvoices-podcast/ourvoices-epis ode-1-whose-data-our-data/

Sturgis, P., Brunton-Smith, I., Kuha, J. and Jackson, J. (2014) 'Ethnic diversity, segregation and the social cohesion of neighbourhoods in London', *Ethnic and Racial Studies*, 37(8): 1286–309.

Sunkara, B. (2019) *The Socialist Manifesto: The Case for Radical Politics in an Era of Extreme Inequality*, London: Verso.

Sutton, S.A. (2019) 'Cooperative cities: municipal support for worker cooperatives in the United States', *Journal of Urban Affairs*, 41(8): 1081–102.

Swain, D. (2019) 'Not not but not yet: present and future in prefigurative politics', *Political Studies*, 67(1): 47–62.

Swain, H. (2020) 'Payback time: academic's plan to launch Free Black University in UK', *The Guardian*, [online] 27 June, Available from: www. theguardian.com/education/2020/jun/27/payback-time-academics-plan- to-launch-free-black-university-in-uk

Swift, R. (2016) *SOS: Alternatives to Capitalism*, Oxford: New Internationalist Publications.

Tarnoff, B. (2018) 'The data is ours!', *Logic*, [online] 1 April, Available from: https://logicmag.io/scale/the-data-is-ours/

Tarnoff, B. (2019a) 'A socialist plan to fix the internet', *Jacobin*, [online] 30 November, Available from: https://jacobin.com/2019/11/tech-compan ies-antitrust-monopolies-socialist

Tarnoff, B. (2019b) 'From Manchester to Barcelona', *Logic*, [online] 7 December, Available from: https://logicmag.io/nature/from-manches ter-to-barcelona/

Tarnoff, B. (2022) *Internet for the People: The Fight for Our Digital Future*, London: Verso.

Taylor, K. (1982) *Political Ideas of the Utopian Socialists*, Abingdon: Routledge.

Thompson, M. (2021) 'What's so new about new municipalism?', *Progress in Human Geography*, 45(2): 317–42.

Thompson, M. (2022) 'Money for everything? Universal basic income in a crisis', *Economy and Society*, 51(3): 353–74, [online] 18 March, available from https://www.tandfonline.com/doi/full/10.1080/03085147.2022.2035930

Tilton, T. (1991) *The Political Theory of Swedish Social Democracy: Through the Welfare State to Socialism*, Oxford: Clarendon Press.

Tong, R. and Botts, T.F. (2017) *Feminist Thought: A More Comprehensive Introduction*, London: Routledge.

Transnational Institute (2017) *Reclaiming Public Services: How Cities and Citizens are Turning Back Privatization*, Amsterdam: TNI.

Treanor, B. (2006) 'Slow university: a manifesto', *lmu.edu*, [online] webpage decommissioned.

Tremblay-Pepin, S. (2022) 'Five criteria to evaluate democratic economic planning models', *Review of Radical Political Economics*, 54(3): 265–80.

Tressell, R. (1965) *The Ragged Trousered Philanthropists*, St Albans: Granada.

TUC (Trades Union Congress) (2007) *The Economics of Migration: Managing the Impacts*, London: TUC.

UCU (University and College Union) (2022) *Workload Survey 2021 Data Report*, London: UCU.

UNHCR (United Nations High Commissioner for Refugees) (2022) *Global Trends: Forced Displacement in 2021*, Copenhagen: UNHCR.

Van Ness, D.W. (2005) *An Overview of Restorative Justice around the World*, Vancouver: International Centre for Criminal Law Reform and Criminal Justice Policy.

Vargas-Silva, C. (2015) *The Fiscal Impact of Immigration in the UK*, Oxford: Migration Observatory.

Vaughan, M. (ed) (2006) *Summerhill and A.S. Neill*, Maidenhead: Open University Press.

Véliz, C. (2019a) 'Privacy is power', *Aeon*, [online] 2 September, Available from: https://aeon.co/essays/privacy-matters-because-it-empowers-us-all

Véliz, C. (2019b) 'Privacy is a collective concern', *New Statesman*, [online] 9 September, Available from: www.newstatesman.com/science-tech/2019/10/privacy-collective-concern

Véliz, C. (2021a) *Privacy is Power: Why and How You Should Take Back Control of Your Data*, London: Corgi.

Véliz, C. (2021b) 'The future of privacy', in D. Edmonds (ed) *Future Morality*, Oxford: Oxford University Press, pp 121–30.

Verdegem, P. (2021) 'Tim Berners-Lee's plan to save the internet: give us back control of our data', *The Conversation*, [online] 5 February, Available from: https://theconversation.com/tim-berners-lees-plan-to-save-the-internet-give-us-back-control-of-our-data-154130

Viktorsson, M.T. and Gowan, S. (2017) 'Revisiting the Meidner Plan', *Jacobin*, [online] 22 August, Available from: www.jacobinmag.com/2017/08/sweden-social-democracy-meidner-plan-capital

Vidal, M. (2021) 'Zapatistas "invade" Madrid to mark Spanish conquest anniversary', *Al Jazeera*, [online] 13 August, Available from: www.aljazeera.com/news/2021/8/13/zapatistas-invade-madrid-to-mark-spanish-conquest-anniversary

Vostal, F. (2016) *Accelerating Academia: The Changing Structure of Academic Time*, Basingstoke: Palgrave.

Wainwright, H. (1994) *Arguments for a New Left: Answering the Free Market Right*, Oxford: Blackwell Publishers.

Wainwright, H. (2017) 'Creating an economy that works for all', in M. Phipps (ed) *For the Many: Preparing Labour for Power*, London: OR Books, pp 21–36.

Wainwright, H. (2018) *A New Politics from the Left*, Cambridge: Polity Press.

Walia, H. (2021) *Border and Rule: Global Migration, Capitalism, and the Rise of Racist Nationalism*, Chicago: Haymarket Books.

Walia, H. (2022) 'Why climate justice must go beyond borders', *Open Democracy*, [online] 20 January, Available from: www.opendemocracy.net/en/oureconomy/climate-justice-migrant-labour-harsha-walia/

Wampler, B., McNulty, S. and Touchton, M. (2017a) 'Participatory budgeting: spreading across the globe', *Open Government Partnership*, [online] 13 October, Available from: www.opengovpartnership.org/stories/participatory-budgeting-spreading-across-the-globe/

Wampler, B., McNulty, S. and Touchton, M. (2017b) 'The participatory (r)evolution: four major PB transformations over time', *Open Government Partnership*, [online] 25 October, Available from: www.opengovpartnership.org/stories/the-participatory-revolution-four-major-pb-transformations-over-time/

Wampler, B., McNulty, S. and Touchton, M. (2017c) 'Participatory budgeting: does evidence match enthusiasm?', *Open Government Partnership*, [online] 2 November, Available from: www.opengovpartnership.org/stories/participatory-budgeting-does-evidence-match-enthusiasm/

Watson, J.L. (2006) 'McDonald's in Hong Kong: consumerism, dietary change, and the rise of a children's culture', in J.L. Watson (ed) *Golden Arches East: McDonald's in East Asia*, Stanford, CA: Stanford University Press, pp 77–109.

We Own It (2019) *When We Own It: A Model for Public Ownership in the 21st Century*, Oxford: We Own It.

Webb, T. and Cheney, G. (2018) 'Worker owned and governed co-operatives and the wider co-operative movement: challenges and opportunities within and beyond the global economic crisis', in M. Parker, G. Cheney, V. Founier and C. Land (eds) *The Routledge Companion to Alternative Organization*, London: Routledge, pp 64–88.

Weeks, K. (2011) *The Problem with Work: Feminism, Marxism, Antiwork Politics, and Postwork Imaginaries*, London: Duke University Press.

Weghmann, V. (2020) 'How Africa is leading the way to a zero waste future', *Open Democracy*, [online] 6 May, Available from: www.opendemocracy.net/en/oureconomy/how-africa-leading-way-zero-waste-future/

Westra, R., Albritton, R. and Jeong, S. (eds) (2019) *Varieties of Alternative Economic Systems: Practical Utopias for an Age of Global Crisis and Austerity*, Abingdon: Routledge.

Wright, A. (1996) *Socialisms: Old and New*, London: Routledge.

Wright, E.O. (2010) *Envisioning Real Utopias*, London: Verso.

Wright, E.O. (2015) 'How to be an anticapitalist today', *Jacobin*, [online] 12 February, Available from: www.jacobinmag.com/2015/12/erik-olin-wright-real-utopias-anticapitalism-democracy/

Wright, E.O. (2019) *How to Be an Anti-capitalist in the 21st Century*, London: Verso.

Ypi, L. (2021) *Free: Coming of Age at the End of History*, London: Allen Lane.

Zaldívar, J.I. (2011) 'Revisiting the critiques of Ivan Illich's *Deschooling Society*', *International Journal for Cross-Disciplinary Subjects in Education*, 1(1): 618–26.

Zamberlan, A., Gioachan, F. and Gritti, D. (2021) 'Work less, help out more? The persistence of gender inequality in housework and childcare during UK COVID-19', *Research in Social Stratification and Mobility*, 73: Article 100583, [online] June, Available from: www.sciencedirect.com/science/article/pii/S0276562421000032?via%3Dihub

Zaunseder, A. (2022) 'Radical democratic citizenship at work in an adverse economic environment: the case of workers' co-operatives in Scotland', *Identities*, 29(1): 88–107.

Zhou, Y.R. (2022) 'Vaccine nationalism: contested relationships between COVID-19 and globalization', *Globalizations*, 19(3): 450–65.

Zuboff, S. (2019) *The Age of Surveillance Capitalism: The Fight for a Human Future at the New Frontier of Power*, London: Profile Books.

# Index

References in **bold** type refer to tables.